THE FINAL MEMORANDA

THE FINAL MEMORANDA

Major General Ralph H. Van Deman, USA Ret.
1865–1952
Father of U.S. Military Intelligence

Ralph E. Weber, Editor
Marquette University

A Scholarly Resources Imprint
WILMINGTON, DELAWARE

The paper used in this publication meets the minimum requirements of the American National Standard for permanence of paper for printed library materials, Z39.48, 1984.

© 1988 by Scholarly Resources Inc.

Published by Scholarly Resources Inc.
104 Greenhill Avenue
Wilmington, Delaware 19805-1897

This book may not be reproduced in whole or in part in any form or by any means, except for brief quotations in reviews or articles, without written permission from the publisher.

Printed in the United States of America

Library of Congress Cataloging-in-Publication Data

Van Deman, Ralph H., 1865–1952.
    The final memoranda : Major General Ralph H. Van Deman, USA ret., 1865–1952 : father of U.S. military intelligence / Ralph E. Weber, editor.
    p. cm.
  ISBN 0-8420-2296-1
  1. Military intelligence—United States—History. 2. Van Deman, Ralph H., 1865–1952. I. Weber, Ralph Edward. II. Title.
UB251.U5V36   1988   87-26508
355.3′432—dc19   CIP

Contents

Foreword vii

A Sketch of a Man and His Times ix

Part I   The Final Memoranda

Memorandum I, April 8, 1949 3

Memorandum II, June 5, 1950 39

Memorandum III, April 10, 1951 79

Part II   The Background

Van Deman, Memorandum for the Chief of War College Division: State of military information work in the War College Division, General Staff, March 2, 1916 103

Van Deman, Memorandum for the Chief, War College Division: Historical sketch of the steps taken by the War Department for the collection, classification and distribution of military information in the Army, March 2, 1916 121

Part III   Appendices

A   Marlborough Churchill to Dennis E. Nolan, June 4, 1918 . . . 157

B^1 Memorandum No. 64, August 28, 1918 158

B^2 Van Deman to William C. Bullitt, April 11, 1919 162

C   Van Deman to Marlborough Churchill, September 4, 1918 . . 165

D   Van Deman to Marlborough Churchill, September 5, 1918 . . 168

E   John J. Pershing to Van Deman, November 29, 1918 171

F   Van Deman to Marlborough Churchill, November 13, 1918 . . 172

G   Van Deman to Marlborough Churchill, November 13, 1918 . . 173

H   Van Deman to Marlborough Churchill, August 13, 1918 175

I   Van Deman to Leland Harrison, October 15, 1918 178

J   Van Deman to Joseph C. Grew, August 4, 1919 185

For Eve

Foreword

Ralph H. Van Deman is the subject of no biography. He wrote nothing for publication during his lifetime about a career to which he devoted, in his own words, "fifty-five years" of his life and which merits for him the title "Father of U.S. Military Intelligence."

In his eighty-fourth year of life, Van Deman began the first of three manuscripts which he styled "Memorandum" and addressed to his successors:

> because very few of the persons connected with the early history of Military Intelligence in our Army are still alive and the writer believes it would be interesting for those now interested in that work to know something of its development as seen by one who was intimately connected with the incidents related.

The first memorandum is an interesting, factual account, written in the third person, of the beginning, here and in the Philippines, of Army Intelligence at the turn of the century.

The last two manuscripts are more than memoranda: they are memoirs, rich not only in history, but in the personality and character of a man who dedicated his life to the security of his country.

Judged from internal evidence, the second manuscript, dated the following year, and the third, dated little more than six months before his death, were dictated, but never edited by their author. They are obviously first drafts, transcribed phonetically wherever a word, or name, is unfamiliar to the transcriber. Punctuation does not observe the conventions of the first Memorandum; syntax is characteristic of an unedited oral text.

For ease of reading and out of respect for the integrity of the text, spelling and typographical errors have been emended in this edition; punctuation and syntax have been allowed to stand. The reader should ever bear in mind that the author did not have the opportunity to edit his first drafts of the second and third memoranda. To do so now would encumber, not elucidate, his narrative.

In this edition we also publish, as background, two memoranda prepared by Van Deman in 1916 for General M. M. Macomb, chief of the War College Division. Both are alluded to in the memoranda written thirty-three years later. The first reveals the state of military intelligence at the time; the second, a daring undertaking for a junior officer, even one addressing a sympathetic superior, together with the work he did under General Joseph E. Kuhn, chief of the War College Division, during the year before the United States entered the war, are the secure bases of Van Deman's title as Father of U.S. Military Intelligence.

We are grateful to Colonel Marc B. Powe, USA, for permission to publish his article: "American Military Intelligence Comes of Age: A Sketch of a Man and His Times."

We are also grateful to the Directorate of Counterintelligence, Department of the Army, and the United States Army Intelligence Center and School at Fort Huachuca, Arizona, for assistance in obtaining clearance for the publication of the Van Deman manuscripts. The memoranda of 1949, 1950, and 1951 are in the archives of the Intelligence Center; the memoranda of 1916 are in the National Archives.

Ralph E. Weber
Laguna Beach, California

A Sketch of a Man and His Times

Colonel Marc B. Powe
United States Army

The student of American military intelligence soon learns that there are two fundamental questions regarding its history – when did it begin and who were its leaders. Curiously, both the American Revolution and World War II have been suggested as the starting points. Not surprisingly, both George Washington and William J. ("Wild Bill") Donovan have been offered as candidates for the title "Father of American Military Intelligence." Washington practiced only tactical intelligence. He did this almost single-handedly, and he seemingly left no legacy. Donovan, on the other hand, showed great imagination in creating a far-flung wartime agency incorporating many new skills. However, while his Office of Strategic Services performed remarkably, it did not break entirely new ground. Thus, we need to look for a link between the two periods and the two leaders.

The bridge can be found in the period from the turn of the century to World War I as the War Department intelligence agency became institutionalized.[1] Furthermore, one man – Ralph H. Van Deman – was largely instrumental in that development. Van Deman (it rhymes with seaman) seems a likely candidate for a starring role in intelligence history, yet he remains little known today. To understand the contribution of this "intelligence genius" and his current anonymity, it is necessary to evaluate the man and his times.

There has been a popular misconception that the highly effective World War I intelligence organizations at the War Department and with the American Expeditionary Forces (AEF) "just happened." This simply is not so. The organizational beginnings of War Department intelligence can be traced to 1885, three years after the founding of the Office of Naval Intelligence.[2] The immediate cause was a request for information on a foreign army from the secretary of war. The adjutant general, R. C. Drum, had to report not only that he did not have the information, but also that there was no effective system for obtaining it. Shortly thereafter, the Military Information Division (MID), Miscellaneous Branch, the Adjutant General's Office, was established with the general mission of collecting "information concerning the coast defenses and interior topography of the harbors of Central America, New Mexico, Cuba, Canada, and probably one or two other countries."

It was envisioned that Army officers would be sent abroad as attaches to "collect such information as would be useful in the event of our Government being called to war with any other nation."³ Even before the attache system was established in 1889, however, orders were sent out to adjutants general of the states and territories directing that they provide information to the MID on National Guard or militia units under their command. Thereafter, officers were detailed to attache duty in five capitals (Vienna, London, Berlin, Paris, and St. Petersburg), with very specific instructions about what information to obtain and send to MID.⁴

During the years before the Spanish-American War, the MIDs prospered and, by 1898, there were more than 20 men assigned to the MID proper, with an additional 16 attaches and 40 officers serving with the militia reporting to the division. The chief of the MID when the war with Spain began was Major Arthur L. Wagner. A founder of the modern U.S. Army Command and General Staff College (USACGSC) and one of the brilliant military men of his day, Wagner had been calling for a military intelligence service in his classes at Leavenworth. Now, he had a chance to put his ideas into practice.⁵

Information collected by attaches had given nearly exact data on the number of Spanish soldiers in Cuba. The MID had put together a very complete picture of Spanish fortifications throughout the island. A similar effort had been mounted to collect information on the Philippines, and the fruits of the total collection effort were used in War Department planning and by President McKinley. A map was maintained by the MID in the White House, and an analysis of the effects of the Cuban climate and terrain on American forces was initiated by Wagner.⁶ Mapping and reconnaissance had been pursued aggressively by the MID since about 1890, and one of the most active officers in reconnaissance was Lieutenant Andrew S. Rowan, who had surveyed for the MID in Canada and the Northwest since about 1891. Rowan was recalled from Canada by Wagner in late 1897 and dispatched with the legendary "Message to Garcia," the Cuban insurgent leader. To gain more information on Puerto Rico, Wagner sent Lieutenant Henry H. Whitney, disguised as a crewman on a British merchant ship, on a highly profitable cruise through the Caribbean.⁷

It was about the time that the MID was beginning its major effort for campaigns to come, in July 1897, that then Second Lieutenant Van Deman was assigned to the mapping section. Evidently working quite closely with Major Wagner, Van Deman was much impressed with the quality of the MID's work and with the professional competence of Wagner. Although he did not get to Cuba until hostilities had ended, Van Deman felt he was doing important work. As an example, he debriefed the American adventurer and former Cuban guerrilla leader, Frederick Funston, who had been captured and released by the Spaniards. The information went to the White House, and Funston, by then a general of the U.S. Volunteers, went on to the Philippines.[8]

While the MID was appreciated in Washington, field commanders seemingly had less interest in combat intelligence. As soon as the expeditionary forces began to assemble in Tampa, the then Lieutenant Colonel Wagner was sent to establish a bureau of military information in the field to support the invasion. Notwithstanding the fact that he had orders from the commanding general of the Army, and much to his disgust, Wagner was informed that there would be no need for such an intelligence bureau. Undaunted, Wagner attached himself to one of the embarking units and managed to participate actively as a cavalryman in the Santiago battle and later in Puerto Rico.[9] He returned to Washington in the fall of 1898 and then departed for the Department of Dakota in December.[10] There can be little doubt that Wagner left a deep imprint on both the MID and the men who worked there.

As for Van Deman, he stayed on duty in Washington until December 1898 when he was dispatched to Cuba and Puerto Rico, apparently to gather information for the MID. In April 1899, he was reassigned to the Philippines as an aide to General R. P. Hughes in the Vasayan District, remaining in that job for two years.[11] Van Deman did some terrain analysis and mapping before being promoted to captain and reassigned to Manila. Having already developed a taste for intelligence, he was pleased to be given the job in July 1901 of helping to establish a Military Information Division of the Philippines. This seems to have been something of a turning point in Van Deman's life.[12]

Who was Van Deman? He was born in Delaware, Ohio, in 1865. An 1888 graduate of Harvard, Van Deman attended one year of law school there before returning to Ohio to enter medical school at Miami University. He accepted an infantry commission in 1891, but the Army allowed him to stay in medical school until graduation in 1893. Following a year of troop duty, he attended Fort Leavenworth's U.S. Infantry and Cavalry School (forerunner of the USACGSC) in 1895, then went to his first assignment with the MID.[13]

By the time Van Deman took charge of the Manila MID, it was a surprisingly modern intelligence operation. Supported by a network of intelligence officers (so titled) throughout the Philippines, the MID supported both operations against the insurgents and the needs of the division commander and Washington. A high priority project in the Philippines – as it was throughout the Army – was mapping. Each intelligence officer prepared sketch maps of his area in accordance with an instructional pamphlet from the MID in Washington supporting it with notes on the area, lines of communication, agriculture, sociology, and the like. The MID in Manila compiled the results and communicated directly with the MID in Washington on this and other intelligence matters.[14]

Van Deman had an opportunity to do combat intelligence work when his confidential agents reported a plot by the insurgents to attack Manila from adjacent swamps and assassinate key officials. Keeping General Arthur MacArthur informed, Van Deman was pleased with the ability of the MID to provide intelligence as a basis for military operations to thwart the guerrillas.

The Manila assignment offered Van Deman his first opportunity to engage in counterintelligence, the field for which he is best known. His office had all the captured insurgent records, and they proved to be a gold mine of information in the antiguerrilla campaign. The MID employed a number of paid agents and received information from attaches stationed throughout the Pacific. Van Deman, fully realizing that counterintelligence is the result of *all* efforts to protect the command from intelligence-gathering by both real and potential enemies, did not focus exclusively on the insurgent's intelligence apparatus. He was concerned by the amount of Japanese interest in the Philippines, and he took the lead in denying the Japanese legal access to the fighting fronts.[15] This concern about Japanese expansion was a recurring theme in Van Deman's career.

In the fall of 1902, Van Deman returned to the United States. Serving successively as an aide to the commanding general, Department of California, and as commander of Company B and the 1st Battalion, 22d Infantry, at Fairbault, Minnesota, Van Deman was one of nine officers selected in 1904 to attend the first class of the Army War College, in Washington, as a classmate of Captain (soon-to-be Brigadier General) John J. Pershing. Van Deman noted that the close relationship existing between the MID (the Second Division of the recently established General Staff) and the War College (the Third Division) had created a demand for information from the files and library of the former. This fact was to have a distinct bearing on the organization of the General Staff during the next decade, since the reference library function was perceived by some as more important than its responsibility as an independent manager of the emerging national intelligence system.[16]

Upon graduation from the War College, Van Deman returned to the Philippines and troop duty with the 21st Infantry Regiment. In June 1906, he was sent with Captain Alexander Coxe on a covert mission to

China to map the lines of communication radiating outward from Peking. Once again, Van Deman encountered what he believed to be an insidious Japanese interest in its neighbors, illustrated by the careful watch the Japanese kept on foreigners in China. For example, Van Deman was more surprised than pleased to have the Japanese postmaster in that country's concession in Tientsin personally deliver a letter to him at his hotel within minutes of Van Deman's return from a three-week trip. Why should an American on an unofficial visit to China receive such service, he asked? "Because the captain has just returned from a three-week trip," the postmaster replied. When asked how he knew to whom to bring the letter, which had been addressed to the American consulate, the postmaster reminded Van Deman that the hotel had a Japanese cook. The two officers were unable to complete the project in the time allotted, and, in fact, they returned in 1910 to try to finish the project only to be expelled after the Japanese government complained to Peking about their presence.[17]

Returning to Washington in March 1907, Van Deman was assigned the chief of the Map Section, MID. Although he does not explain his own role, Van Deman notes that President Theodore Roosevelt had tasked the MID in early 1907 to provide him with weekly reports on worldwide Japanese activities. Roosevelt later told Van Deman's boss he worried about a Japanese move against the United States. The MID seems to have played a useful role in the voyage of the "Great White Fleet." At the same time, the MID's Map Section was engaged in an aggressive mapping program which gave the War Department good maps of much of the world before World War I.[18]

A turning point for the MID occurred in June 1907 when the War College Division (WCD) was moved from downtown near the War Department Headquarters to Washington Barracks (now Fort McNair). Because the Third Division (WCD) was so dependent on the Second Division (MID) for its maps, library, and files, the MID soon joined them at Washington Barracks. This move was strongly protested by the chief of the Second Division, doubtless with Captain Van Deman's encouragement, on the grounds that the MID should be accessible to all of the War Department (not just the WCD), as well as to the White House, Navy and State departments. Although the MID was supported in this view by an ad hoc committee of the War Department division chiefs, the chief of staff ordered them to move. Within a few months, the Second Division was merged with the Third, forming a new War College-dominated Second Section. As Van Deman later noted in a successful plea for reestablishment of a separate MID, the result of merging the information and War College functions demanded too much, and one function or the other must suffer. Intelligence did.[19]

Although a similar view was communicated to the chief of staff in 1908, it was to no avail, and the new combined section was created. As it turned out, the problem remained for Van Deman to rectify eight years later.

When Van Deman's normal three-year General Staff tour was completed in 1910, the chief of the Second Section had him extended for six months to finish cataloging the "mass of maps that have accumulated for years." That project apparently completed, Van Deman went out to the Philippines for duty with the MID in Manila once again.

During his two years in Manila, Van Deman remained intimately involved in the mapping project for China. Of long-range importance, he noted that the direction of this mapping project – and all other intelligence work in the Philippines – was handled exclusively by the MID in Manila since there was no longer an organization in Washington to plan for field intelligence activities. He became convinced that this decentralization of a national strategic collection effort must be corrected.[20]

Having established a name for himself in mapping, Van Deman was assigned as an instructor teaching "topographic and maps" in the 21st Infantry Regiment at Vancouver Barracks, Washington, after his regiment returned there in May 1912. In mid-1914, he was reassigned to inspector general duties with the Second Division.[21] He took part in the concentration of the Second Division in Texas which was intended as a demonstration of military preparedness aimed at Mexico. The effort, which was more effective than the first attempt (in 1911) to field a "maneuver" division, was to aid mobilization for war three years later. Unfortunately, there was no provision for intelligence in these field forces – despite the potential for war with Mexico – until 1914.

Reassignment orders reached Van Deman in early 1915, sending him back to the General Staff – a new major – for what was to be the period of his greatest contribution to the Army and to military intelligence.

The nature of the military intelligence (MI) problem facing the War Department, and more particularly Van Deman, is summarized by General Peyton C. March (who is actually commenting on the relatively improved intelligence situation which existed in early 1918 when he became Chief of Staff):

> I found the Military Intelligence an unimportant section of another General Staff division. It is unbelievable, but when we entered the war it consisted of two officers and

two clerks. Every other army of importance in the world had a General Staff division devoted to gathering military intelligence, and on a par with the other General Staff functions of military plans, operations and supply.[22]

In fact, the situation Van Deman found when he arrived for duty with the WCD in July 1915 was much worse than March had pictured. He found that none of the functions of the former MID, and, in fact, no intelligence work whatsoever was bring done in Washington. What little work was being done in the field and overseas was entirely self-directed. In spite of the fact that the war in Europe had been going on for nine months and American observers were sending in detailed reports, no system existed to present information about the war to the General Staff, subordinate elements of the War Department or the national government. Moreover, Van Deman found a table "piled high" with information reports from the Mexican border which were not even being filed. In short, the entire War Department intelligence effort consisted of the haphazard accumulation of reports.[23] Realizing that no management of intelligence activities was being performed by the Army despite the danger of war and that the Army was losing most of the information being received by the WCD, Van Deman submitted various memoranda through the president, WCD, to the chief of staff advocating the re-establishment of a Military Information Division in the General Staff. "These memoranda were approved by the president of the Army War College but were entirely ignored by the Chief of Staff." The most important of these papers was his "Historical Sketch" of the growth of the military information function in the Army, dated 2 March 1916. This document provided an excellent summary of events from 1885 until its writing, as well as a brilliant analysis of the importance of having a separate, equal intelligence division.[24]

Under the existing arrangement of subordinating the intelligence function to the War College, the "system" was entirely passive. There existed no centralized or initiatory authority for intelligence work in the Army. The root of the problem was (and still is):

> the most necessary and essential kind of information, the information without which no war plan can be made that is worth the paper it is written on, does not come in of its own accord or as a matter of routine. It must be actively sought and traced out and proved up.[25]

The hard-hitting, thirty-two-page "Historical Sketch" arrived at a rather bluntly stated conclusion: Intelligence work had declined steadily since 1908, and, from the intelligence viewpoint, the General Staff was worse off than anytime since 1903.

Brigadier General M. M. Macomb, the chief, WCD, an experienced intelligence collector himself, not only approved Van Deman's remarks before forwarding them to the chief of staff but also added his own comment that the job of heading up the war plans element was too big for one man. Although the desired result – a separate MID – did not occur immediately, it did produce an improvement in field intelligence. In April 1916, department commanders were directed to create an intelligence officer on their own staffs and throughout their subordinate commands "as is deemed necessary by the circumstances."[26]

During the year remaining before the United States was thrust into the war, Van Deman and the new chief, WCD, Brigadier General Joseph E. Kuhn, collaborated in coming to grips with the intelligence problems. Kuhn, who also had collected information for the old MID, proved to be as sympathetic as his predecessor to the need for intelligence. In late 1916, Kuhn decided to cancel the current War College class in order to use those officers "in making an extensive study of military intelligence reports from abroad, so the information compiled might be imparted to the troops." He also sought and received authority from the chief of staff, General Hugh Scott, to initiate a program of identifying and training qualified National Guard officers for tactical intelligence work. This action provided a nucleus of intelligence officers when mobilization occurred.[27]

The most significant help that General Kuhn gave, however, was letting Van Deman use his own initiative within the nascent intelligence framework of the WCD. Kuhn informed the chief of staff on 11 April 1917 (one week after the declaration of war) that, in fact, his Intelligence Section had been engaged in secret intelligence work for the past year. Working with various departments of the civil branch of the government such as the State Department, the Department of Justice and the Treasury Department, which had information collection functions, Van Deman had reestablished a War Department's intelligence agency. Furthermore, Kuhn and Van Deman had persuaded the secretary of war to obtain a congressional appropriation of $1 million for "Contingencies – Military Information Section, General Staff Corps." Thus, Van Deman had a framework of ideas, support from other government agencies, and money to operate with as soon as the war began.[28] What he had done, in short, was lay the groundwork for the first *national* intelligence system.

Oddly enough, even the declaration of war did not lead to the reestablishment of the MID as a separate agency. With the consent of

General Kuhn, Major Van Deman went to see the chief of staff to present his case. He found General Scott unsympathetic. He could see no reason for the U.S. Army to have any such thing as a military intelligence service. If the British and French armies had such organizations and were receiving the necessary information concerning the enemy, there was no reason why we should not say to them "Here, we are now ready for service – we would be pleased if you hand over to us all the necessary information concerning the enemy which your intelligence services have obtained." After two or three interviews, Scott became exasperated and ordered Van Deman to cease his efforts with the organization of an intelligence service.[29]

But there was no denying the combined efforts of Kuhn and Van Deman. Through a variety of pressures, including Van Deman's use of a mutual friend, the problem was brought to the attention of Secretary of War Newton Baker. Orders were issued on 11 May 1917, directing the establishment of a Military Intelligence Section of the WCD, as proposed by Kuhn. It was a brilliant victory for Van Deman and Army Intelligence. Moreover, it revitalized Elihu Root's concepts for a General Staff made up of separate coordinating agencies for intelligence and operations.[30] The war, however, would not allow time for any victory celebration.

What shape should the new MI Section take? What should be its method and mission? Where would it get people? Recognizing that "we have never even attempted in any previous war to carry out the duties which must now be undertaken," Van Deman declared that they would have to play it by ear. In general, the new section would have an administration branch to manage intelligence collection, an information branch to handle espionage and counterespionage, and a censorship branch.[31]

Van Deman soon produced an extremely lucid statement of what national-level wartime intelligence would entail. He introduced the terms "negative" intelligence (that is, denying intelligence to the enemy) and "positive" intelligence (that is, the use of all available sources to gather information about the enemy) into American military usage. This memorandum outlines the need for a coordinate intelligence apparatus between the various U.S. military and civilian agencies, as well as friendly foreign agencies. It concludes that, since the information in question was of a military character and since the only organization with a charter to operate on so wide a spectrum was the War Department General Staff, the coordinating function should belong to the MI Section, WCD. This was, in fact, the way American intelligence was managed during the war.[32]

Since the war would end about eighteen months after America entered, the reader may wonder what intelligence practice could be accomplished in such a short time that had not been possible during the previous thirty-two years of departmental existence. Writing after the war, Van Deman's successor, Brigadier General Marlborough Churchill, would write:

> The field assigned to Military Intelligence in the War Department is so broad that there is a tendency on the part of officers either to have only a very hazy idea of its scope, or to understand but one phase of intelligence work and to disregard the many other phases . . . for example, if an officer has served with combat troops in France, he is likely to think only of combat intelligence . . . on the other hand, if an officer has been unfortunate enough to remain during the war on duty in the United States, he is very likely to think of Military Intelligence only as a bureau of investigation, or sort of military secret police . . . (while both of these play their parts, there is additionally) the duty of maintaining a complete foreign map collection and complete terrain handbooks covering areas in which we are likely to carry on military operations. . . . The other major function which has been assigned to MID consists of playing the part in our Government Information Service . . . (of obtaining) . . . data on foreign armies.[33]

At the time of the armistice, the MID employed 282 officers, 29 sergeants, and nearly 1,000 civilians in a network "which was not only of paramount value to the War Department, but covered the world in furnishing information to the State Department, the Department of Justice and other government departments, bureaus and war boards."[34]

Yet there were "never more than six officers of the regular service on duty in the branch at any one time." Where did the rest come from? Van Deman, a lieutenant colonel by mid-1917, had obtained authority to appoint qualified civilians as commissioned officers of the national Army, and he made very effective use of this power. An interesting insight into this procedure is provided by Herbert O. Yardley, an early American code and cipher specialist and chief for twelve years of what came to be known as the American Black Chamber. Yardley, a State Department code clerk when war was declared, was convinced that this country must establish a cryptographic bureau, like those of the European countries, to gather information from enemy communications. But to whom could he present the idea? He soon learned that a Major Van Deman was trying to establish an intelligence service. He obtained an interview; Van Deman instantly hired Yardley, commissioned him as a first lieutenant, and put him in charge of Codes and Ciphers (MI-8).[35]

The problem perceived by Van Deman and his original assistant, Captain (later Colonel) Alexander B. Coxe, was threefold: coping with "the manifold domestic problems arising from the fact of our mixed population"; protecting the morale of American troops; and furnishing the AEF "with whatever information was usable in the conduct of its campaigns." In plain English, they were concerned about pro-German and latent anti-British feeling in America creating a climate for espionage, sabotage, and subversion, and they had to support the AEF with both information and qualified intelligence personnel.[36]

The problem of security was a real one. Sabotage had occurred by the summer of 1917, and there were also concrete examples of espionage against the United States before the country even went to war. In a fever of anti-German sentiment, dozens of organizations devoted to running down spies sprang up in America. Van Deman saw a potential for this huge super-patriotic force, aided in consolidating them under a single umbrella organization (the American Protective League) and coordinated their work and reports in the MI Branch. He established an alert guard system for War Department offices, identification card systems, and a variety of other steps to enhance security (including passport controls, port and industrial security organizations, and a system for maintaining files in Washington to support an Army-wide security program). Subordinate offices of the MID, manned by mobilized civilian police officers, were established in eight U.S. cities to conduct personnel security investigations.[37]

To provide French-speaking specialists in intelligence and security for the AEF, a force of fifty sergeants was recruited and designated as the Corps of Intelligence Police (CIP), predecessor organization of the Counterintelligence Corps (CIC).[38]

Information gathering and presentation was an area with which Van Deman was familiar because of his years of intelligence experience, although the scope of the effort and number of agencies available was unprecedented. From the WCD, he inherited the maps and photographic gallery and control of the military attaches. As mentioned before, there were intelligence officers serving throughout the United States, and there were, of course, intelligence reports coming in from both the AEF and the Allied governments. Coordination was effected with the new aviation corps for its intelligence potential. Dissemination was a priority; information was provided to the staff and the AEF on a regular basis, and briefing maps were maintained by the MID in both the White House and Capitol.[39]

Yardley's cryptographic bureau (MI-8, the predecessor of the U.S. Army Security Agency) soon proved a valuable asset. MI-8 developed codes for use by the U.S. government which proved to be effective throughout the war. Yardley also placed mobile radio intercept stations on the Mexican border to keep track of German attempts to establish a clandestine wireless station in that country. Another important MI-8 function was in discovering secret writing used by German agents leading, for example, to the only death sentence for espionage handed out in America during World War I.

In June 1918, Van Deman, who had been promoted to colonel the previous August, was ordered overseas as a replacement for the AEF G2, Colonel Dennis E. Nolan. As he himself realized, he had reached the pinnacle of his Army service. To recapitulate Van Deman's contributions, it may be said that he created – for the first time in American military experience – a complete intelligence system, coordinating at national level all available assets. Perhaps his most important legacy was the development of a doctrine which gave the intelligence system life, even through the hard years between world wars. Van Deman's MID centralized the services of the forebearers of a number of such modern agencies as the U.S. Army Map Service (now the Defense Map Service), the attache system, the U.S. Army Intelligence Agency (formerly the U.S. Army Intelligence Command and before that the CIC), the U.S. Army Security Agency, the National Security Agency, the Defense Investigative Agency, the Industrial Security Organization, the U.S. Army Intelligence Center and School, and, of course, the entire tactical intelligence organization within the Army. Although he was to be promoted to major general and command a division before retirement, Van Deman believed his best period was in World War I.

For today's Military Intelligence Branch, this period was crucial: If it was born in the early days of the Republic, it only reached maturity during World War I. If Van Deman was not the father of the branch, he certainly was its godfather. The establishment of intelligence officers as equal members on all staffs, the recognition of a need for professional intelligence men, the birth of the CIP and MI-8, and the outstanding performance of duty by the MI men ensured their reputation. Thereafter, the Army always provided for an intelligence effort, even though it was often less than completely effective. The creation of the MI Branch, delayed for forty years, was the inevitable fruit of the work done by Van Deman, Churchill, and Nolan.

In Europe, Van Deman visited the Intelligence School at Langres, France, and units in the line to prepare himself to replace Nolan. The war ended first, and Van Deman was Pershing's natural choice to be the senior American intelligence officer and chief of Allied counterintelligence for the Paris Peace Commission. During the ten months he held this position, Van Deman developed an abiding distrust of Bolshevism, a common reaction for military men of the period who were seeing daily the most blatant subversion inspired by Moscow. For example, circulars appealing to American forces to mutiny were discovered in early 1919 and traced to an American Communist living in a part of Germany not occupied by the Allies. This appeal, and others circulating at the time within the AEF, were intended to create dissension between officers and their units and between Regular Army and temporary officers.[40]

One of the interesting ideas that Van Deman proposed, without success, was the creation of an internationally backed League of Nations intelligence agency. He wrote to Churchill in 1919 that nobody he talked with

> seems to be impressed with the necessity for having any such service. . . . How under the sun they expect to function without it, I can't imagine and am sure they will have to come to it in the end. Just now, however, they seem to have exceedingly vague ideas of what the organization of the League is going to be.[41]

Returning to Washington in August 1919, Van Deman served briefly as deputy to Churchill in the MID, then returned to the Philippines in March 1920 as commander, 31st Infantry and Post of Manila. He occupied this position until April 1923, except for a three-month period of detached service with the British Army in India "for observation and study." Returning to the States, he served with the National Guard for several years, first in Washington in the Military Bureau, then as an instructor in Berkeley, California. Promoted to brigadier general in October 1927, he assumed command of the 6th Brigade. The last two years of his active duty were spent on the West Coast at Fort Rosecrans in San Diego, California, and as commanding general, 3d Infantry Division, at Fort Lewis, Washington. He was promoted to major general in May 1929. After thirty-eight years' service, Van Deman retired in San Diego in September 1929 but did not stack arms.[42]

Long-established interests and an ardent patriotism combined to keep

Van Deman engaged in intelligence work for the remainder of his life. Although he was married and highly active in civic affairs such as the San Diego Harbor Commission, the Red Cross, and the Chamber of Commerce, the picture that emerges from the few public references to him during the 1930s and 1940s is of a man obsessed with the security of the country. He continued his longtime interest in mapmaking, and, at the behest of the War Department, he made the first military maps of southern California since the Civil War.

Van Deman's primary intelligence function after he retired, however, was maintaining files on "subversives." Working with the knowledge and cooperation of the War Department, Navy, and Federal Bureau of Investigation, he developed a voluminous library of Communist literature, a photo gallery, newspaper clippings, and information reports. He provided information to various federal agencies and local police departments. His motives were quite simple: He believed American national defense rested on good intelligence, and he could help provide it.[43]

During World War II, the old general became an adviser to the War Department G2. His exact duties are now unclear, but he received a Legion of Merit in 1946 for "accumulation and evaluation of confidential intelligence information" from 1941 to 1946.[44]

On 22 January 1952, Van Deman died at home in San Diego. His passing was as quiet and unobtrusive as much of his life had been. He is little discussed today – despite the current flurry of interest in intelligence – but the fact remains that no individual contributed more to American intelligence organization or doctrine than Van Deman. He quite literally led American intelligence into the twentieth century.

NOTES

[1] It is important to recognize that much in American life was becoming institutionalized at this time as illustrated by Robert H. Wiebe's pathbreaking, *The Search for Order: 1877-1920*, Hill and Wang, NY, 1967. For more information on the War Department's development in this area, see Marc B. Powe's M.A. thesis, "The Emergence of the War Department Intelligence Agency: 1885-1918," Kansas State University, Manhattan, KS, 1974.

[2] *The Army and Navy Journal*, 10 October 1885, 1. Personnel from the Office of Naval Intelligence Division. Also of note in this and other newspaper accounts at this time, the new office was referred to as an "intelligence" bureau although it was not officially so designated until 1917.

[3] *Ibid.*

[4] Memorandum for the assistant secretary of war, "A Brief Outline of the Origin, Growth and Work of the Military Information Division, Adjutant General's Office," signed by W. A. Simpson, assistant adjutant general, 21 February 1902, cited hereinafter as Simpson Memo and found in the National Archives, Washington, D.C.

[5] Arthur L. Wagner wrote the first American book on tactical intelligence, *The Service of Security and Information*, Hudson-Kimberly, Kansas City, MO, 1893.

[6] Ralph H. Van Deman, *Memoirs*, unpublished manuscript 1949-1951, Part I, 3-8, author's files.

[7] Simpson Memo.

[8] Van Deman, 5-8.

[9] Arthur L. Wagner, *Report of the Santiago Campaign*, Hudson-Kimberly, Kansas City, MO, 1907, 138-40.

[10] George W. Cullum, *Biographical Register of the Officers and Graduates of the U.S. Military Academy*, Riverside Press, Cambridge, MA, 1901.

[11] Van Deman, 5-8.

[12] Department of the Army letter, "Statement of Military Service of Ralph Henry Van Deman D362," Office of the Adjutant General, Washington, DC, 26 April 1973, cited hereinafter as Statement of Military Service.

13 *Ibid.*

14 *Annual Report of the Lieutenant General Commanding the Army, 1901*, War Department, Washington, DC, Part II, November 1902, 203-4.

15 Van Deman, 10-13.

16 Ralph H. Van Deman, Memorandum for the Chief of Staff, "Historical Sketch," National Archives, Washington, DC, 2 March 1916, 7.

17 Van Deman, *Memoirs*, 17-20.

18 Van Deman, "Historical Sketch," 12-13.

19 *Ibid.*

20 Van Deman, *Memoirs*, 26-30.

21 Statement of Military Service.

22 Peyton C. March, *The Nation of War*, NY, 1932, 226.

23 Van Deman, *Memoirs*, 30-31.

24 Van Deman, "Historical Sketch," 19. As Van Deman noted, this problem had been seen by General Wood in 1913 when he was chief of staff. He suggested improvements that would have resulted in better intelligence management, but the War College Division did not comply.

25 *Ibid.*, 32.

26 For an analysis of this problem, see Powe, especially Chapter IV.

27 Memorandum for the Chief of Staff, 11 April 1917, "Organization for Intelligence Work," War Department, National Archives, Washington, DC.

28 *Ibid.*

29 Van Deman, *Memoirs*, 33-34.

30 Memorandum for the Chief of Staff, 11 May 1917, "Proper Organization of a Military Intelligence Section, General Staff." War Department, National Archives, Washington, DC.

31 *Ibid.*

32 Memorandum for the Chief of Staff, 13 May 1917, "Method of Handling Secret Service Matters," War Department, National Archives, Washington, DC.

[33] Marlborough Churchill, "The Military Intelligence Division, General Staff," *Journal of the United States Artillery*, April 1920, 293-95.

[34] March, 226.

[35] Herbert O. Yardley, *The American Black Chamber*, NY, 1931, 34-35. This sensational book, written after Secretary of State Stimson closed the Black Chamber in 1929, caused a number of countries to change their code systems.

[36] Van Deman, *Memoirs*, 50-54.

[37] *Ibid.*, 56.

[38] Memorandum for the Chief of Staff, 11 August 1917, "Intelligence Service," War Department, National Archives, Washington, DC.

[39] Van Deman, *Memoirs*, 39 and 58-63.

[40] *Ibid.*, Part III, 8.

[41] *Ibid.*, 19-20.

[42] Statement of Military Service.

[43] *New York Times*, 9 July 1971, 5.

[44] *San Diego Tribune*, 20 July 1946, 10.

PART I THE FINAL MEMORANDA

Memorandum I

Memorandum: San Diego, California

April 8, 1949

The following memorandum is in no sense to be considered an official document. Nor is it to be considered as a personal history of the writer. It is not for publication. It consists of certain incidents pertinent to the history and development of the Military Intelligence service of the United States Army which can now be remembered by the writer after nearly fifty-five years experience in intelligence work. It is more than possible that there may be some minor discrepancies in this work, since, with the exception of a few dates, the writer has had to depend entirely on his unaided memory, without notes of any kind, in its preparation. It has been written because very few of the persons connected with the early history of Military Intelligence in our Army are still alive and the writer believes it would be interesting for those now interested in that work to know something of its development as seen by one who was intimately connected with the incidents related.

                                                           R. H. Van Deman

                                                        Maj. Gen., U.S.A., Ret.

       Anyone who is interested in Military Intelligence work in the United States knows there was no government organization or group charged with the collection and filing of information concerning foreign countries at any time in our history up to 1885. Nor was there in existence an organization whose function was the preventing of the collection of confidential military information concerning our own country by foreign governments.

       In 1885 the then Secretary of War asked the Adjutant General of the Army for information concerning the armed forces of a certain foreign power. The Adjutant General replied that he had no such information. The Secretary then suggested that it would be well if a bureau be set up by the Adjutant General for the purpose of collecting and filing information concerning foreign governments which would be of interest to the government of the United States. Whereupon, the Adjutant General detailed one officer and supplied a clerk whose duties would be to gather and file information concerning the military organizations of foreign countries in which, for one reason or another, the United

States might become interested. This was the beginning of what was later to be known as the Military Information Division of the Adjutant General's Office.

In 1889 Congress passed a law authorizing the sending abroad of officers of the Army for the purpose of gathering and forwarding to the War Department military information concerning the countries to which they were sent. This was the beginning, of course, of the system of military attaches which has been so valuable to the Military Intelligence service. Eventually the duty of picking these officers for detail and their preliminary instruction before going abroad was assigned to the Military Information Division of the Adjutant General's Office and all additional instructions as sent to them from the War Department and their communications and reports all came to the Military Information Division.

The writer's first contact with the Military Information Division of the Adjutant General's Office was in June 1897. At that time the office occupied three rooms on the main floor of the old State, War and Navy Building almost directly opposite the main entrance to the building. The first room was occupied by the Chief of the Division, at that time Colonel Arthur L. Wagner. The second room was occupied by the commissioned personnel and the third contained the files of the Division, including such maps as had been collected for its use, and the civilian clerks, stenographers and draftsmen. The number of commissioned officers, including the Chief, at that time consisted of some seven or eight individuals.

At this time the Division was occupied particularly in gathering and processing information concerning Cuba and the other Spanish possessions in the Caribbean. This, of course, was due to the fact that it was perfectly evident that it would not be long before the United States would be involved in a struggle with Spain to free Cuba and the other Spanish possessions in the Caribbean from the domination of Spain. The Division was also engaged in gathering topographical and other information concerning several other foreign countries and for this purpose was sending each year a limited number of officers to those countries for the prosecution of this work. The system of military attaches had been established some years before and the information obtained by these military attaches was received and processed by the Military Information Division of the Adjutant General's Office.

The blowing up of the battleship Maine, 15 Feb. 1898, finally made it evident that the declaration of war against Spain could not be very long delayed and the entire force of the Military Information Division was put to work at adding to the information already on file in the Division concerning Cuba and the other island possessions of Spain. One of the most important subjects to be investigated was the probable health of the northern troops who might be required to serve in Cuba and the Division prepared a carefully documented report based upon all the information obtainable at this time with respect to this problem.

It will be remembered that at this period the cause for Yellow Fever was not known and that northern troops exposed to this disease were particularly susceptible. The then Secretary of War (Russell A. Alger) believed that an army should be raised as soon as possible and sent at once to invest the Cuban capital of Havana. The report on the probable health of northern troops serving in Cuba during the summer months was presented by the Chief of the Military Information Division, Colonel Wagner, at a meeting at the White House called by the President of the United States at which the President, The Secretary of War and numerous high ranking officers of the Army and Navy were present. After Colonel Wagner had read this report the President (McKinley) decided that the plan to send United States troops into Cuba during the summer months would not be carried out. Whereupon, as Colonel Wagner was leaving the room to return to his office, the Secretary of War said to him, "Colonel Wagner, you have made it impossible for my plan of campaign to be carried out. I will see to it that you do not receive any promotions in the Army in the future."

The Secretary made his promise good. For, although Colonel Wagner was later appointed a Brigadier General the notice of his appointment reached him on his death bed and it is very doubtful whether or not he ever realized his life's ambition had been achieved.

It will be interesting to note that the total force of the United States Army up to the reorganization upon the advent of the Spanish-American War consisted of 25,000 men. The make-up of the Army at this time was as follows: The Adjutant General's Department, and Inspector General's Department, a Judge Advocate General's Department, an Ordnance Department, a Commissary Department, a Quartermaster's Department, a Corps of Engineers, an Artillery Corps (embracing both coast and field artillery), a Signal Corps, ten regiments of cavalry (the enlisted men of the 9th and 10th consisting of Negroes), 25 regiments of Infantry (the enlisted men of the 24th and 25th regiments composed of Negroes.) A regiment of Infantry consisted of a Colonel, a Lt. Colonel, a Major, an Adjutant (Captain), a Quartermaster (Captain), a Commissary (Captain), ten companies consisting of a Captain, a First Lt., a Second Lt., and approximately 50 enlisted men. Each regiment was authorized to have a band but the musicians composing this band had to be detailed from amongst the enlisted men from among the various companies. The organization of a Cavalry regiment and of the Artillery regiments was similar.

It will be remembered that Lt. Rowan was sent to Cuba to contact General Garcia, the commander of the rebellious Cuban troops. This incident received great publicity through the article written by Elbert Hubbard. Lt. Rowan was one of the members, at this time, of the Military Information Division and it was upon the recommendation of Colonel Wagner that he was sent to contact the insurgent leader in Cuba. Another of the officers then on duty in the Division and also a lieutenant was sent to investigate conditions in Puerto Rico. This was Lt. Harry Whitney. Whitney was very nearly captured by the Spaniards while he was on a fishing boat off the Puerto Rican coast.

One of the sources for information concerning the insurgents in Cuba and the topography of certain vital areas was an American who had been serving with the Cuban insurgents as an artillery officer. He was captured by the Spanish but was finally released through the efforts of the United States government and allowed to return to the United States. This man was sent from Philadelphia, Pennsylvania to the Military Information Division in Washington for the purpose of giving what information he could and was interviewed exhaustively by one of the officers attached to the Division concerning his knowledge of matters in Cuba. This gentleman was Frederick Funston who shortly afterwards was appointed a Colonel of a volunteer regiment and later a Brigadier General of Volunteers. General Funston, of course, was the officer who captured Emilio Aguinaldo in northeastern Luzon and so brought to an end the Philippine insurrection.

As is generally the case with bureaus that are attached to larger divisions of government, matters which had no connection whatever with military information were assigned to the Military Information Division. One of these was the allocation of volunteers by regiments to the various states upon the call for the 75,000 volunteers. Unbelievable as it may seem, this call for volunteers did not include volunteers for the medical department, the commissary department, the quartermaster corps, the engineers, the ordnance or artillery. It included only infantry and cavalry and the cavalry was to consist of only two squadrons. In making the apportionment the cavalry was allotted to those states known to be, at that time, raising horses, such as North and South Dakota and Montana. When the allotment was returned to the Division from the Secretary of War's Office, it was noted that the cavalry as allotted had been entirely blue penciled and in the place of the original allotment as given by the Division, a full regiment of cavalry was to be organized in the state of Texas. Upon inquiry of the Adjutant General of the Army as to why this change had been made it was ascertained it was because of the President's desire to give to the Army medical officer who was then the President's official physician the command of a regiment of cavalry. As

THE FINAL MEMORANDA 7

is of course well known by everyone, this man was Leonard Wood who afterwards became Major General Wood and who is well known to every American. The Lt. Colonel of this regiment was, of course, Theodore Roosevelt at that time the Assistant Secretary of the Navy. The regiment was known as the Rough Riders.

In preparation for the coming hostilities the Division had prepared, by the map section, a map of Cuba on a fairly large scale and had it printed on cloth as a map for use in the field. It is doubtful as to whether or not this map was of very material use since it was not a topographical map.

Most officers of the Division were very soon detailed to other duties or they were returned to their regiments then under orders to proceed to training camps in Florida. Eventually only one officer was left in the Military Information Division in Washington. This was Lt. Willis Scherer who proceeded to handle such military information work as he was able during the continuance of the Spanish American War. One of the important things that Lt. Scherer accomplished was the publication of a pamphlet on the Philippines and its distribution to the services.

In February of 1901 the writer was serving as an ADC on the staff of Brigadier General Robert Hughes then in command of the Department of Visayas of the Philippines. In this month he was promoted to the grade of Captain which automatically removed him as an ADC from the staff of General Hughes. He was then ordered by the commanding general of the Philippine Division, Major General Arthur MacArthur, to proceed to Manila for service in the Bureau of Insurgent Records. Upon arrival in Manila, he was instructed that upon the relief of the officer in charge of the Bureau of Insurgent Records, Captain John R. L. M. Taylor, who was under orders to return to the United States, to take over the Bureau and reorganize it into the Military Information Division of the Philippines. At this time the Bureau of Insurgent Records was housed in the old Spanish ordnance headquarters in the walled city which afterwards became first the Army and Navy Club and later the Manila Public Library. Soon after the departure for the United States of Captain Taylor the Bureau of Insurgent Records was moved to quarters on the groundfloor of the Estado Mayor which, as everyone who has served in the Philippines knows, was located on the left bank of the Pasig River in the city of Manila not far from the zoological gardens. The second floor of this building was occupied by the Commanding General and his staff and officers.

Carrying out instructions, the Military Information Division of the Philippines was set up. The organization following very generally that of the Military Information Division of the Adjutant General's Office in

Washington, D.C. The Insurgent Records constituted one of its sections since they contained very valuable information concerning insurgent activities and the personnel of the insurgents who had been engaged in armed insurrection against the United States. The Division also contained a map section and was supplied with two very efficient Filipino draftsmen. It was also supplied with several clerks detailed from the enlisted personnel of the Army. In addition it was provided with several undercover agents all of whom were Filipinos with the exception of one American. This American eventually became a member of the Philippine Commission. He died of cholera during the epidemic of 1903.

In addition to the office organized in Manila, information officers were also ordered appointed by each commander of a separate post in the Philippine Islands of which there were at that time some 450. These post information officers were required to submit a sketch map covering the territory around their post for a distance of at least ten miles with a report of the topography and the important natives living in their vicinity. These maps were retraced in the Manila office and blue printed and made available to the authorities, military and civilian, who desired them. The reports on the topography accompanied the blue prints and the reports on the Filipino personnel were made available to the Commanding General and his staff.

There was, of course, no connection between the Military Information Division of the Philippines and the Military Information Division of the Adjutant General's Office in Washington at the time the Philippine Division was set up and it was some years before the Philippine organization was made a branch of the Washington office.

In 1902 there was still active fighting on the part of the Philippine insurgents in various parts of the Philippines, particularly in Southern Luzon. In that year the undercover agents of the Military Information Division discovered an active plot for an attack on Manila and for the proposed assassination of all of the important military officers in the city. The attacking force was concealed in certain swamp land but was kept informed constantly with matters in Manila. The Commanding General and the then acting Chief of Staff were, of course, kept informed of what was going on and precautions were taken to make impossible the carrying out of this plot. As a matter of fact, means were taken to disperse the proposed attacking force and to make impossible the carrying out of the assassination plot within the city.

It will be remembered that when Emilio Aguinaldo and the other insurgent leaders were expelled from the Philippine Islands in 1895 by the Spanish government all of the group, with the exception of one man, took up quarters in Hong Kong and set up what was known as the

Philippine Revolutionary Junta. The one man who did not remain in Hong Kong proceeded to Tokyo. The writer cannot remember the true name of this individual but his alias was Robinson. This man became extremely friendly with certain high officials of the Japanese government particularly the officer in charge of the Military Information Division of the Japanese Army. This was made comparatively easy, by the fact that Japan was already very much interested in the prospect of taking over the whole of Asia with Japan as the suzerain power. Robinson, of course, kept in touch with that revolutionary group in Hong Kong and also with certain of his old friends in the Philippines. Sometime after the end of the revolutionary activities in the Philippines, Robinson desired to return to the Islands and a little later in this report an incident will be noted with respect to his proposal to return to the Philippines.

In 1902, as noted before, there was still sporadic fighting in various parts of the Philippines particularly in Southern Luzon. One morning the officer in charge of the Military Information Division of the Philippines came into the office of the aides of the Commanding General which opened into the room used for receiving callers. Seated in this reception room he noticed a Japanese officer in full uniform wearing a sword and white gloves. Believing that this man might be from some Japanese ship which had recently arrived, he asked one of the aides present who the Japanese officer was. He was told that it was Captain Tanaka, a Japanese Military Attache accredited to Manila.

Since military attaches are only accredited to embassies or legations, that of course, was impossible since Manila was entitled only to a counselor agency. It was suggested that the aide ascertain for what purpose the so-called military attache was calling on the Commanding General which he promised to do. After the interview of the Japanese officer with the Commanding General, it was ascertained that what he wanted was a permit to allow him to travel to certain places in the Philippine Islands and upon being required to name the places that he desired to go it developed that it was only to those localities in which actual fighting between Filipino insurgents and the United States Army was in progress. The Japanese was told to return the next day for his answer and, upon the advice of the Military Information Division, he was told that permission to travel in the Philippines was refused because the Commanding General did not desire to place any obstacle in the way of the officer's leaving the Philippines at the earliest practical moment. Captain Tanaka left the Philippines within two or three days. Inquiry developed the fact that Captain Tanaka was an officer belonging to the General Staff of the Japanese Army and it was perfectly evident that he had been sent to the Philippines for the purpose of gathering information concerning the Islands and the inhabitants and perhaps getting in contact with the insurgent elements. It also developed that another officer of the Japanese General Staff had been killed while actually engaged in serving with the Philippine insurgents in southern Luzon a few months before. A few days after the departure of Captain Tanaka, the confidential agents of the Military Information Division of the Philippines discovered that an additional Japanese officer was in Manila posing as an agent for a boat building firm. Upon interviewing this gentlemen, it developed that he had blue prints for a comparatively small sailing schooner and that was all the equipment he had which would entitle him to pose as an agent for the boat building firm. It was hinted to this gentlemen that his presence in Manila was no longer desired and he also quietly disappeared.

The desire of the man known as Robinson who was living in Tokyo to return to the Philippines Islands was mentioned above. This man evidently believed that it was necessary for anyone who had been formerly connected with the insurgent movement to show proof that he was not now hostile to the United States before he would be allowed re-entry to the Philippines. He, therefore, forwarded to the Army headquarters in Manila a large amount of correspondence and other documents connected with his activities in Tokyo, applying at the same time for permission to return to the Philippines permanently. Permission was given him to return which he did and shortly after reaching the Philippines he discovered that it would not have been necessary for him to submit any of the correspondence as proof of his loyalty to the United States. Upon discovering this, he applied to have the papers returned to him. He made this application to the Provost Marshal of the Philippines who at that time was General Franklin Bell, afterwards Chief of Staff of the Army. General Bell believed that these papers should be returned to Robinson and so advised the Commanding General. When this question was put up to the Military Information Division it was pointed out to the Commanding General that there was much important information in the correspondence showing the activities of the Japanese Government in connection with probable plans for activities against the Philippine Islands by Japan and that these papers should be retained. As a compromise it was proposed to return to Robinson those documents which were considered of little importance and copies of those which were known to be of importance, the originals being retained in the files of the Military Information Division of the Philippine Islands. Across the face of the original documents returned to Robinson was written in red ink, "Copies on file in the Military Information Division of the Philippine Islands" and across the face of the copies which were returned to him was written also in red ink, "Originals on file in the Military Information Division of the Philippine Islands." This decision was not at all pleasing to General Bell and from that time on he was never favorably inclined to the Military Information Division.

THE FINAL MEMORANDA 11

This incident is noted for two reasons. First to show how interested the Japanese Government was, even at that period, concerning the future of the Philippines and to note the effect which the incident had on the attitude of General Bell toward the Military Information Division which had far-flung results in the future.

During 1902 after much letter writing and other correspondence the Military Information Division of the Philippines was made a branch of the Military Information Division of the Adjutant General's Office of the Army. Upon the establishment of the General Staff system in 1903 it automatically became a branch of the Second (Military Information) Division of the General Staff. When the latter was merged with the Third (War College) Division in 1908 the Military Information Division of the Philippines continued to function as a military information unit, its reports being forwarded to the War College Division.

In 1904 the first class of the War College Division was convened. At this time the Army War College building was under construction but not yet ready for occupancy and the Army War College occupied a private house on Jackson Square. This building was replaced, of course, many years ago by the office building which now stands at this location. The first class consisted of only five or six officers, one of these was General John J. Pershing, although he did not finish the course because he was made a Brig. Gen. from the grade of Captain and ordered to the Philippines to take charge of the operations then in progress against the Moros at Mindanao and the Sulu archipelago. During this session the Army War College found it most convenient to call upon the Second (Military Information) Division of the General Staff for material which had been gathered, filed and carded over the years by the Military Information Division of the Adjutant General's Office.

The writer remembers that practically every morning a push cart would appear at the quarters of the Army War College loaded with books and documents which had been requested by the authorities of the Army War College for use of the college. This material, of course, was returned as soon as it had answered its purpose. This incident is mentioned because of the bearing it had on the abolition of the Military Information Division of the General Staff in 1908.

It will be remembered that following the Boxer Rebellion in China various nations including the United States established garrisons in Peking and Tientsin with detachments on the railroad between Tientsin and Mukden. This of course was for the purpose of protecting foreign nationals and making it possible for them to escape to the seaboard in case of another anti-foreign uprising similar to the Boxer Rebellion. In 1906 it was decided that a topographical map and report should be made of the routes, both rail and road, which led from Peking and Tientsin to the sea. At this time no topographical map of this area was available and it was considered a military necessity that one be available for use in case of need.

For this purpose two officers were sent from the Military Information Division of the Philippines to China leaving Manila in July of this year and returning in December. These officers covered the railroad from Peking via Tientsin to Taku at the mouth of the Pai-Ho, as well as the Pai-Ho from its mouth to a point just east of Tungchow. Also the railroad from Tungchow to Mukden which runs parallel to the coast was mapped from Tang-Ku to Shan-Hai-Quan where the railroad passes thru the great wall of China into Manchuria. In addition the old highway from Peking to Shan-Hai-Quan via Tungchow was also mapped.

As illustrating the close watch which agents of the Japanese Government residing in countries other than their own, kept on the activities of other people in these countries the following incidents are interesting.

While working out of Tientsin the writer lived at a pension in the British Concession of the city using his own name, but, of course without any title or anything else which would indicate that he was a member of the military service. The only address which he gave was his own name in care of the American Consulate in Tientsin. Upon returning from a trip the writer was favored with a visit from the postmaster of the Japanese postoffice in Tientsin. Upon being asked why he was favored with this call the postmaster produced a letter addressed to the writer in care of the American Consulate in Tientsin. When asked why the Japanese postmaster was bringing this letter in person instead of sending it to the point at which it was addressed, the postmaster replied with a knowing smile, "Well, I knew the Captain had been on a trip for three weeks and I thought he would like to have his mail as soon as he returned so I bring it over." When asked how he knew that the writer was at this particular pension he replied with another knowing smile, "You have Japanese cook."

Another incident which occurred during this mission in China which is interesting and to a certain extent instructive as to the attitude held by well-informed Chinese officials toward the American government at this period. While working around the territory in the neighborhood of Shan-Hai-Kwan the writer lived at a hotel kept by an ex-British soldier and his wife just east of the tracks of the Tientsin-Mukden railroad. Taking his meals at this hotel was a Chinese gentleman usually appearing in European clothes and evidently a man of education. While working out of Shan-Hai-Kwan to the south, the writer used the railroad in order to reach points at a distance from Shan-Hai-Kwan which had to be

THE FINAL MEMORANDA   13

covered. The only early-morning train available was a freight and that obliged him to occupy the caboose on that train. The third morning on which the writer took this train he found attached to the caboose a day coach which was entirely empty. When he attempted to board the caboose the conductor motioned him down and ushered him into the day coach saying that it had been provided for him. That evening while at supper at the hotel the hotel proprietor came to the writer's table and said that the Chinese gentleman, who occupied a table in a different part of the room desired to talk to him, which request, was, of course, granted. When the Chinese gentleman introduced himself in perfect English as Captain S. H. Yung saying that he had been captain of one of the Chinese war vessels which was destroyed by the Japanese fleet during the Chinese-Japanese War in 1895. He said he came from a Canton family which was well-known and liked by the Empress Dowager and that after the war was over he was given the position of station master at Shan-Hai-Kwan which position he was still occupying. He said that while he did not know what the writer was doing in China he was quite sure that it was for the purpose of gathering informations which would be of use to the American Government under certain contingencies and that if that were the case he was very much pleased that such action was being taken because he knew enough of the Americans and the principles under which the American government was established to know that the United States was China's friend and that any information concerning China would not be used to her detriment. The writer, of course, did not acknowledge that the Chinese man's supposition was correct but neither did he try to deny it. When asked if he was responsible for the placing of the day coach on the freight train he said that he was and that the caboose of a Chinese freight train was no place for an American gentleman.

Some years later another group of Army officers was sent from the Military Information Division of the Philippines to China for the purpose of mapping the territory as outlined by the work of the party in 1906. In some way the presence of this group of officers became known to the Japanese who informed the Chinese government of the fact that there was a group of American Army officers gathering military information in North China. Whereupon the Chinese government inquired of the United States government as to what this group of Army officers was doing in China and it thereupon became necessary to remove them before very much work had been accomplished. As will be stated later, this work was completed in 1911 by a group of officers sent from the Military Information Division of the Philippines for that purpose.

At the request of President Theodore Roosevelt, the Military Information Division, then of course the Second (Military Information) Division of the General Staff, was charged with the preparation of weekly memoranda concerning the activities and apparent intentions of the Japanese all over the world. A copy of these reports were furnished to the President of the United States, the Secretary of War and the Secretary of the Navy. This series of reports began in early 1907 and very largely as the result of the information contained in these reports the President in the late spring or early summer of 1907 called a meeting consisting of the Secretary and Assistant Secretary of War, the Secretary and Assistant Secretary of the Navy, the Chief of Staff of the Army, the Chief of Naval Operations, the ranking Admiral of the Navy and the President of the Army War College. To this group the President explained that he was convinced that Japan was preparing for a hostile move against the United States at sometime in the not too distant future and that it was his opinion that the Fleet should be sent from the East Coast to the Pacific and be based on the West Coast of the United States.

Upon the completion of the President's talk, the Assistant Secretary of War rose to his feet and said, "Mr. President, do you believe that the Japanese would dare attack the West Coast of the United States? Why, Mr. President, the women of the Pacific Coast would drive the Japanese into the sea with their broom sticks." In reply the President gazed at the Assistant Secretary with his well-known grin and said, "Oh, sit down, sit down." The President then asked the Admiral in charge of the Fleet how soon he could start the Fleet around the Horn to the Pacific. The Admiral said in three weeks. Whereupon, the President issued verbal orders directing that the Fleet prepare and sail for the Pacific Coast at the end of three weeks.

Shortly after the close of this meeting, after the Admiral had returned to the Navy Department, he called the President and said that his estimate for the Fleet to prepare for the move was entirely too short because preparations for refueling and other measures on the South American coast would be necessary and those arrangements could not be made within the time he had specified. So the President authorized an extension of such time as would be necessary to make the preparations for fueling, etc., which would be required for the trip around the Horn.

While this move was supposed to have been kept as a secret, within a few weeks it leaked out and the pressure which was brought to bear on the President by business and political interests of the Eastern seaboard was so strong that eventually he had to modify the orders concerning the Fleet. These orders were changed to require the Fleet to make a trip around the world including, of course, in this trip certain ports of Japan. This was the real story of the well-known voyage of the United States Fleet around the world which began in Dec. 1907 and ended in Feb. 1909 and as will be realized there was no intention originally to make this world trip but only to shift the Fleet from the East to the West Coast. This incident was related to the writer by the President of the Army War College, General Witherspoon immediately upon his return from the meeting.

In 1903, when the General Staff was organized, the Military Information Division of the Adjutant General's Office was transferred to the General Staff as the Second (Military Information) Division. The offices, clerks and material of the Division including its records, a very considerable library and a very well manned photograph gallery were transferred bodily to the Second Division of the General Staff.

At this time the Military Information Division was quartered on the second floor of the Lemon Building on New York Avenue a very short distance from the old State, War and Navy Building. The photograph gallery was housed on the top floor of a building on 17th street almost directly across from the main entrance of the old State, War and Navy Building. This building is now occupied by the National Council for the Prevention of War.

In June of 1907 the Army War College Division with its personnel, property and records was moved from its temporary quarters in the private house on Jackson Square to the now completed War College building. When the War College Division began operations in its new location it discovered that the information which had been compiled by the Military Information Division of the Adjutant General's Office and which was now in the possession of the Military Information Division of the General Staff was very badly needed. It had been easily obtainable while the War College Division was quartered in the house on Jackson Place but now it was five miles from the Lemon Building and the obtaining of this information daily as had been the custom was impossible. At this time there was only one automobile in use by the War College Division and that was a White Steamer which was assigned to the President of the Army War College. Had there been sufficient automobile transportation it is possible that the disastrous incident about to be related would not have occurred. About May of 1908 the President of the Army War College went to the Chief of Staff (at that time General Franklin Bell) and suggested that the Military Information Division be moved bodily to the War College Building. He said he made this request because the information compiled by the Military Information Division of the Adjutant General's Office and the maps which had been collected were of extreme value to the College in its work and he desired to have this material where it was of easy access to the officials and students of the War College. The President of the Army War College said that there was no reason why the two Divisions, the Third (Army War College)

Division and the Second (Military Information) Division, could not function in the same building and remain completely separate organizationally. To this proposal the Chief of Staff agreed and shortly afterwards the Military Information Division was moved bodily to the Army War College Building.

Not more than a month after the Military Information Division had been moved into the War College building the President of the Army War College again went to the Chief of Staff and said that the housing of two completely separate organizations in one building had not worked out as well as he had believed it would; therefore he proposed that the Military Information Division be abolished and that its personnel and material be merged into the Army War College Division which would then be renumbered as the Second Division. Probably because of his prejudice against military information work which, as mentioned before, he acquired while Provost Marshal of the Philippine Islands, the Chief of Staff readily agreed to this second proposition and orders were issued to effect it. On June 24, 1908 the Second (Military Information) Division of the General Staff was dissolved and incorporated into the War College Division of the General Staff.

This resulted in the placing of all the personnel and material of the Military Information Division in the War College Division. The officers were transferred as a part of the personnel of the Army War College Division. The clerks were placed in the pool of the Army War College under the Chief Clerk of the War College Division. The map section and the draftsmen connected with it were placed under the Executive Secretary of the War College Division. All of the records and correspondence of the old Military Information Division of the Adjutant General's Office were placed in the War College files. The photographic gallery which was then quartered in the basement of the War College Division was placed under the Chief Clerk of the War College Division. The handling of the military attaches was placed under the Secretary of the War College Division. The only semblance of a military information service which remained was the establishment of a committee of the War College, the chairman of which was the President of the Army War College, to deal with military information matters. The membership of this committee consisted of practically every officer on the War College staff.

Everyone who is familiar with the workings of large committees can realize what happened and it goes without saying that a committee of this size and of this composition was not in any position to handle Military Information and as a matter of fact from the time of the consolidation no military intelligence work was accomplished either in the

THE FINAL MEMORANDA 17

United States or abroad except the reports of the military attaches continued to be received and filed in the War College files. These reports were sent around on inter-office memoranda to the various officers of the War College Division but none of the information was made available to the service at large as had been done by the Military Information Division before its demise. In the summer of 1909 or 1910, a group of officers then serving in the Philippine Islands were sent by the Military Information Division of the Philippine Islands to China to continue work on the topographical map in the Peking area which was begun in 1906. It will be noted that this work was being carried on by the Military Information Division of the Philippines and not the Military Information Division of the General Staff in Washington since at this time that organization had ceased to exist.

The group of officers sent to China in 1909 or 1910 had only been at work a comparatively short time when the State Department in Washington received a communication from the Chinese Government inquiring what this group of United States Army officers was doing in China. This inquiry, of course, led to the speedy recall of the officers then engaged in the mapping work as the United States government had no explanation to offer as to why these officers were working in China. Unquestionably this inquiry by the Chinese government was prompted by the Japanese who were keeping an extremely close watch upon the movements of Americans in China and other parts of Asia.

In July of 1911 a third group of officers then serving in the Philippines was sent to continue the work on the topographical map of the Peking area. Great caution was taken by this group in leaving Manila in order that it might not be known to the Japanese agents then active in Manila and the Philippine Islands. This group proceeded by steamer from Manila to Hong Kong and thence by steamer to Shanghai and so up the Yangtze to Hankow. Upon reaching Hankow it was discovered that the revolution against the Manchu Dynasty had broken out further up the Yangtze River and it was necessary to leave Hankow without delay. By the friendly advice of a British officer in the service of the Pehan railroad the group was notified of a special train from Hankow to Peking and was warned that this was probably the last train that would be permitted to leave Hankow for an indefinite period. Taking advantage of this information the group was able to board the train and proceed to Peking whence it proceeded at once to Tientsin by rail. In Tientsin bicycles were purchased and two houseboats were hired together with two interpreters and the group separated into two parties and proceeded up the Pai-Ho River working out from the river to complete the map in that region. Contact was maintained with the Consulate General at Tientsin although the Consul never was informed as to who the individuals of the group were or what their business was in China. Contact was also maintained with an official of the British American Tobacco Company and arrangements were made which would allow the individuals of the group to act as employees of that company should their activities be questioned. With the exception of a portion of the territory which was flooded by the cutting of certain dikes by the Chinese, the area included in the railway from Tientsin to Peking, the Manchurian highway from Peking to Tungchow and the Pai-Ho river from Tungchow to Tientsin was filled in. This work was completed in December of 1911 and the group returned to Manila.

In this third expedition it was found necessary, in order to obtain the names of the various villages which were mapped, to have the chief officer of each village write the name in the conventional Chinese signs. It was found to be impractical to get the pronunciation of the names correctly. Upon returning to Manila it was believed it would be possible to find an educated Chinese man from North China then living in Manila who would be able to transliterate the Chinese ideographs and so obtain the English spellings of the names. However, application to the Chinese Consul in Manila revealed that amongst the 60,000 Chinese then living in Manila there was not a single man from North China. It therefore became necessary for the officer charged with the work of this particular expedition to learn how to use an English-Chinese dictionary in order to transliterate into English the Chinese names of the villages. This was done later in Washington, D.C.

In May of 1915 the writer was again detailed a member of the General Staff Corps and assigned to duty with the War College Division and, like every other officer on duty in the War College Division placed on the Military Information Committee. It will be remembered that the Second (Military Information) Division of the General Staff was merged with the War College Division on June 14, 1908 and so passed out of existence. To make the picture of the present situation clear it would be well to recall some of the duties formerly performed by the Military Information Division of the Adjutant General's Office and by the Second (Military Information) Division of the General Staff during the brief period of its existence. One of the vital functions of that service, which we now designate as military intelligence was the distribution to the armed services of the information concerning foreign countries covering the military and economic conditions and all other information which would be of military value to the United States. This information was distributed by the publication of pamphlets prepared by the Division from information gathered by it and was frequently accompanied by maps compiled in the map section of the Division. Certain information was also made available to the armed services thru the two service papers, the "Army

THE FINAL MEMORANDA 19

and Naval Journal" and the "Army and Navy Register" and thru publication in the various magazines of the armed services. In addition to this of course information considered too confidential for publication was communicated to bureau chiefs and commanding officers by documents prepared by the Military Information Division and sent directly to these individuals. With the absorption of the Military Information Division by the War College Division this activity ceased completely since there was no organization formed with duties of this character. During the existence of the old Military Information Division of the Adjutant General's Office and of the Second (Military Information) Division of the General Staff, officers especially selected for the purpose were sent to certain foreign countries for the purpose of obtaining topographical and other information which could not be obtained thru the ordinary channels or by the military attaches assigned to those countries. With the exception of work performed by the Military Information Division of the Philippine Islands on its own this work also ceased upon the disappearance from the scene of the Military Information Division of the General Staff.

In May of 1915, war had been in existence in Europe for about nine months. Reports about it of course were received from all the military attaches concerning operations within their observation. In addition the United States had sent a military mission to France which was constantly returning reports on the military situation and activities. These reports all came to the War College Division and were filed with the War College records. Most of the reports were of course circulated to the various members of the War College Division before being filed. None of the information was distributed to the armed services as had been the custom previously.

It will be recalled that at this period General Pershing was operating in Mexican country with the consent of course of the Mexican government for the purpose of capturing Pancho Villa after the latter had raided the town of Columbus, New Mexico. An information officer was serving with General Pershing's headquarters and made frequent and copious reports which finally reached the War College Division, many of them in the form of telegrams. Whether or not they were ever filed in the War College Division the writer doubts since in May when he joined the War College Division he found a large table piled high with these telegrams which had never been filed. An officer had been assigned to read these telegrams and as far as could be ascertained, that was about all that was done with them. Some of the activities of the Intelligence officer with General Pershing's headquarters were extremely interesting but hardly orthodox.

Upon his assignment to the War College Division in May of 1915 the writer discovered that he was the only officer in the War College Division who had had any training or experience in what we now designate as military intelligence. Realizing that no intelligence activities were being performed by the Army, that the United States was rapidly approaching its entrance into the war and that the Army was being deprived of practically all of the information being received by the War College Division from our military attaches and other agents abroad, numerous memoranda were submitted thru the President of the Army War College Division to the Chief of Staff of the Army calling attention to the present state of affairs and advocating the re-establishment of a Military Information Division in the General Staff. These memoranda were approved by the President of the Army War College but were entirely ignored by the Chief of Staff. It was suggested to the President of the Army War College who was, it will be remembered, the chairman of the Military Information Committee, that an attempt be made to make at least some of the information coming into the War College Division available to the Army. The President agreed that this was a desirable thing to do but insisted that everybody in the War College Division was too busy to read and edit the material so that they could be made available for publication. He finally suggested that it might be possible that the Command and Staff School at Fort Leavenworth might be able to take some of these reports and themselves publish them for distribution to the Army. The Commandant of the School was communicated with and agreed that the school would be glad to carry out such a plan. To this end a report was selected (by whom is not known by the writer) and sent to the school at Leavenworth which proceeded to carry out its promise. Upon the publication of this report the British Government very strongly protested to our government the publication of the report since it had been obtained by our military attache in London from the Corps of Engineers of the British Army under promise of complete secrecy. The report contained some of the most confidential information concerning the engineering operations in the possession of the British Army. After that experience, no more reports were sent to the school at Leavenworth and the reports coming in from abroad detailing the information concerning the war which was now becoming a real war were filed in the War College files without any of it being made available to the military services at large. The only thing which was accomplished was the issuance of an order in 1916 which made possible the assignment of officers to each department headquarters in the United States with military information duties.

On April 6, 1917 the United States entered the war against Germany and immediately thereafter both the British and French governments sent missions to Washington to consult with our government authorities on

THE FINAL MEMORANDA   21

the proper future proceedings. Each of these missions contained an officer representing the military intelligence organization of that country, who was referred to the War College Division since that was the only organization in the Army at that time which was even remotely connected with what we now know as military intelligence. However, since there was no organization in existence to handle such matters, these activities consisted entirely in conversations.

Upon the declaration of war and with the consent of the President of the Army War College the writer went to the Chief of Staff and explained the situation with respect to military information as it existed in the army at that time. The Chief of Staff said he could see no reason for the United States Army to have any such thing as a military information service and that if as explained the British and French armies had such organizations and were receiving the necessary information concerning the enemy there was no reason why we should not say to them, "Here, we are now ready for service – we would be pleased if you hand over to us all the necessary information concerning the enemy which your intelligence services have obtained." No amount of talking or argument could change the Chief of Staff's opinion and after two or three such interviews, he became exasperated and ordered the writer to cease his efforts with respect to the organization of a military information service. He also gave him strict orders that he was not to approach the Secretary of War on the subject. By the middle of April it became perfectly evident that no action could be expected from the Chief of Staff. This seemed to pretty well block any chance of the Army's obtaining a military intelligence service but the matter was so vital that the writer decided to employ other means to accomplish the objective if possible.

The then Chief of Staff was a fine officer and later in the war became a member of the Supreme War Council in Europe. However, he apparently knew nothing whatever about the vital importance of an intelligence service or how impossible it was to carry on a war without the necessary information concerning the enemy organization and efficient service for the discovery and elimination of spies and saboteurs within our own country and armed forces. Unfortunately this could also be said concerning many of the higher officers of the Army at that time and it is also applicable to many of the officers of higher rank during the period between the First and Second World Wars. As has been mentioned before, the writer was the only officer then on duty in the War College Division who had had any previous experience or training in intelligence matters and for this reason he felt responsible that a suitable organization for intelligence work be created and put to work at the earliest possible moment. As no action to this effect could be expected from the Chief of Staff it was evident that other means would have to be employed if this was to be effected.

At this particular time one of the best known and respected women novelists of the United States appeared in Washington. She had been engaged for some weeks in visiting various training camps of the Army at the request of the Secretary of War and had come to Washington to make a report to him on the matter. Merely by chance, the writer was detailed to escort this lady to certain of the installations in the immediate vicinity of Washington. In conversation she mentioned the fact that she had lately been in touch with an American young man who had been serving with the British Military Intelligence in Europe and was quite audible on the subject of the importance which the Allied military authorities in Europe placed on the work being accomplished by their intelligence services. The writer explained to this lady that there was no military intelligence service in the United States Army and there had not been since 1908. He also explained to her the methods that had been employed to persuade the Chief of Staff to take the matter up and provide an intelligence service and how these methods had failed and that in addition that he had been forbidden to go to the Secretary of War in the matter. She became quite excited and said that she should certainly report this matter to the Secretary of War that very day. Further events revealed that she had done just this.

About a week before this occurrence the writer ascertained that the Secretary of War took breakfast each morning in a certain club with the Chief of Police of the District of Columbia. This latter gentleman was well known to the writer and with the hope that information concerning the military information situation might be conveyed to the Secretary of War by the Chief of Police. He explained to the latter what the situation was and the problem involved and asked him if he would talk to the Secretary of War concerning it. This the Chief of Police promised to do and did.

On the 30th day of April a telephone message from the office of the Secretary of War to the President of the Army War College directed that the writer report to the Secretary of War at once. When he reported to the Secretary he was asked to describe briefly what was being done in the way of military intelligence work in the British and French armies in Europe and what the United States Army organization for intelligence was. After about a half hour's conversation the writer was told that within 48 hours an order would be sent to the President of the War College Division directing that an organization of intelligence be set up at once. As a result the War College Division on May 3, 1917 issued instructions for the formation of an intelligence branch of the Army War

College for the purpose of handling Military information for the Army. Because he was the only person immediately available with any knowledge whatever of military intelligence organization and activities, the writer was detailed in charge of this branch and directed to organize it as rapidly as possible.

As it appeared that our forces would operate most closely with the units of the British Army it was decided to base the organization for the United States on the Military Intelligence organization of the British Army and for that reason our organization was named Military Intelligence instead of the former name of Military Information. Most valuable assistance was rendered by the British Intelligence officer who accomplished the British Military Mission sent to the United States. The intelligence officer who accompanied the French Military Mission to the United States was also frequently consulted and much valuable advice obtained from him. However it was not advisable to base our organization on the organization of the French Army since the counter espionage activities in France are handled by the Surete, a non-military organization, the personnel of which was composed of civilians. This organization was not under control of the French War office completely.

Very fortunately the officer selected to prepare Tables of Organization for the United States forces to be sent to Europe was sent down to the Army War College where he did his work. This officer was among the few officers at the time who really knew the importance of military intelligence service and so wrote into the Tables of Organization which he was preparing for our overseas army the combat intelligence organization for corps, division, brigade, regiment and battalion.

Without attempting to go into the details of the organization of the Military Intelligence Branch it is believed that it would be interesting and perhaps instructive to give a brief resume of how the organization was effected and the reasons for the methods employed. In order that the provisions of the order establishing the Branch might be promptly carried out certain authority was given to the officer in charge of the Branch. He was allowed to request the detail of a limited number of officers of the regular service for duty with the Branch. The first officer selected was a man who had served in the Military Information Division of the Philippines and had been on at least one confidential mission to China. He was appointed Secretary of the Military Intelligence Branch and remained in that position until he was sent overseas to be attached to the Intelligence Section of General Pershing's Headquarters in the early fall of 1918. To this officer should be given a major amount of the credit for the organization and the accomplishments of the Military Intelligence Branch. His name was Alexander B. Coxe.

There were never more than six officers of the regular service on duty in the Branch at any one time. The vast majority of the officer personnel consisted of civilians commissioned in the National Army and detailed for duty in the Branch. In order to secure the officer personnel for the Branch the officer in charge was given authority to request that selected civilians be commissioned in the National Army and immediately detailed for duty in the Military Intelligence Branch. He was also authorized to obtain from the Civil Service the necessary clerks, stenographers and other personnel necessary to carry on the work. In order that the best possible material in the way of officer personnel might be secured, a group of men who were known to have very wide acquaintance throughout the United States along various lines were first selected and commissioned and assigned to the Branch. Then, with the advice of these men, additional civilians were selected and commissioned in the National Army and detailed for duty in the Branch as the necessity for their particular service arose. No officer was commissioned until there was a plain need for his service in the particular field for which he had been recommended. This plan was continued during the entire period of the organization of the Branch. In order to set up such special sections as the Code and Cipher Section and the Translation Section as well as the group of civilians who handled the organization of Plant Protection, the Intelligence Branch was authorized to select civilians and then have them placed in the ranks of the Civil Service in a temporary status.

The Map Section, formerly a part of the Second (Military Information) Division of the General Staff was assigned to the Military Intelligence Branch as was the Photograph Gallery. In addition, the supervision of the personnel and reports of military attaches was also assigned to the Military Intelligence Branch. However, the Library and files of the old Military Information Division of the Adjutant General's Office remained in the War College and so far as is known are still there.

The authorization for the establishment of the Military Intelligence Branch had scarcely been made before demands were made on it for service which in many instances had really nothing to do with military intelligence matters. However, they were matters which needed immediate and serious attention and there seemed to be no other organization in the War Department which could be made available to handle them. The first of these questions to come up was the subject of the guarding of the various offices of the War Department not only those in the State, War and Navy Building but also those in the countless offices which had been occupied in various office buildings in the city of Washington by the various branches of the Army. In the State, War and Navy Building there was a desk manned by certain uniformed guards who interviewed and assisted visitors in finding the particular office which they desired to

THE FINAL MEMORANDA

visit, but there was no attempt whatever to ascertain whether or not such visitors were enemy agents or not. In the buildings occupied in the various parts of the city there were no guards whatever either during the day or night except for the presence perhaps of a janitor.

It would seem that this situation was one which would have appealed to the authorities of the Army as needing correction but that was far from the case. It required considerable pressure from the highest authorities of the Army to accomplish this objective. Finally after considerable delay and after the following two incidents a system of checks and guards was established over all of the offices occupied by the War Department in the city of Washington which dealt with what is now known as classified information.

The incident referred to was as follows: In a certain office building the Ordnance Department had established an office under charge of a civilian which among other records contained those of the places where quantities of high explosives were stored in the Western part of the United States and the amounts stored at each place. One day a young officer in the uniform of a captain of the United States Ordnance Department appeared at that office announcing that his name was so-and-so and that he came from Colonel so-and-so, who was the officer in charge of the particular section to which the office pertained. This young ordnance officer demanded a list of the localities in which high explosives were stored in the Western United States together with the amounts. The civilian in charge of the office asked permission to phone the Colonel of Ordnance in charge of the office to confirm this request of the young ordnance officer and permission to give him the records he requested. Whereupon the ordnance officer became extremely indignant and wanted to know whether or not his uniform was not recognized by the civilian in charge of the office. He finally became quite abusive but the civilian stuck to his guns and refused to give the information until he had been allowed to telephone to the Colonel for the permission. Whereupon the ordnance officer left the office. The civilian then telephoned to the Colonel and gave the name and a description of the young officer who had just visited him and was informed that there was no officer in the Ordnance Department answering to that name or description and that the Colonel had not authorized anyone to seek information from the civilian on the matter of stored high explosives in the Western United States. Whereupon the matter was reported to the Military Intelligence Branch which, with the aid of the Army and of the police of the city of Washington threw a cordon around the city of Washington with instructions to pick up anyone having the description as given by the civilian in charge of the Ordnance office and hold him for investigation. However, no such person was ever discovered and in fact the pseudo ordnance officer had disappeared. There seemed to be little doubt but that this young man was an enemy agent.

The second incident was as follows: one evening about six o'clock, two carefully selected officers of the Intelligence Branch were ordered to report to the officer in charge of the Branch. They were given a list of certain offices occupied in the city of Washington by the Military. They were instructed to visit these offices between eight o'clock in the evening and four o'clock the following morning and obtain any confidential papers or other confidential information which would be of value to an enemy agent. They were to don civilian clothes and in visiting the offices were to conduct themselves as an enemy agent might. The confidential documents which they were able to obtain were to be marked very carefully showing the office from which obtained and the time at which they were taken. These two officers were directed to report to the officer in charge of the Military Intelligence Branch the following morning in the Branch office with the articles which they had obtained and the time at which they were taken. These two officers were of course enjoined upon to maintain complete secrecy. The following morning the two officers reported with the selection of confidential documents and communications which they had obtained under the instructions which have been outlined above. The documents were obtained from unlocked desks and from tables in the various offices and some of them from safes the combinations of which had been found on cards in unlocked drawers in these offices. Upon the arrival of the usual time of offices to open the following morning the officer in charge of the Military Intelligence Branch began calling up the officer in charge of the office which had been visited and asked them if they had certain documents in their possession. Upon being informed that they had they were asked to see if they had them. A search of course revealed that the document in question was missing. Whereupon they were told where the documents were, that they would be returned and why and how they had been obtained and under what circumstances.

When these two incidents became known to the heads of departments it aided greatly in convincing the Army authorities that guards over offices had now become a necessity.

The Civil Service was pouring into Washington literally thousands of clerks and stenographers from the various Civil Service offices throughout the country. Upon arrival all these clerks were assigned to various offices in the government as requests for service were made. Nothing whatever was known concerning these clerks except the fact that they had been appointed by the Civil Service. Even the heads of the offices had no way of knowing whether or not they were being served by the same individual two days in succession – the only thing they knew was that they had been given instructions to report to a certain office and that they had done. It was therefore necessary to provide for these clerks at least some sort of identification card so that only those persons authorized to be in a certain office building would be admitted and after much argument and no little pressure from above an identification card with photograph was provided for the employees. The question, however, as to loyalty was never taken up although certain measures were approved which made it possible to observe those who because of their associations or activities became subject to investigation.

From the beginning of its activities the Military Intelligence Branch cooperated with all of the various investigatory agencies of the government particularly with the Federal Bureau of Investigation which had been established not so many years previously. It also worked very closely with the secret service section of the Department of State although the Department of State had always denied that it possessed any such section. The only investigating organization of the government which did not cooperate was the United States Secret Service which was specifically forbidden to take part in any such activity much to the chagrin of the then head of the service.

As everyone in the Army will remember, the "Army List and Directory" was a monthly publication which gave the name, rank, and address of every officer in the Army together with considerable information concerning the location and duties of various organizations of the Army. Very early in its work the Military Intelligence Branch discovered that certain suspected persons were using the "Army List and Directory" for the purpose of sending information overseas to the Central Powers and the Military Intelligence Branch felt that the publication of the "Army List and Directory" should be suspended for the duration of the war. That met with very determined opposition on the part of the Adjutant General but it was finally suspended. It also developed that menus for Thanksgiving dinner and Christmas and New Year's were being prepared for the various organizations and training camps throughout the United States; in many instances these menus gave complete roster of the company together in some cases with photographs of the officers and non-commissioned officers of the camp. The Military Intelligence Branch suspected that enemy agents were collecting these menus and that they were being shipped overseas in several different ways. When it was recommended that the publication and distribution of these menus be stopped it was discovered that the preparation of them had been taken in hand by various large corporations and considerable amounts of money were involved. Naturally much pressure against the recommendation that they be abolished arose at once. The matter was finally compromised, allowing the preparation of the menus but making sure that they were held before distribution until the units about which they pertained were safely in Europe.

In the early summer of 1917 the Government authorities in Copenhagen picked up a very large shipment of objects intended for transmittal to the United States for use by saboteurs. These objects consisted of imitations of lumps of coal, dispatch cases, field glass cases, fountain pens, and other such objects all loaded with TNT and provided with fuses. There were also large quantities of carbonundum in the shape of crayons which were intended for use in putting automobile and airplane engines out of commission as well as for use in the axles of railroad cars. Samples of these objects with the TNT still in them but with the fuses removed were sent by the Danish authorities to the United States and were transmitted to the office of the Military Intelligence Branch. For several days enough TNT was on the floor under the table of the officer in charge to blow that part of Washington into bits had there been a means of exploding it.

It will be remembered that a very large number of cargo ships sailing from eastern ports of the United States for France were burned at sea because of the ignition of the cargo. Investigation soon developed the fact that these fires were caused by incendiary bombs placed in the cargo by enemy agents working on the docks where the ships were loaded. Intensive effort to discover the top enemy agent handling this matter was inaugurated and the man who made the incendiary bombs became frightened and escaped to Cuba. He had been in Cuba only a short time until his suspicious actions excited the interest of the intelligence service of the Cuban Army and he was arrested. The Department of Justice through the Federal Bureau of Investigation took the matter up and this man was deported from Cuba and was held as a prisoner by the Department of Justice. He was placed in a small laboratory near Washington and required to produce the same sort of incendiary bombs that he had made for use on board the ships. In one of his experiments an explosion injured him rather severely but he eventually recovered. The man was never tried, for what reason is not known, and in the latter part of 1917 or early 1918 he contracted pneumonia and died.

In the early summer of 1917 the Federal Bureau of Investigation informed the Military Intelligence Branch that an individual had been detained by the customs authorities in the port of New York who was believed to have in his possession certain secret ink and the Federal Bureau of Investigation wanted to know if the Military Intelligence Branch desired to have him brought to Washington for an interview. In compliance with a request from the Branch, the individual was brought

THE FINAL MEMORANDA

to Washington and interviewed by an officer of the Military Intelligence Branch. He proved to be a young man, the son of a woman still in Europe, who had been caught in Germany by the declaration of war. He had gone to the German authorities and asked to be allowed to leave Germany but for a long time was refused such permission. Finally he was told that if he would do certain things after he arrived in the United States that this permission would be given him and he finally agreed to carry out the instructions. What he was expected to do was this, he was to be furnished with certain articles of wearing apparel which were impregnated with a secret ink and he was given instructions as to how to obtain the ink from these articles. After obtaining the ink he was to make reports of certain matters which the German Government desired to know and using this ink for the reports he was to take them to Cuba where they were to be transmitted to Germany.

He took ship from Germany to Copenhagen whence he proposed to proceed to the United States. While on the ship between Germany and Denmark he realized that he was being watched by a German agent. This so alarmed him that when he arrived in Copenhagen he went to the American embassy and acknowledged that he had in his possession articles of wearing apparel impregnated with secret ink which he had agreed to use in making reports to the German government after he reached the United States. He gave to the Embassy representative one of the impregnated handkerchiefs which he had been furnished. It was because of this that his identity was known when he reached the port of New York where he was picked up by the customs authorities and turned over to the Federal Bureau of Investigation. He still had in his possession some impregnated shoe strings and a handkerchief or two. These articles he willingly surrendered to the officers of the Military intelligence Branch who interviewed him and an attempt was made by the Branch to obtain the secret ink using the method described by the young man who had carried the articles.

At this time no individual in the Military Intelligence Branch had any expert knowledge concerning secret ink and while an attempt was made to develop the ink by soaking the articles in distilled water no results whatever were obtained. A short time before this occurrence the Harvard Chemical Laboratory had offered its services to the government for any use to which the government might wish to put it. It was therefore decided to send a sample of the fluid obtained from the impregnated handkerchief to the chemical laboratory for analysis. Within a few days a report was received from the laboratory to the effect that there was nothing in the fluid sent for analysis but pure H_2O and a few grains of starch. In the summer of 1917 when the writer was in the Secret Ink Laboratory of the British Military Intelligence service the officer in charge asked him to sign his name in a book using a perfectly clear fluid for the purpose. After having signed his name the officer in charge brushed a reagent across the signature which then came out as black as the ordinary commercial ink. It was then explained that this was the best secret ink that the German government had used and that it had been sent to the British Intelligence from the United States by the Military Intelligence Branch of the Army for the purpose of investigation and experiment. The British officer in charge then said, "The young officer who sent this sample to us is here in the laboratory now." He called to a young man in the Uniform of the United States Army who was in another part of the room to come over. It developed that this was one of two young men of the Harvard Chemical Laboratory who had attempted to analyze the fluid sent them for analysis and who had reported pure water and starch grains were contained in it. His face was very red when he had to acknowledge that the methods used by the Harvard Chemical Laboratory in analysis were inadequate and that the only reason they did not discover the chemical of which the secret ink was composed was that the method used was not precise enough to discover the very minute quantity which the fluid contained. This ink figured very prominently in the very noted case of a German agent confined in the Tower of London for a considerable period before his execution.

We had scarcely entered the war before dozens of organizations sprang up in various parts of the United States which were to be devoted to the running down of spies. Of course, this sort of thing was an extremely dangerous development and it was evident that these organizations must be stopped in their activities at once. However it was realized that if one of these organizations could be developed into a national group that could be trusted to obey orders and do nothing except what they were told to do that they might be of great value to the government. With this possibility in view a very careful investigation was made of a number of these organizations and one of them with headquarters in Chicago was selected for a more thorough examination. The man in charge was brought to Washington for an interview and after careful investigation it was explained to him what it was expected that an organization of this character could accomplish. He agreed that his group could be so organized as to meet the requirements. He was therefore authorized to go ahead with his organization and make it into a national one on an entirely voluntary basis and that every individual in it was to understand that they were to do absolutely nothing except what they were requested to do by the Military Intelligence Branch in Washington. This was the reason for the organization of what is known as the American Protective League which at one time contained some 65,000 members scattered all over the United States and so placed that any important community of any size had a section of the organization. In the beginning, there was a little trouble in getting some of the members to understand exactly what orders meant and some of the smaller groups did make more or less trouble in questioning the loyalty of persons in their communities. However, that was dealt with a pretty strong hand and within a short time such activities ceased.

Early in 1918 the State Department began calling on the Military Intelligence Branch for the information concerning persons applying for passports to visit European countries in order of course to prevent individuals of suspicious loyalty from reaching Europe. To handle this problem the American Protective League was utilized and a group consisting of the head of the League and some five or six of his assistants were brought to Washington and commissioned. They were assigned to duty in the Military Intelligence Branch and thru this group questions concerning individuals applying for passports could be made very rapidly and that information when obtained was forwarded to the State Department.

Early in 1918 it became apparent to the Military Intelligence Division of the American Expeditionary Force that the information concerning the topographical and other information on Germany and other countries of the Central Powers was far from adequate. To remedy this condition the Military Intelligence Branch in Washington was requested to collect and forward to the Military Intelligence Section of General Pershing's Army in Europe such information as could be gathered in the United States which would be of Military value when time came for the invasion of the territory of Germany and the other Central Powers. Again the services of the American Protective League were called in and books, magazines and published reports were gathered all over the United States by this organization from citizens in the communities in which the organization existed. These were shipped to Washington, and by the Military Intelligence Branch forwarded to the Military Intelligence Division of the American Expeditionary Force. Literally tons of the material was gathered and shipped. The books, magazines and other articles were donated by the individuals who owned them.

At the beginning of the first World War the manufacturing of munitions and other war materials was being conducted almost exclusively in government plants; however, it immediately became evident that this work would have to be taken up by civilian manufacturers and the government rapidly allotted the manufacturing of certain war materials to various individual institutions. While the government plants were under strict guard, no provision had been made for the guarding of the civilian plants when they took over the manufacture of government supplies. It was therefore necessary not only to see that guards were provided but also that means be taken to uncover any suspected disloyal persons in these plants who might engage in sabotage. In order to accomplish this purpose a civilian was selected who was believed capable of handling the matter and he was told to select whatever group of individuals he believed necessary to visit these various civilian plants manufacturing war materials and set up from among the proven loyal employees, undercover operators who would carefully observe the employees of the plant and be in a position to discover any attempts at sabotage. The man who was chosen selected twelve other men and that group proceeded to complete the organization of what came to be known as the Plant Protection System.

The chief of this Plant Protection System declined a commission in the Army because he said he believed he could work better as a civilian than he could as an officer in the Army and so none of the twelve men under him were commissioned. This group of men did a very excellent job of work and their services had never adequately been acknowledged.

The Tables of Organization prepared for the National Army, of which mention was made above, provided the personnel for the collection of combat information. Through this personnel also was distributed to the military authorities involved such military information as it was desired to have distributed by the military intelligence services. Instructions concerning the collection of combat information were issued by the Military Intelligence Branch and that which was necessary to distribute to military commanders and units was so distributed by the Branch. However, the organization provided by the Tables of Organization did not cover the personnel required for the handling of subversive individuals within the ranks of the National Army. To provide for this service it was directed that the intelligence officer in regiments and similar units select enlisted men in the proportion of about one to every fifty enlisted men in their organization. These men were to be selected with extreme care and were then to be instructed by the intelligence officer in accordance with instructions issued by the Military Intelligence Branch. All information concerning individuals in the Army suspected of disloyal or other connections with the enemy forces was forwarded promptly to the Military Intelligence Branch. Close association of the Military Intelligence Branch with the British and French intelligence services made possible the exchange of information concerning all suspects between three services.

This information was carefully carded and constituted what was known as the Suspect List. Lists of suspects in printed pamphlets were frequently received from the Military Intelligence services of both Great

Britain and France and the Suspect List before the end of the war consisted of many hundred thousands of cards. It was very soon found necessary to set up organizations in all of the principal ports of the United States groups known as Port Control Organizations. The personnel of these organizations consisted of officers engaged in intelligence work but also of officials and personnel of both the Immigration and Customs Bureaus. It was the duty of these Port Control Organizations to keep a close watch on the individuals passing in and out of the United States not only as passengers but also those in the crew of the various vessels. Reports of their findings and information gathered was, of course, forwarded directly to the Military Intelligence Branch.

As the necessity for investigations all over the United States became more and more pressing, it became evident that the work would be accelerated if we would set up branches of the Military Intelligence service at various strategic points in the country and authority to do so was requested and obtained. Groups consisting of commissioned officers and civilian clerks were set up in New York City, Philadelphia, Chicago, St. Louis, Salt Lake City, New Orleans, San Francisco and Los Angeles. The size of the group depended upon the work to be done in that particular area.

As the necessity for undercover investigations of individuals and organizations grew, particularly in the Washington, D. C. area, it became evident an organization composed of men who were experts in this sort of work should be set up. To meet this need a number of men whose work in civil life was along these lines, the majority of them selected from the Metropolitan Police of New York City, were brought to Washington and quartered in a private dwelling house in Southeast Washington. These men wore civilian clothes and every precaution to see that their presence in Washington was unknown was taken. They were commanded by a captain also selected from the New York Police Department. The only members of the Military Intelligence Branch who even knew of their existence were the officer in charge of the Branch, the executive officer and the officer who handled the finances of the Branch. This was probably the beginning of the organization later known as the Counter Intelligence Corps.

In the fall of 1917 it became evident that agents of the Central Powers were circulating among the Negro people of the United States. The method of agitation used was by word of mouth and it was evident that measures to counteract the influence of such propaganda must be taken if we were to avoid serious trouble with the Negro population. For this purpose two extremely capable and reliable Negro men were selected after most careful investigation. These men were instructed to circulate among the various communities where unrest was being reported among the Negro population. They were to remain long enough in each community to determine for themselves what the real trouble was and then by conversations and formal talks in Negro churches and other meeting places to persuade the Negroes in the community that the actions being suggested to them by persons who had previously circulated among them would lead to very serious consequences if not abandoned. In order to cover as large an area as possible these two men did not travel together but during the continuance of the war they covered practically the entire United States although their principal work lay among the Northern States. Neither of these men have ever had any public acknowledgment of the very fine constructive work which they accomplished.

On February 7, 1918 instructions were issued changing the Military Intelligence Branch from the War College Division to the Executive Division of the General Staff and in March of 1918 the Military Intelligence Branch was moved bodily, personnel and material, to the Monroe Courts on the corner of 15th and M Streets, Washington. This was a seven-story house and was entirely occupied by the Military Intelligence Branch with the exception of a few rooms in the basement which were occupied by a section of the Quartermaster Corps.

In the late spring of 1918 the Quartermaster General asked that a suitable man be recommended to him who could set up an organization for the investigation of suspected dishonest activities connected with the work of the Quartermaster Corps. This was done and a man who was believed to be fully competent to handle such work was brought to Washington and reported to the Quartermaster General. After the writer had been sent overseas, it developed that this man was unable to carry out his assignment and the Quartermaster General requested that the Military Intelligence Branch set up an organization of its own which would handle such work which was done. This will explain why such an organization was set up in the Military Intelligence Branch. It was not the proper work for the Intelligence Branch but was done as a matter of emergency.

After the troops of the American Expeditionary Force took their places in the battle lines two large scale maps were prepared on which all battle lines were placed. One was in the White House and the other at the Capitol and an officer detailed for the purpose made all the changes as rapidly as they were reported to the Military Intelligence Branch in order to keep the President and the members of Congress posted on the location and movements of the battle lines of the Allied and the Central Powers.

During this period on each Wednesday evening a meeting, usually composed of all of the commissioned officers on duty in the Military Intelligence Branch was called for the purpose of discussing any particular problems which needed general discussion and in order to hear visiting officers from the European theatre of war who were in a position to give talks on the intelligence work being accomplished by the Allied forces in Europe. At these meetings it was stressed that no officer connected with the intelligence service should ever either in public print or in a public speech reveal any of the activities of the intelligence service for the reason that such knowledge belonged to the government and not to the individual. In only one instance so far as the writer knows was that promise violated in spite of the fact that undoubtedly much pressure must have been brought on many of the officers for articles giving their experience in the intelligence service.

As has been indicated in the first part of this memorandum constant effort was made to have the Military Intelligence service re-established as the Second or Military Intelligence division of the General Staff where it belongs. However, it was not until August 26, 1918 that this was accomplished and the Military Intelligence Branch became the Second (Military Intelligence) Division of the General Staff and thus was restored to its proper place after a lapse of about 10 years.

During the entire war, organizations composed of Irish men in the United States engaged in operations which they hoped would harm Great Britain. Many of these activities, while of course operating against Great Britain also harmed the United States and the other Allied powers as well. One typical case of the kind of activities by Irish organizations in the United States was the attempt to destroy a copper mine in the western part of the country on which the Allies were depending for a large quantity of that most important war material. The plot to destroy this mine was discovered thru the development of a secret ink letter which was intercepted by the Post Office censorship and turned over to Military Intelligence. The leader of the plot was the head of one of the Irish organizations in this country and was caught in Buffalo just as he was boarding a train. There were many other incidents of attempts to interfere with Allied operations in the United States which the leaders of the various Irish organizations hoped would make trouble for Great Britain. The attempted Irish Rebellion led by Sir Roger Casement with German help provided by submarine is, of course, well known.

The Code and Cipher Section, in addition to its work in deciphering, in the latter part of the war provided the codes with which government communication between Washington and General Pershing's headquarters were carried on. These codes were changed very frequently and at irregular intervals. This rather unusual procedure became necessary because it developed that the diplomatic and War Department codes had become known to the Central Powers. In this connection an incident which is of considerable interest and which so far as the writer knows has never had any mention publicly was as follows: When German submarines were discovered operating in the immediate vicinity of our Eastern coast the question arose as to why they did not cut our trans-Atlantic cables. It was surmised that they might be utilizing the cables in some way for obtaining information which they could not otherwise obtain. Just how this information was obtained was a question. The matter was discussed with an officer then in the Signal Corps of the Army who was previously one of the chief engineers of one of the cable lines and it was suggested that it was possible that German submarines might be able by induction to take off messages passing over the cable. To test this theory, the Signal Officer in question rigged up an apparatus to see whether or not by contacting a submarine cable under water he would be able to obtain messages off of it by induction. He actually made contact with one of the trans-Atlantic cables a short distance off shore and was able to take off messages passing over the cable. Whether or not this was the real reason for the failure of the Central Powers to cut our trans-Atlantic cable it certainly would have explained what was otherwise an enigma.

In the fall of 1917 it became evident that attempts were being made by a wireless station south of our Mexican border to communicate with Europe. At that time there was only one wireless station in the world capable of sending messages across the Atlantic and that was at Nauen, Germany. However, our wireless listeners began catching very strong and high frequency messages coming from some point in Mexico. Investigation revealed that the Germans were erecting a very strong wireless station in Chapultepec. However, it soon developed that this station was not strong enough to reach Germany and reports soon reached us that the Germans were beginning a much stronger station some place on the northern coast of South America. In addition to the messages coming from the station at Chapultepec there were other wireless messages emanating from various parts of the Republic of Mexico all of which were being sent in code but which were not very strong. In order to keep touch with this development three Army wagons were equipped as listening-in stations and operated along our southern border all during the latter part of the war. That the Mexican government, presumedly friendly to the United States, should have permitted this activity by German agents within her territory might seem strange. However if we remember the Zimmerman case of 1916 this action by the Mexican government does not seem so strange. It will be recalled that Zimmerman, the secretary of state of Germany, proposed to President Carranza of

THE FINAL MEMORANDA

Mexico that he throw in his lot with the Central Powers and declare war against the United States. Pres. Carranza did not inform the United States of the receipt of this message until after it had been picked up by the British Intelligence and by our Immigration office at Nogales where two men and a woman were arrested trying to enter the United States. They had sown into the garments which they were wearing the same coded message. It appeared later that Pres. Carranza knew of this attempt to get this message into the United States and did not stop it. We can thus understand why the United States watched any activities of Mexico during this period with great suspicion.

Perhaps the most spectacular piece of work which the Code and Cipher Section accomplished although it was by no means the most important, was the decoding of a message found on the person of a German agent attempting to cross from Mexico into the United States on a Russian passport. This was a man by the name of Luther Witke, Jr. with an alias of Pablo Waberski. The message which this man carried in code was addressed to all German agencies in Mexico directing them to furnish the bearer with amounts up to one thousand pesos in gold and to give him such assistance as he might require. Also to send such messages and cables as he might request. The message was signed by the German Counsel General. Witke was detained at the border and placed in jail and the coded message found on his person sent to the Military Intelligence Branch where it was submitted to the Code and Cipher Section and decoded during a single night. This led to the trial and conviction of Witke who was sentenced to death although his sentence was commuted to life imprisonment by President Wilson. At the end of the war he was released.

In 1918 Colonel Nolan, the G-2 of the AEF, wrote the Chief of the Military Intelligence Branch asking him to select a group of men who spoke French, were entirely trustworthy and had some investigational experience for duty abroad. The Chief of the Branch called together the heads of three of the largest and most important detective agencies in the United States and asked them for the names of men who would fulfill the qualifications. The results of this meeting were not promising, in fact Mr. Pinkerton said when he [was] told the requirements, "there ain't no such animal." He finally did send officers to various cities which he believed to have a considerable population of French-speaking individuals, and finally got together the necessary number. Sometime later it was learned that very few of them were acceptable for the principal reason that they were either Belgians or in some way connected with Belgium and at the time no Belgians were considered trustworthy unless they had been examined. This was, of course, the beginning of the organization later known as CIC.

As stated at the beginning of this memorandum this is not an attempted history of all of the activities of the Military Intelligence Branch of the General Staff which accounts for the fact that very few incidents of what we in those days called "positive intelligence" have been given. This is not because the Branch did not carry on many activities connected with collection, processing and distribution of military intelligence but because such activities were purely routine and would be of no particular interest in a memorandum such as this.

The writer was ordered overseas in June of 1918 and upon arrival was assigned to the G-2 Division of General Pershing's Staff. Incidents connected with this service will be taken up in an additional memorandum.

Memorandum II

San Diego, California   June 5, 1950

Memorandum

As stated in the memorandum dated April 8, 1949:

> The following memorandum is in no sense to be considered an official document. Nor is it to be considered as a personal history of the writer. It is not for publication. It consists of certain incidents pertinent to the history and development of the Military Intelligence service of the United States Army which can now be recalled by the writer after nearly fifty-five years experience in intelligence work. It is more than possible that there may be some minor discrepancies in this work, since, with the exception of a few dates, the writer has had to depend entirely on his unaided memory, without notes of any kind, in its preparation. It has been written because very few of the persons connected with the early history of Military Intelligence in our Army are still alive and the writer believes it would be interesting for those now interested in that work to know something of its development as seen by one who was intimately connected with the incidents related.

However for the information contained in this memorandum the writer has had access to a diary which he kept during his tour of duty in Europe which gave names of places visited and individuals contacted together with dates, but which gave practically no information concerning what had actually been done. He also had the help of various letters on intelligence matters received and written during this period.

This may seem to be an unusual way to cover this period but it seemed to the writer that if the meetings which were held with various officials and the investigations of office procedure and methods which were made were given in chronological order and then tied in with the various historical events as they took place, it would give a clearer and more understandable picture. A picture not only of the operations of our Military Intelligence services in the European area but its connection with the Intelligence services of the Allies and of the Washington office M.I.

This also seems to be a convenient place to make the following observation: The writer has not been in sufficiently close touch with the present organization of the Military Intelligence Service to warrant him in either criticizing or making suggestions concerning it. However, there is one point in connection with the matter of officer personnel which I feel it my duty to call to the attention of all the intelligence officers who may read this memorandum. This is: It is my carefully considered opinion after being closely associated with Military Intelligence matters over a period of some fifty-five years, that the Army will never have a really efficient intelligence service until it is made into what is known as a "career" service. In other words, until the officers who have proved themselves to be competent and efficient intelligence officers are allowed and encouraged to make military intelligence their army career. This should, of course, only apply to the higher ranking intelligence officers since the efficiency of all intelligence officers must be based on the thoroughness of their training in the military service and this requires years of both study and actual experience.

R. H. Van Deman

Maj. Gen., U.S.A., Ret.

THE FINAL MEMORANDA 41

As I had to rely purely on memory in writing the first memorandum, it was to be expected that many incidents which should have been included were omitted and I think it would be advisable to simply name a few of these although I will not try to go into detail. In the first place the incidents occurred during the period when there was no Military Intelligence organization and therefore, as far as I know, they are not officially recorded in any intelligence files.

The details of one of these incidents was given to me by the German Assistant Military Attache to the United States who was sent from Washington to Los Angeles for the purpose of handling the undertaking. At the time he gave me this story, many years after the war was over, he had become an American Citizen and his son had become a reserve lieutenant in the United States Army. Before we entered the First World War, Germany had determined that it would be possible to stage an uprising in India and had made extensive plans to that end. It was necessary however that arms and ammunition be supplied and for this purpose a considerable quantity of rifles and ammunition was therefore purchased and stored in Los Angeles, California. A small schooner was obtained which was to carry these arms and their accompanying ammunition to a point near an island near the Mexican coast where a steam ship known as the "Maverick" was to meet the schooner and take over her cargo. However, when the schooner arrived off the island the Maverick was not there and as there was no water supply on this island and the schooner was about out of drinking water she was sailed to the nearest Mexican port. By this time our State Department had discovered what was going on and the schooner with her load of rifles and ammunition was held at the request of our government by the Mexican government. When the Maverick arrived off the island rendezvous and after sailing around the island and being unable to find a trace of, or a message from, the schooner she sailed for Manila. There it was attempted to purchase a number of revolvers without success and finally the Maverick departed for her ultimate destination which was Karachi, India and that was the end of that incident.

As was suspected at the time, the German Government had made plans for an uprising in the United States if it could be engineered. This, of course, was to be handled through the German agents and organizations in the United States. No action concerning this matter was undertaken until after the war had been declared against Germany and then a search was made in New York City in an attempt to locate a cache of arms which rumor had it the Germans had concealed there. When the subbasement of the building in which the "German Club" was located was searched, it was found that a considerable number of packing cases had been stored in the basement but had been removed and there was certain evidence that these packing cases had contained arms. Whatever became of these rifles is not known although it is rumored that they were shipped into the Middle West and there concealed.

There was another incident connected with arms of a little different character which Military Intelligence endeavored to solve after its organization had been effected. Before the Bolshevik revolution in 1917, the Russian Czarist Government had purchased a considerable number of rifles and bayonets which her agents attempted to ship to Russia. This was perfectly well known, but the place of storage of the arms was not known to Military Intelligence nor was it ever possible to discover what became of these rifles and bayonets. That they were not shipped out of the port of New York seems probable although it is possible that an agent of the Soviet Government did manage to get them out of the city and to ship them under cover from some other port. Recently, a newspaper account of the death of Franz von Rintelen reminds me that in describing the placing of incendiary bombs on ships carrying munitions from the United States to France in the first memorandum, I failed to mention that von Rintelen was the German agent in the United States who was responsible for this activity.

As all intelligence agencies now know, the headquarters in the United States for German Intelligence and secret service work in the First World War was the German Embassy in Washington. This method was also used by the other Central powers both in this country and in Great Britain. During the period between World War I and II the same system was again used by both Germany and Italy and was continued up to the time of the Second World War. This same system is now being used by Soviet Russia in this country and in all countries outside of the Iron Curtain.

Some little time before the German Ambassador and his entourage were sent out of the United States at the beginning of the First World War, an American who was an employee of the German Embassy in Washington and who happened to know that the writer had been engaged in intelligence work brought to me certain cards which he had abstracted from the files in the Embassy. These cards contained a brief history of various officers of the regular Army of the United States including a fairly full personal and military history of the officer, a brief history of his wife and her family if he were married and ending with a statement as to whether or not the reporting agent believed he could be bribed. These cards had, of course, to be returned in order to protect the employee who brought them to me and we were never able to see more than a dozen or so altogether although the man who brought them to me stated that there were many more and included at least all officers of the grade of Captain and above who were in the regular Army of the United States at that time.

I also failed to mention the obtaining of the briefcase of Mr. Albert one of the high ranking officials of the German Embassy which was obtained a short time before the German Ambassador and his entourage were ousted from the United States. This briefcase contained an astonishing amount of information concerning the activities of the intelligence and secret service work then being carried on through the German Embassy. In this incident a Mr. Voska, later a captain in the Military Intelligence, was responsible.

I should also have mentioned the many visits paid to the Intelligence offices by Ignaz Paderewski the noted pianist who later became the first premier of Poland. Paderewski was most anxious that the United States should incorporate his Polish Legion as a unit of its armed forces for the war.

When I was ordered overseas in June of 1918 I was relieved by Lt. Col. Marlborough Churchill. Churchill had been a member of the Military Intelligence of the American Expeditionary Forces in France for a short time and had been ordered back to the United States for the purpose of training some of the officers of the National Army then being formed. He had had little experience in Intelligence but was favorably known to the Chief of Staff, General Payton C. March, who selected him as the best officer known to him to take over the intelligence work. That the Chief of Staff made a very excellent selection is amply proven by the work that Lt. Col. Churchill did as the head of the Military Intelligence Branch of the Executive Section of the General Staff as well as that performed following the restoration of the Military Intelligence to its proper place in the General Staff organization and his promotion to Brigadier General.

Too little has been said concerning the most excellent work done by Marlborough Churchill from the time he took over the head of the Military Intelligence Branch of the Executive Section of the General Staff up to the time that an attack of sleeping sickness acquired from a clerk in his office caused his retirement. As an evidence of the fine character of this man and as showing that patriotism and devotion to what he believed to be his country's interests, a letter written by him to General Nolan, the G-2 of the A.E.F., is hereto appended marked "Appendix A." In reading this letter it must not be forgotten that he was urging the return to Washington of the man who would supplant him as head of the Military Intelligence.

I do not believe that I have mentioned in the first memorandum the name of the officer who was the Executive Secretary of the Military Intelligence Branch. This officer was Alexander B. Coxe and to him should be credited more than to any other one officer, in my opinion, the excellent work accomplished in the organizing of the Military Intelligence Branch of the War College Division. He remained as Executive Secretary when the Military Intelligence Branch became a Division of the General Staff and continued his excellent work until he was sent overseas. Coxe was not only a most able officer but had had considerable experience in intelligence work. He was with the writer on the first expedition into China for the purpose of preparing an up-to-date topographical map of the region.

I left Washington, D.C. for New York City on June 5, 1918 arriving at New York on the morning of the sixth where I was met by Major Nicholas Biddle, the officer in charge of the New York intelligence group. During the next few days Maj. Biddle went over with me the set up of his office – he also accompanied me to the Port of Embarkation at the docks of the old North German Lloyd Steamship Company in Hoboken, New Jersey where arrangements had to be made by all casual officers going overseas. The intelligence officer at the Port of Embarkation was Major Dunham.

Major Biddle had been an official in the New York Metropolitan Police and was selected to head the New York Intelligence group on the recommendation of the Police Commissioner of New York City. A better choice could not have been made, Biddle did an excellent job and should be credited with a very large part of the work which was accomplished by the New York office during the war. He selected the officers who composed his group and his fine judgment of men was evidenced by the character of the men he selected. Biddle's office was excellently organized and ran with smoothness and efficiency.

While completing my arrangements for transportation at the Port of Embarkation at Hoboken, I ran into Major Sherman Miles who had been one of the intelligence officers on duty in the Military Intelligence Branch in Washington almost from its organization. Miles was one of a number of General Staff officers ordered at this time for duty overseas. He told me that all of the others with the exception of myself and Col. Hamilton S. Hawkins had been assigned to English ships and would therefore land first in England.

I boarded the transport to which I was assigned on the morning of June 9 and met Col. Hawkins who was assigned to the same transport. We pulled out into the stream about nine that evening and anchored in the lower bay. German submarines had been on our coast the last week or two and one had been discovered in the eastern entrance to New York bay during that day. We were therefore ordered to proceed directly to sea from the lower bay and sailed about midnight during a violent thunderstorm. The transport was about 40 percent overloaded and for that and several other reasons the voyage was not a particularly comfortable or happy one.

The convoy consisted of four transports all, of course, commanded and manned by the Navy. There was no escort until we had reached a rendezvous point two days out of Brest where we were joined by a number of destroyers. Upon approaching the harbor of Brest a blimp joined the escort group. The voyage was without incident. We reached Brest on the morning of June 19th and landed at five in the evening.

On the morning of June 22nd orders came through directing Col. Hawkins and me to proceed to Blois which was the post to which casual officers were sent to wait assignment in the American Expeditionary Forces. The direct rail route from Brest to Blois is through Paris, but as at that time the Germans were beginning their attack on the Marne and Paris was evacuating many of its activities, the confusion on the rail line was so great that military personnel were being shipped around the city instead of being sent through it. We reached Blois on the evening of June 23rd and were sent to the Hotel du Blois which was reserved for casual officers awaiting assignment.

The next day I reported to Casual Officers Headquarters and registered and telephoned to Colonel Dennis E. Nolan who was the G-2 of the American Expeditionary Forces at the headquarters in Chaumont. I did this after discovering that casual officers were sometimes held in Blois from two weeks to a month before being assigned. Colonel Nolan told me over the telephone that he knew that I had been ordered to France but did not know that I had arrived and that I was to come down to headquarters and that he would see that orders to that effect were issued at once. Nolan said I was to continue in intelligence work and asked that I go over the intelligence work at the posts and camps which were under the charge of Lt. Campanari whom I had met while registering at Casual Officers Headquarters.

The first of these camps was in a little town called St. Aignan where a replacement division was located. This division at this time was commanded by General Alexander. From there we drove to Remorantin where there was a replacement depot and labor camp under Colonel Charles J. Symmonds and the aviation assembling camp under Colonel Kendrick and then back to Blois, arriving there at 8 P.M. The next day I went with Lt. Campanari to Tours. At Tours was located the headquarters of the Service of Supply and here were some of the largest depots and shops which we had in France. Here also were the Chief Quartermaster, the Chief Surgeon, the Chief of Engineers, and the Chief of the Air Service and several other offices. These offices were located in an old French barracks consisting of three four-story brick buildings on three sides of a square. General Francis J. Kernan was in command.

I here met for the first time Capt. Cabot Ward who was the intelligence officer for the Service of Supply and who also had an intelligence office in Paris. I was to see considerable of this officer later. After going over the intelligence office of Capt. Ward at Tours and visiting briefly some of the officers of the S.O.S., Lt. Campanari and I returned to Blois with the understanding that I would return to Tours and go more thoroughly over some of the intelligence problems as soon as my orders for Chaumont arrived.

The next morning, June 26th, the orders for Chaumont arrived and I proceeded to Tours. After breakfast the following morning, June 27th I met the officer in charge of the three large buildings composing the salvage plant and went with him to visit the plant. It was at this plant that clothing was deloused and if possible repaired for re-issue. All material found on battle fields and along the highways except ordinance material was taken to this salvage plant where it was cleaned and repaired or made into other articles. Campaign hats which could not be reblocked were made into slippers for the patients in the hospitals. Shoes that could not be repaired were made into patches or shoe laces. The work in this establishment was done almost exclusively by French women, there being only a few soldiers employed there.

After going over this plant, I caught the 8 P.M. train for Chaumont. This train was known as the "At-ta-boy." It received its name from General William W. Atterbury who was the officer in charge of all the railways under the AEF in France. This particular train was entirely manned by American soldiers who were ex-railway men, even the pullman car porter being an ex-Red Cap. We reached Chaumont at 12.40 P.M. the following day, June 28th, two hours late.

Captain Ward, who had gone to Chaumont on routine business, met me at the station and took me to intelligence mess Number One where I met Major A. Moreno, Major N. W. Campanole, Major Wiley Howell, Captain Frank Moorman and Captain T. H. Hubbard. Colonel Nolan and Colonel Arthur Conger were at the front. The house in which the Mess was located was a rather small private house at 25 Boulevard Gambetta. Nolan, Moreno, Moorman and Major Bruce Magruder lived as well as messed there and Howell, Conger, Major E. W. McCabe, Major R. G. Alexander and Campanole and Hubbard messed there as did Major A. James, who was in charge of the accredited newspaper correspondents, when he was in town. Many interesting and important people were entertained at this Mess at either luncheon or dinner and many subjects important to the intelligence service were discussed.

We had luncheon at the Mess and then went to the AEF headquarters. These offices were located in a French barracks consisting of three four-story stone buildings built around three sides of a square on a high plateau overlooking a river.

The offices of the Commander-in-Chief and those of the General Staff were located in the center building, the Adjutant General and his assistants in the building to the right and those of the Engineers, the Tank Corps and others in the one to the left. I reported to the Adjutant General and then went to Colonel Nolan's office where I was told that General Pershing wanted to see me. I went to General Pershing's office at once and had nearly an hour's conversation with him. He told me that he wanted me to continue with intelligence work and that he had talked with Colonel Nolan concerning the matter. He said that after I had familiarized myself with the intelligence work of the AEF, particularly the front line work and the intelligence work of the Allies that he thought I should return to Washington and continue my old job as head of the Intelligence Branch of the Executive Division of the General Staff. I told him I had talked with Colonel Nolan over the telephone and in addition Colonel Nolan wanted me to look over the Military Attache's offices in the neutral countries. General Pershing agreed that this should be done.

After this conversation with General Pershing I went to see the Chief-of-Staff who was General James W. McAndrew. He said the orders assigning me to duty in the G-2 section of the AEF were then being issued. I then returned to G-2 headquarters where a desk was allotted me so that I could begin work the following morning. The next day, June 29th, I began the first part of my work which was to familiarize myself with the various offices of the G-2 section. Office hours for all of the offices except the Intelligence section were from 9 A.M. to 12:30 P.M. and from 2 P.M. to 7 P.M. The intelligence section had these same hours but, in addition, went back to their offices after dinner and worked until 11 P.M. This, of course, was because of the character of the work which the Intelligence had to handle and which required that the reports of each day's operations and activities should be processed at the end of each day. This included the issuing of the summary of the day's operations of the AEF which was handled by Colonel Nolan personally.

The office buildings were lighted by electricity and heated with coal-burning stoves. All windows were provided with black cloth curtains which had to be pulled down as soon as the lights were turned on. This was, of course, for the purpose of making it more difficult for the enemy bombing planes to locate the buildings. Strange to say, neither Chaumont nor the headquarters buildings were bombed during the entire war. Just why, it is difficult to say for the headquarters buildings were located on a high plateau along the river and on moonlight nights, must have stood out like a sore thumb. While we had many "alerts" no bombs were ever dropped in the Chaumont area during the entire war.

The work accomplished by the G-2 Section of the AEF was very large in amount and most excellent in quality. When it is remembered that none of the personnel of the Section had ever had any previous training or experience in intelligence work the character of its work is really remarkable. The Section had no existence until General Pershing and his staff reached Europe. The story of its organization has been written by General Nolan and that description as well as details of its set up are on file and available. However, a very brief sketch of its organization at the time I joined it might be interesting. As was the case in all military intelligence organizations at that period the Section was a "Service" as well as a staff section. It was basically divided into three main sub-sections, designated A, B and C. The A sub-section handled what, in those days, we called positive intelligence – that is, the collection, processing and distribution of military information. The B sub-section handled what we then called negative intelligence and now designate as counter-intelligence – that is, all the activities involved in preventing the enemy and its agents from obtaining military information concerning our forces and activities or of interfering with those activities by sabotage. The C sub-section was the map section which was charged with the collection, production and distribution of maps of the terrain occupied and over which it was planned to operate. Eventually this sub-section was equipped with mobile map producing trucks.

Colonel Dennis Nolan, Major General later on, was the Assistant Chief-of-Staff, G-2 and in charge of the section. Colonel Arthur Conger was in charge of the A sub-section, Major A. Moreno in charge of the B sub-section and Major R. G. Alexander in charge of C sub-section.

In addition to its intelligence work, the G-2 section was also charged with looking after the newspaper correspondents who were duly accredited to the AEF. This meant seeing that they had quarters provided for them together with mess facilities and that they were taken to the places where operations were in progress and that they were not allowed to wander at will through the AEF. The handling of this group was not an easy job and the lot of the officer who was in charge of the group was not a happy one.

One of the most important jobs of the A sub-section was the keeping up-to-date of the "Battle Map." This consisted of a large scale

THE FINAL MEMORANDA   49

map covering the front lines and showing the location of the various divisions of both our own and the enemy's troops. This was an important job and required the constant attention of the group entrusted with its handling. To realize the importance of such a map, it must be remembered that this was mainly a war of trenches and position and it was most important for the commanders of Divisions and higher units to know what the location of the enemy divisions directly opposing them were.

At this time the A and C sub-sections were both busy in preparing data and maps for a planned invasion of Germany which the Allied forces planned for the following spring. In this work they were utilizing the information which had been sent over from the United States in such volume and which was mentioned in my first memorandum.

On July 2nd Nolan returned from his trip to the front and we had a long talk, principally on just what I was to do and the order in which it was to be taken up. Nolan knew the Secretary of War expected that I would be sent back to my old job in Washington as soon as I had completed the work I was directed to do in Europe. He also knew that General Pershing concurred in this plan. At this and several subsequent talks the work which I was to accomplish and the general order in which it was to be done were decided upon. It was decided that I should first go over the various sections of G-2 AEF in order to get an understanding of just how they worked. Having completed this task I was then to take up the examination of the offices of the Military Attaches in France, England, Switzerland, Holland, Denmark and Norway, Italy and Spain. In addition to checking on the office set-up I had another job with regards to the Military Attaches' offices. Some of the Military Attaches had not been carrying out carefully the instructions which had been issued by the Washington office sometime before. These instructions required all Military Attaches in Europe to transmit at once to the G-2, AEF, all information which came into their hands in addition to transmitting it to the Washington office. Some of the Military Attaches did not seem to understand what this was for or why it was considered so necessary that this type of information should be sent immediately to the G-2 of the AEF.

The order in which these offices were to be visited would depend on circumstances. I was then to visit both the intelligence sections of the British Expeditionary Forces and the French Field Forces and then go over the British Intelligence set-up in London and the French Deuxieme Bureau in Paris. While in Switzerland I was also to look into the manner in which the various vice-consuls were working in cooperation with the offices of our Military Attaches. Having finished all of this work I was then to visit our front line troops and study the work of the various intelligence sections covering Army, Corps, Brigade and Regiment. All of this, of course, was for the purpose of coordinating the work done by our various Military Attaches and intelligence units with that of the G-2 AEF and the Military Intelligence Branch in Washington as well as to gain whatever assistance might be possible from the intelligence services of the French and British. The knowledge gained from this work was not only for the benefit of the intelligence service of the AEF but also for that of our intelligence service in the United States. The information gained from all these investigations I of course reported to both the G-2 section of the AEF and to the Military Intelligence Branch in Washington.

On the morning of July 6th, Major Callan O'Laughlin came into the office and I took him over to luncheon so that he might have a chance to have a quiet talk with Colonel Nolan. There had been considerable disturbance among the accredited correspondents lately and I knew Nolan wanted to talk to O'Laughlin about it. O'Laughlin was a well-known newspaperman who was known to have much influence with newspaper men. He subsequently became the editor and publisher of the Army and Navy Journal. Soon after this talk with Nolan he was detailed in the G-2 Section for special work.

As it was necessary for me to obtain a passport for Switzerland and also since I was directed to go over the office of our Military Attache in Paris, I left Chaumont the morning of July 10th taking Majors O'Laughlin and Campanole with me and proceeded by automobile to Paris. Arriving in Paris in the early afternoon, we went to the Ritz Hotel where by appointment I met Gurnee Munn one of the assistant Military Attaches in the Paris Embassy. It will be remembered that at this period the Germans were making a determined attack on the Marne and there was much fear on the part of many officers that Paris would be attacked and might fall. Because of this situation the towns through which we passed on the way to Paris from Chaumont were full of troops.

After luncheon I went to the Embassy with Munn and there met Major Barclay Warburton, the Military Attache, and his other assistants, Capt. McFadden, Lt. Mavrick, Lt. Hoffer and Lt. Sanger. I also met Robert Bliss the councilor of the Embassy and Hugh Gibson one of the secretaries and had a long talk concerning intelligence matters in France in which the Embassy was particularly interested. The offices of the Military Attache were at the top floor of the building occupied by the Embassy.

The next day both O'Laughlin and myself went to the Provost Marshal's office as required and registered. This permitted us to draw our sugar and bread cards without which neither could be obtained at any restaurant or hotel. After registering, I returned to the Military Attache's office and discussed matters connected with the work of the office. A letter which I wrote to Churchill dated Oct. 20, 1918 goes into the matter of the relationship of the Military Attache's office and G-2 Service of Supply in considerable detail and an extract from that letter follows:

"You ask me about the Paris situation and Cabot Ward and Warburton and say, 'have never had a clear idea of that'

"Cabot Ward, as you know, is an Assistant Chief of Staff of the Service of Supply and is the G-2 man on the staff of the Commanding General of the S.O.S. He has the same relation to G-2, G.H.Q. as the G-2 man of an Army does. In other words, while he is a staff officer of the S.O.S., he gets his instructions as to his particular work from G-2, G.H.Q. Of course, the only Intelligence work that S.O.S. handles is counter-espionage within the area of the S.O.S. That means all of France occupied by our activities back of the Zone of the Armies, as well as the handling of American military interests in England which is Base No. 3 of the S.O.S. The headquarters of the S.O.S. is in Tours but it was found that most of the activities of the S.O.S. counter-espionage service centered in Paris and therefore Ward moved his main office there, leaving a representative in Tours, Major Henretin, with whom he is in constant telephone touch. He also visits Tours frequently.

"Under the S.O.S. counter-espionage Service come the Port Control officers at the Ports of Debarkation. There are also Port Control officers at London, Liverpool and Cardiff, England and counter-espionage officers at the aviation camps in England and Ireland. There are also officers in certain other important towns and in camps and centers engaged in U.S. Army activities. This includes the large labor camps, the airplane assembling camp, the salvage plants, etc., which are controlled by the S.O.S. In all of these places Ward maintains a counter-espionage service. Where divisions are located in the S.O.S. area, close liaison is maintained between the S.O.S. counter-espionage service and the troop counter-espionage service, although the S.O.S. does not exercise any authority over them, the troop counter-espionage service always remaining under G-2, G.H.Q. The closest liaison is maintained by the S.O.S. counter-espionage service with the Provost Marshal and with the French 2nd Bureau and Surete, also with local French civilian police agencies in the towns in the S.O.S. area. Also with the Paris police and with the counter-espionage service of the Allies and with the office of our Military Attache. Before the S.O.S. was established and Ward established an office in Paris, the Military Attache handled a great deal of the activities now under Ward's office. When I first went to Paris I found there was a great deal of confusion in the minds of both Ward and Warburton as to just what each covered, and that there was scarcely any touch between the two offices and not a little friction purely because of that confusion. It only took a short time to straighten that out and now they are in very close personal touch and things are working nicely.

"One of the functions which was passed from the Military Attache to the S.O.S. counter-espionage service was the Passport Visa matter. It was perfectly evident that the S.O.S. counter-espionage service was in much better position to handle this than the Military Attache and it was arranged that it should be so handled even before the Passport office was established in Paris by the State Department.

"I think that will give you a rough idea of the functions of the S.O.S. counter-espionage service and the relation of Ward's office to that of Warburton. It is really only in connection with the Passport Control that any functions of the Military Attache have passed to the S.O.S. In connection with cable communications from S.O.S. to M.I.D. and vice versa you will have received my memoranda on the subject in a recent letter. In addition to this, if you ever want to get any counter-espionage information from S.O.S., in a hurry, you can cable Warburton and he will get it from Ward at once and send it to you. Or, if you want to communicate with G-2, and don't want it to go by the regular cable, you can use Warburton's office."

After completing the talk with Major Warburton, the Military Attache, I went to see Capt. Stickney who was our representative on the French Postal Censorship. This visit was for the purpose of getting an understanding as to just what this office was doing as well as to make the personal acquaintance of the officer in charge. From there I went to make a courtesy call on Col. Gourgen in charge of the French Deuxieme Bureau (Intelligence) and from there to the office of Colonel Walner the immediate assistant of Col. Gourgen and in charge of counter-espionage. I had met Colonel Walner several times before and in the opinion of both our Intelligence and that of the British he was considered the best and most efficient intelligence officer that the French had. The fact that he spoke such perfect English was, of course, always a help with dealing with either ourselves or the British.

The following day I set about obtaining some civilian clothing for use in Switzerland. All American officers in France were, of course, required to wear uniform and I had not therefore brought with me from the United States any of my civilian clothing. But it was not considered advisable that I appear in uniform in Switzerland or in the other neutral countries to which it was proposed that I be sent. After attending to this matter I had another long talk with Mr. Robert Bliss at the Embassy. These talks with Mr. Bliss and those with High Gibson were valuable in

THE FINAL MEMORANDA   53

connection with intelligence work not only in France but in the adjoining
neutral countries as well.

On the following day, I made my regular application for a passport
for Switzerland and for Spain. It was believed that it might be well if I
continued on into Spain after finishing in Switzerland as there were
several matters to be looked after in connection with the espionage agents
of the Central Powers in Spain which Colonel Nolan wanted checked on.
I returned to the Military Attache's office after making my application
for the passport and found a long cablegram from Leland Harrison in
Washington. Leland Harrison was the official in charge of the Secret
Service of the State Department and I had worked very closely with him
all during the time I was in charge of the Military Intelligence Branch in
Washington. The State Department always denied that it had a Secret
Service but it had one nevertheless. This cablegram from Harrison dealt
with a matter which I will take up in describing the work which I had
to do in Berne.

At luncheon at the Ritz that day General Harry Rogers of the
Quartermaster Department introduced me to a woman who figured quite
prominently in certain underhand proceedings which concerned General
Pershing and which I will mention later in this memorandum.

At dinner that night I ran into General James Harbord who had
recently come out of the fighting at Belleau Woods where he had
commanded a Marine Brigade. Harbord and I had been classmates in
infantry and cavalry school in 1893-95 and he had come over to Europe
as General Pershing's Chief of Staff but had been allowed to go into
active combat work at his own earnest request.

Major Warburton had obtained tickets for Major O'Laughlin, Major
Campanole and myself to attend a review of troops which was part of
the celebration of Bastile [sic] Day, July 14th. So the next morning we
three proceeded to the reviewing field. In the reviewing stand were many
high-ranking French officers and civilians together with a number of our
own including General Tasker H. Bliss and his staff. General Bliss, of
course, was the American representative on the Supreme War Council.

There were detachments from all of the various countries represented in the Allied forces taking part in this review and although none
of the detachments were large they were an extremely fine-looking lot of
men. That applies particularly to the detachment representing the American forces who had been so recently moved from the front line that they
had not even had time to remove the mud from their shoes and clothes.
Moving pictures of this review covering both the troops and the reviewing
stand were taken and were a week or so later displayed at the War

Department in Washington as well as in a small theatre in North-west Washington.

After luncheon I went to Hugh Gibson's apartment where I found Hugh Wilson, the First Secretary of the Legation at Berne. This was fortunate meeting with Hugh Wilson because he was able to give me a lot of information concerning affairs in Berne and Switzerland which I would otherwise have had to dig out of someone after reaching Berne. Following this conversation with Gibson and Wilson I returned to the Ritz where I met Captain Voska.

Voska had been an editor of a newspaper in Austro-Hungary and had gotten into trouble politically and had because of this come to the United States some twelve years before the war broke out in 1914. He was the real organizer of the Bohemian National Alliance in the United States. He worked for the British Intelligence in 1914-15 and 16 and did some exceedingly clever work himself as well as utilizing his Bohemian organization to a large degree. It was Voska who got the handbag from Dr. Albert, the German propagandist as mentioned previously. Through the Bohemian Alliance, Voska was in constant touch with affairs in Austro-Hungary and had a good many agents there whom he had sent in from the United States. All of the expenses incident to these agents were borne by the Alliance. When the United States entered the war, Voska stopped the activities of the Alliance in the United States because he said that now he felt that its activities should be directed by the United States and that meant military control.

I had heard of Voska and his work early in the game and had had him looked up and reported upon. He came to see me just before Secretary of War Baker left the United States for his first trip to Europe and laid the whole matter before me and suggested that he be commissioned or taken over by the Military Intelligence as a civilian agent and sent to France to work under the immediate supervision of G-2, GHQ. The State Department urged us to do this and highly recommended Voska's honesty and loyalty. After talking at length with Voska, I went to Mr. Baker the day before he left Washington and proposed that we commission Voska and five or six other members of the Bohemian National Alliance who were already enlisted men in our Army. One of Voska's propositions was to continue the work of the Alliance in fomenting revolution in Hungary and also to continue certain lines of sabotage in which they had been engaged. It was on this latter activity that the Secretary struck and declined to take on the proposition. So I let the matter rest intending to take it up again when the Secretary returned from Europe, as I was sure he would have a very different angle on things then. This proved to be the case for when I took it up a few days after his return, he agreed to the entire proposal. We then commissioned Voska and six others and sent him and five of his men to France to Nolan for duty. When I got to G-2, GHQ, Voska had been sent to Italy to get in touch with his agents in Austro-Hungary through the Italian lines, leaving two of his officers in Paris in touch with Mr. Edward Benes foreign affairs minister of the Czechoslovakian provisional government. Voska had made his contacts in Italy and had returned. I had a long conversation with Voska in which he explained just what he had been doing and it was agreed that I should discuss matters with Colonel Nolan and then decide whether there should be any changes in the work in which he was engaged.

The next morning, July 15th, I left Paris by automobile with Major O'Laughlin and Major McIlvane for the headquarters of General Hunter Liggett who commanded the First Corps at La Ferte. We went via Meaux where I had been a few days previously with Major O'Laughlin because some of the accredited correspondents who were at that time quartered at the hotel in Meaux had been getting a little out of hand and Colonel Nolan wanted O'Laughlin to have a talk with them. When we reached Meaux we drove to the hotel in which the correspondents were quartered to make inquiries about the road ahead and found that the correspondents had all departed. Just as we entered the hotel a high explosive shell dropped just around the corner. We then found out that there had been shelling all along the Marne that morning and that it was evident that the Germans were making an attack in force. Some more shells fell in the town before we left it to proceed to La Ferte. As we continued we could see shells exploding on the ridge to our right and we found that the Germans had been paying particular attention to shelling bridges and intersection points along the Marne all that morning. We reached General Liggett's headquarters at 11 A.M. and found that the chateau in which the headquarters was located had been under fire and airplanes bombing all night and as a consequence nobody had had any sleep. The shelling had continued all morning but fortunately no shells or bombs struck the chateau. General Liggett was an old personal friend so I went into see him as soon as we arrived and had a long talk. He was quite upset because a large naval gun had been placed on the ridge just outside of La Ferte and was shelling the Germans and had been doing so all night. What effect this shelling had had the General did not know but he complained that it had been drawing hostile fire all morning. The G-2 of General Liggett's Corps was Colonel Williams and as actual fighting was then going on at Chateau Thierry as well as other points along the river, prisoners were coming in in rather large numbers. This gave me my first opportunity to observe a G-2 Corps during combat.

Examination of prisoners was extremely interesting. The very high degree of both the intelligence and instruction of the German non-commissioned officers as evidenced by their ability to read a topographical map, to explain on the map the position of such troops as they knew about and other details connected with the forces to which they belonged, was rather remarkable. While we were observing the work of the G-2 section, the Chief of Staff of General Liggett's Corps, General Malin Craig came in. I wanted very much to go down to Chateau Thierry but General Liggett said no and as O'Laughlin had developed a very high temperature and it was evident that he was coming down with the flu and it would be necessary to get him back to Chaumont as there were no facilities there, we left in the early afternoon for Chaumont. The roads leading directly in the direction of Chaumont were too crowded with troops and supply trains to transverse and we therefore proceeded via Montmirail, Suzanne, Troyes and Bar-sur-Aube reaching Chaumont at 7 P.M. After dinner I proceeded to the G-2 office as usual.

The town of Chaumont was very well supplied with basements or stone arched cellars which acted as refuges in case of shelling or airplane bombing. Upon warning of the approach of hostile airplanes an alert was given by a vehicle of the Fire Department racing about town with a bugler blowing the French Army call "Alert." Thereupon all civilians were required to vacate the streets and proceed to one or another of these cellars where they had to remain until the same Fire Department vehicle raced around the streets while the bugler sounded the French Army call corresponding to our recall. Then they would all troop out and rush to their homes. Sometimes there were two and even three alerts in one night and it certainly must have been anything but pleasant for the civilians though as mentioned before no bombs ever fell in the town of Chaumont or any place near the AEF headquarters. In addition to the vaulted cellars which the French called "caves" there were rather deep trenches in the immediate vicinity of the headquarters buildings where troops or other employees could take refuge.

On July 21st I proceeded to the town of Langres where we had an intelligence school and where most of the AEF staff schools were located. Langres is a very old town, as a matter of fact it was an old Roman town during the time the Romans occupied this portion of France and many of the old Roman ruins were still to be seen in the valley and on the ridge. It was also part of the French Fortified Defense and several of the forts which comprise this line were plainly visible from the town. As this was more or less a pleasure trip I took General Omar Bundy and his aide with me. It was a Sunday and therefore there were no classes being conducted so the only thing we got out of the trip was to meet a few old friends who were there.

THE FINAL MEMORANDA

The next day Lt. Colonel W. F. H. Godson, our Military Attache at Berne, drove up by appointment in order to take me to Berne. He brought with him Mr. Dennett, the Red Cross Director in Switzerland. In the evening I had a long talk with Godson concerning the activities of his office.

On the afternoon of July 23rd, Nolan and I had a long talk with Capt. Voska concerning the work in which he was engaged. For some time, Voska working out of Italy with his contacts in Austro-Hungary had been fostering trouble for the Central Powers in Austro-Hungary and gathering information vital for our military forces. He was frequently dropped in Austro-Hungary from an airplane and later picked up by the same means and returned to Italy. Naturally the Italian Army Intelligence Service cooperated in this work and it is almost the only instance which I can remember that the Italian Intelligence rendered us any particular service. It was decided at this talk with Voska that he should continue as in the past with his work, keeping in close contact from time to time with Mr. Benes and Mr. Thomas Masaryk, the first president of Czechoslovakia.

On July 24th, after luncheon, I left Chaumont for Berne, Switzerland in the automobile of Col. Godson with Mr. Dennett. The route we followed went through Langres, Gray, Besancon, and then to Pontalier which we reached at 6:45 in the afternoon.

Pontalier is a small town lying about three miles from the Swiss border and is of no particular importance or interest except that it is here that the main and only route for many miles crosses from France into Switzerland both by road and railway. The French have a control station here under the Second Bureau and very closely examine everyone going in either direction. The control group here is a part of what is known as the Belfort Service. That is, Belfort is the headquarters and Pontalier is one of the substations. The Belfort Service is credited with training and providing some of the best spies France has sent into Germany and Austro-Hungary. It was through this service that the information of the German offensive in July 1918 was received. This information made it possible for the Allies to take such measures to meet the offensive that it not only failed but that they were enabled to launch a counter-attack which was really the beginning of the end of the war. We had several of our own intelligence officers and intelligence police (sergeants) serving with the French at these various frontier stations, principally at Belfort, Pontalier, Annemasse and Evian-Les-Baines.

We had been in telephone communication with the officer in charge of the Pontalier station before we left Chaumont and he had asked us to have dinner with them at their mess. We got our rooms at the hotel and then went up to the mess which was only a short walk away. The mess was in the same house in which the offices were located. Here I met Lt. Libalier and Lt. Le Conte of the French service and Lt. Quimby of ours. Almost all of the French officers belonging to the Belfort service were Alsatians and had, of course, been in the German Army at the outbreak of the war. At the first opportunity these men deserted and were at the time I met them officers in the French Army with prices on their heads. Some of them had had very remarkable adventures in making their escapes from the German lines and they were, almost without exception, under assumed names.

We had an exceedingly pleasant dinner and as both of the French officers spoke a little English I managed to get along very well. We had intended to start for Berne early in the morning but Lt. Libalier had had a telegram from the Chief of the Belfort service asking that I stay over for luncheon the next day, saying that he was most anxious to see me and would come over to Pontalier if I would stay. As I was most anxious to meet him, for both official and personal reasons, we decided to stay over and to put in the next morning a visit to a very famous old fort called Fort de Jeux, which lay between Pontalier and the Swiss boundary and directly under which the road and the railway into Switzerland passed.

We went back to our hotel about 11:30 P.M. and the following morning Godson, Dennett, Quimby, Le Conte and I started in the car for Fort de Jeux. This old fort was situated in and on an enormous mass of rock which appeared to have broken away from the main ridge to the south and rolled into the valley. As I said before, the main road to Switzerland lead past this conical rock mass and between it and the main ridge to the south. The top of the rock was chosen by one Seur de Jeux in the Tenth Century as a site for his chateau. This chateau was still standing and in use by the garrison stationed there as it was a part of the works of the fort. The Seur de Jeux was, of course, a "Robber Baron" and his chateau was certainly ideally located for his business since the road was absolutely commanded by it and was the only road leading to the south for many miles. There was barely enough room between the rock and main ridge for the road and the railway to pass. At a guess I should say that the top of the rock was fully 400 feet above the valley and the chateau was built on the extreme summit, one wing actually overhanging the road. A fairly good road led from the main road up and around the rock to the top and to the fort. Beginning with the old chateau and using it as a part of them, fortifications had been built at various periods on the top and around the sides of the rock. The last addition is, of course, Vauban. The fort mounted several modern guns with command of the valley for several miles. One of these guns was mounted in a chamber cut out of the interior of the rock and the opening through which it fired was blocked by a large boulder which swung aside when necessary. We passed through the sally port of the Vauban part of the fortifications into the interior of the fort on the summit of the rock on the north side, which was some 30 or 40 feet lower than the south end. After entering we went up and across a very deep moat over the old draw bridge built in Louis XIV's reign. It was in the buildings in this part that the officers' quarters were located.

At this time, of course, the fort was garrisoned by a small caretaking detachment most of whom were wounded soldiers. From the officers quarters we passed through a tunnel into the interior of the rock where the kitchens were located, and then up through the old chateau on the top of the rock. The walls of this building were about five feet thick. The interior was lighted by slits of windows and the only heat was from minute fire places and not many of them. On the side farthest from the Swiss frontier the chateau overlooked the valley of a small stream on the further side of which was a high steep ridge. From this old chateau we went down some steep dark stairs and so into the interior of the rock. After getting a smoky lantern, we went down a flight of spiral iron stairs straight through the center of the rock for about 200 feet. At the bottom of these steps we came into galleries where the ammunition and stores of the fort were kept. Here in one of the central chambers was the opening of a well or cistern cut through the rock to a depth of about 200 feet, which must have brought the bottom of the well to about the level of the valley floor. The officer who accompanied us lighted a newspaper and dropped it in. It went down and down until it was a mere speck of light. Into this well the Prussians threw all the records of the old fort, records that went back almost [to] the period of old Seur de Jeux, after they captured the fort in 1870. The French had not, at that time, tried to get these records out, although they said they expected to do so someday. A typical French attitude – always plenty of time! From here we climbed back up for some distance and then went through a horizontal tunnel and came out into the Vauban portion of the fort where the casements were located and where the garrison was quartered when the fort was fully garrisoned. While we were in the officers' quarters one of the officers picked up an article from the mantelpiece and held it out to me. It proved to be the top of a human skull. The officer said that it was the top of the skull of the Negro, Toussaint L'Ouverture, who led the uprising against the French in Haiti and who was responsible for the wholesale murder of almost the entire French population of that island. He was imprisoned here until his death and then some cheerful soul had a drinking cup made out of the top of his skull!

From the casemates [sic] we made our way back to where we had left the car and drove back to the mess in Pontalier. It was a most interesting trip. Pontalier used to have the largest absinthe factory in France. The factory was still there and so were thousands of bottles of absinthe but the law prohibited not only the manufacture of absinthe but its sale as well. In fact, it was a misdemeanor to even give it away. The little plant from which absinthe was distilled grew in great profusion all around Pontalier; I even saw it growing between the paving stones in Fort de Jeux.

At luncheon, besides our party and officers belonging to the mess, we had Major Anglier, Chief of the Belfort Service, who had asked us to delay our trip so that he could come over; the British Consul, whose name I have forgotten and Captain Hamilton of the British Intelligence whose station was in Berne. Hamilton had just been spending two weeks in Belfort for the purpose of studying methods in use in that service. In fact, the French had a sort of Intelligence School there for instruction in certain kinds of intelligence work and both our people and the British had two or three officers there under instruction.

We left Pontalier at 2:30 P.M. Our route led over the road we had gone over the morning of our visit to Fort de Jeux and so through the defile between the rock on which the fort was built and the ridge to the south and around the foot of the ridge toward the Swiss frontier. About a mile beyond Fort de Jeux we came to the Boundary. Here we found the French frontier guard with an officer in charge who examined our passports and papers and then let down the chain which was stretched across the road between two posts and we drove on about fifty yards to the Swiss barrier, a chain of the same kind. Here our passports had to be again examined. There was no officer here at all – only a Swiss soldier who could speak neither French nor German but only a patois which none of our party could understand at all. However, he made no difficulty and obligingly signed the passports when he was shown where to sign. There is a very small village on the Swiss side and a Customs House but we had no difficulty with the Customs at all and drove on through the village to a hotel on the further side where Captain Hamilton telephoned to Berne to announce our arrival.

We got to Berne at 6 P.M. and after dropping Hamilton and Dennett at the hotel, went on to Godson's apartment. It had been arranged that I was to stay at Godson's apartment so that I would not have to register at the Police Headquarters, which I would have been compelled to do had I gone to an hotel. As Berne was loaded with German, Austro-Hungarian and Turkish spies it was thought best that I keep as quiet as possible.

The following day I went to the office of the Military Attache and

THE FINAL MEMORANDA

met the office personnel. Besides Colonel Godson, his commissioned personnel consisted of Captain Ernest Schelling, Captain Davis, Lt. Devalle and Lt. King. At the office I discussed the counter-espionage work with Lts. Devalle and King. I then proceeded to make my courtesy call on Mr. Pleasant A. Stovall who was the United States Minister to Switzerland.

I have previously mentioned the receipt of a cablegram from Leland Harrison concerning the affair of the consul general at Zurich and it now seems about time to explain what this affair was all about. Our Consul had a daughter living with him at this time who was married to a captain of the German Navy then serving at the German Naval Headquarters. This officer was in the habit of visiting his wife at the home of the Consul over the week-end. This fact was, of course, well known to both the Swiss and Allied personnel living in and near Zurich. These people did considerable talking and the remarks made concerning the Consul's judgment in allowing the visits of an enemy officer to an American Legation were very severely critical. Sometime before Colonel Godson was sent to Berne as Military Attache, this Consul started to make a visit to Spain but was taken ill just as he reached the French-Spanish border and returned to Paris. Here the authorities insisted that he remain for the time being because of the reports which had come out of Switzerland concerning the activities of his Consulate in connection with the visits of his son-in-law. The Consul blamed all of this on Colonel Godson and the cablegram from Leland Harrison requested that I investigate the matter and let him know the result. I made a very careful investigation of the whole situation and interviewed all the vice consuls in that portion of Switzerland, Colonel Godson and his staff, and the United States Minister, Mr. Stovall. The result of this investigation showed very conclusively that Colonel Godson had had nothing to do with the charges made against the Consul and that the whole affair was engineered by the visits of the German naval officer to the Consul's daughter. As a result of this investigation the Consul was convinced that the Military Attache had had nothing to do with the predicament in which he found himself and the matter was adjusted. As the State Department believed that the Consul was obtaining valuable information concerning the activities of the German Navy through the conversations which the Consul had with the German naval officer and it was anxious that the status quo be not interfered with, nothing was done to interfere with these visits. The loyalty of the Consul was never questioned at any time.

The day after I arrived in Berne, by invitation of Captain and Mrs. Schelling, I drove to the chateau the Schellings owned on Lake Geneva for the week-end. I found here Hugh Wilson of our Berne legation and we had an extended conversation concerning certain phases of intelligence work. On Monday morning I returned to Berne and had luncheon with our Minister, Mr. Stovall, and discussed intelligence matters, particularly the incident which I had been directed to investigate in Zurich.

On July 30th, with Captain Schelling, I drove to Basel where we stayed at the house of the Consul, Mr. Holland. In addition to other matters I discussed with Mr. Holland the work his office was doing in cooperation with the Military Attache's office in connection with certain phases of intelligence work. The next day we proceeded to Zurich where I saw the Consul, Judge McNally, and the vice-consul from St. Gaulle, Mr. Cherborough with whom the usual intelligence work was discussed. The next day we drove to Lucerne and discussed matters with the vice-consul, Mr. Ray.

We returned to Berne on Aug. 2nd and that evening I talked with High Wilson of the Legation on intelligence matters and matters concerning war trades.

The next day I called on Mrs. Vera B. Whitehouse who handled our public information set-up in Berne and had a talk with her concerning matters connected with intelligence work of which she had knowledge. I then got Mr. Dannett and we looked over his Red Cross storehouse and from there I went to the office of the French Military Attache who showed me through his offices and explained its workings. The next week-end I again spent at the Schelling's chateau and met there Captain Gharde, U.S.N. of Washington, D.C. who had previously sent word that he wanted to see me. His business was the affair of the Consul of which I have already spoken.

Upon my return to Berne on Monday, I visited the office of the British Intelligence in Berne and discussed with Major Fischer, Major Langley and Captain Hamilton matters of mutual interest. On Aug. 9th I left Berne to return to Chaumont traveling, of course, via Pontalier. At Pontalier I was met by Franklin P. Adams, then a Captain in the American Expeditionary Forces, with a car and proceeded via Besancon and Bersoul.

The two following days I spent in the intelligence office making reports including a personal letter to General Churchill which described my trip to Switzerland and certain incidents connected with my stay there which I think would be interesting to intelligence officers and I have therefore appended it hereto marked "H." On the second day the G-2 of the Headquarters of the British Expeditionary Forces, Colonel Drake, who had come to deliver two lectures on intelligence at our intelligence school at Langres arrived. The next day I proceeded to Langres with Col. Moreno and Adams and heard Col. Drake lecture, once in the morning and again in the afternoon.

THE FINAL MEMORANDA

On Aug. 13th I proceeded with Moreno and Magruder and Col. Drake to the headquarters of the British Independent Air Force. Here we met the young Col. Church of the British Air Forces in command of the station who took us to the airdrome a short distance away. At this airdrome we saw one of the Hedley Page bombing planes. At this time the Hedley Page was the largest known plane and they really did seem enormous!

The next day I had luncheon with Brig. General Samuel D. Rockenbach who was then in command of our first tanks. After luncheon I proceeded to General Joseph E. Kuhn's headquarters and looked over the intelligence set-up of his outfit.

On Aug. 15th orders directed me to proceed to Holland via London were issued and I left the following day for Paris where I remained until the 19th when I proceeded to Montreuil then the headquarters of the British Expeditionary Forces in France. Here I met Col. Drake, the Intelligence officer at British headquarters. I also met Major Fowler of our service and went with him to the Headquarters of the First Corps at Fruges, where I looked over the Corps Headquarters' intelligence set up and returned to Montreuil.

At Montreuil I was the guest of Colonel Drake. The Intelligence Section of the headquarters of the British Expeditionary Forces occupied a chateau just around the corner from the plaza in Montreuil where the intelligence mess was also located.

As a hint to intelligence officers who will come in contact with Englishmen a warning which Colonel Drake gave me might well be remembered. Drake said, "When you go into breakfast tomorrow morning just say good morning and nothing more. Don't try to carry on a conversation until after breakfast is over and you have left the dining room."

The following morning I went to Colonel Drake's office and he went over with me the set-up for the intelligence at the British headquarters. The counter espionage records were kept at a little town just south of Dieppe and I went over these records and the method of handling them very carefully.

On August 21st accompanied by Colonel Drake, I went to Fruges for luncheon and then proceeded to St. Omar where the headquarters of the Second Brigade of the First Corps was located. Here we went into the intelligence set-up of a brigade. Then we returned to Montreuil and that night just after dinner eight bombs were dropped in and about British Headquarters in Montreuil. One of these being just around the corner from the chateau in which we were quartered. These bombs killed one French officer and a nurse and several men were killed or wounded.

The following morning I left Montreuil with Colonel Drake and proceeded to Boulogne where the British had a port control section under Major Combar who in civilian life was a don at Cambridge. We went over the set-up of his office and at five in the evening Colonel Dansey arrived from London and Dansey, Drake and I returned to Montreuil. Colonel Dansey was the intelligence officer on the British Mission which came to Washington immediately after we had declared war against Germany and whom I mentioned in the memorandum dated April 8, 1949, as working very closely with me in setting up the Intelligence Branch of the War College Division. He was at this time a member of the little group in the British Intelligence of the War Department in London which analyzed the various intelligence reports, summarized them and recommended lines of action to superior authority. To this group was attached an officer of the British Navy whose advice was most valuable in connection with naval matters.

The following day Dansey, Drake and Col. Menzies of the British Intelligence Service and I talked over the possibility of cooperation between the British and American Intelligence services after the war was over. After this conference I proceeded by motor to Boulogne where as mentioned before the British have a very efficient port control service. As an evidence of what close control is exercised over traffic between Boulogne and British ports, it was necessary for me to have a warrant which authorized transportation on boats and railways to London, my orders had to be stamped by our debarkation officer at the dock and this officer had to issue a card giving permission to land.

I sailed from Boulogne at 3:15 and reached Folkestone at 4:30 and proceeded by car to London. The next day I went to the office of our Military Attache, Colonel Stephen L. H. Slocum, where I also met Captains Cutting and Marsden, the Assistant Military Attaches. I also called on General John Biddle who then commanded American troops in England. Later in the day I visited Colonel Turner, the Service of Supply counter intelligence officer, and talked over passport control. Appended hereto marked "Appendix I" is a letter to Leland Harrison on the subject of passport control which goes fairly well into the situation and is submitted as being a fairly accurate description of conditions as they existed together with recommendations on the solution of the problem.

On Aug. 27th, by previous arrangement, I went to the M.I.-5 section of the British Intelligence Service and was shown through the office by Colonel M. M. Halcane. M.I.-5 is the British Intelligence Section which handled counter espionage matters.

The next day I went to the Ritz to meet the Assistant Secretary of the Navy, Franklin Delano Roosevelt, and went with him to the Naval office. Secretary Roosevelt and his party continued their trip for a visit to the High Seas Fleet that evening.

I returned to the office of the Military Attache where I received a cable from General Churchill in Washington telling me that the Military Intelligence Branch had been transferred back as the Second (Military Intelligence) Division of the General Staff. A copy of a memorandum signed by Churchill giving the set-up of the Division at this time is appended hereto marked "Appendix B[1]."

Later in the day I visited the office of M.I.-9 which was the postal censorship set-up and was shown its organization and functions by Colonel G. S. H. Pearson of the British Intelligence Service. I here also met Mr. F. V. Worthington, the Deputy Chief Censor who showed me the workings of the secret ink bureau. It will be remembered from the first memorandum that it was in this office that I met the young officer who had been in the laboratory of Harvard University and had tried to analyze the secret ink which we sent in from the Intelligence office in Washington.

On August 30th I had a very interesting talk with a Mr. Smith whose initials I do not now recall, who had been a representative on the War Trades Board and had recently talked with King Alfonse of Spain. This same day Captain Herbert O. Yardley who was the chief of our code and cipher section of the Military Intelligence in Washington came in. He was one of several of our intelligence officers who had been sent to Europe for the purpose of giving them an opportunity to see at first hand what was going on.

On August 31st I attended a luncheon which was held at the Navy Club at which the following were present: Major General G. M. W. Macdonogh, director of British Military Intelligence, General Bocanveil, the French Military Attache at the Hague; Colonel C. E. Dansey of the British M.I.-1-c and Captain Mansfield Cummings of the Royal Navy and the same office as Dansey; Colonel Drake, Military Intelligence officer of the British Expeditionary Forces, the British Military Attache from the Hague, two Belgian intelligence officers; Colonel Walner of the French Second Bureau in Paris. Immediately following the luncheon we proceeded to the smoking room of the club and held a conference for the purpose of obtaining better cooperation among the Allied agencies in Holland.

The result of the conference was that it was agreed that the Military Attaches of France, Great Britain and the United States and Belgium should form a committee in Holland and by absolute frank co-operation in the employment of agents, to bring about a condition when we will get co-operation instead of competition and avoid the use of agents who have been found untrustworthy or useless by one or another of the services. In addition to this a committee was to be formed in London to which all questions of policy should be referred and also all questions which the Holland Committee could not act upon. The London Committee was to consist of a representative from the Intelligence Service of each of the above mentioned countries.

On the afternoon of September 2nd I went to the British Intelligence office of M.I.-5 where I had a long conversation with Major H. E. Spencer on port control and passport control. The next day I met Yardley and sent him to Col. C. N. French's office. French was in charge of the Secretariate Section, M.I.-1 of the British Military Intelligence. I then proceeded to purchase my ticket for Holland and returned to the office of our Military Attache and wrote a long letter to General Churchill on the subject of port control. As has been previously noted the United States had no real port control up to this time and it was most important that one be established. The letter mentioned above goes into the necessity of this activity as I saw it at the time and it is interesting as it shows conditions. I therefore have appended it hereto marked "Appendix C."

After completing the above-mentioned letter I was driven by Col. Slocum to a German prison hospital near Belmont where a class of intelligence officers was interrogating German prisoners. This class was made up of both British and American officers and Colonel Hewitt was in charge.

The following morning I met Major Riggs who had arrived from Archangel the day before and had a talk with him over conditions in Russia of which he was cognizant. I then had luncheon with Colonel French and talked over general intelligence matters of interest to both us and the British.

The next day I wrote another letter to General Churchill on the subject of the use of Intelligence Officers aboard transports and other ships which is interesting as showing conditions at that time and is therefore appended hereto marked "Appendix D."

On Sept. 6th, Mr. Robert Bliss of the State Department arrived in London from Paris. I had that morning received a message from General Nolan informing me that Bliss was arriving in London and asking me to get in touch with him. This I did and had a long talk with him concerning matters of mutual interest.

The same day I received a telephone message from the British Intelligence office directing me to be at the Cannon Street Station in time to take a train at 6:15 A.M. the following day. This was by previous arrangement, of course. The British were extremely careful in maintaining secrecy concerning the exact time a ship from England to Holland left England. On the date that a ship left England all the Naval forces stationed along the Southeast coast moved out into the North sea several miles and remained there for defensive purposes until the ship for Holland arrived at The Hook. The British Intelligence maintained an extremely effective port control office at Gravesend which was the port in southeast England from which the ship for Holland sailed. The necessity for such a station is evident when it is realized that this was the only direct means of communication between England and Holland during this period of the war. When I arrived at the Cannon Street Station I was met by a man in civilian clothes who introduced himself to me by name saying he would show me to my compartment on the train. When we entered the compartment he also seated himself and informed me that he was also on his way to Holland. It was not until I returned from Holland that I found out that this man had been detailed by British Intelligence to go with me and see as far as possible that nothing happened to me until I reached the shores of Holland. A part of the reason for the solicitation [sic] on the part of British Intelligence was to make sure no preventable accident should interfere with putting into effect of the decisions of the conference concerning intelligence matters in Holland which I was charged by our G-2, AEF, of promulgating upon my arrival in The Hague.

We left Cannon Street Station at 6:15 A.M. and arrived at the port of Gravesend at 7:30 A.M. I was here met by Captain Smith in charge of the port control station, who took me through the station set-up and explained in detail the methods of screening passengers and cargo. We boarded the ship and sailed about 1 P.M. During the voyage we were required to remain fully clothed and to wear our life belts. We reached The Hook about 2 P.M. the next day.

The man from the British Intelligence office who was my companion telephoned to our Legation at The Hague and they sent a car to meet me. When the automobile arrived we proceeded to The Hague and I went to the office of Colonel Davis, our Military Attache at The Hague. A room was engaged at the Neudoylen for me. Davis dined with me at the hotel and we had a long talk concerning the general intelligence situation.

On the evening of September 10th I attended an entertainment by the British internees who had escaped from the enemy territory or had landed inadvertently with their airplanes in Dutch territory. They were quartered in the village of Schrirengus in very considerable number.

On the 11th Colonel Davis, Captain Waldo, the assistant Military Attache and I proceeded by motor to Rotterdam where I called on our Consul-General, "Col" Listoc with whom I discussed various matters concerning our intelligence in Holland. In the evening Mr. Engert of our Legation had dinner with Mirza Mahmud Khan, Charge D'affaires of the Persian Legation, and myself, and in a long conversation I obtained considerable information concerning affairs in Persia which, of course, is now Iran.

On the 13th I called on the French Military Attache, General Bocanveil and discussed with him the decisions of the conference which he had attended with me in London.

On September 14th I saw the man in charge of the Legation passport work and had a long talk with him. His office was handled efficiently but in my opinion the work should have been more closely tied in with the Military Attache's office than it was.

On the 16th I had a long talk with Engert on conditions in the East particularly in Persia concerning which Engert was very well informed.

On September 17th I went by rail to Amsterdam with Captain Waldo and called on our Consul and discussed matters with which his office was concerned, returning to The Hague that evening.

On the 18th I was notified that I must be aboard the ship on which I was to return to England that night and I proceeded to say my good-byes to the members of the Military Attache's office as well as those of the Legation and proceeded by train to The Hook.

In going over the situation at The Hague, I found that there had been a good deal of confusion in connection with the direction to forward to the G-2, AEF intelligence information. This confusion was easily explained away and things put on a workable basis. There were one or two rather valuable agents of the Military Attache's office who worked back and forth between Holland and Germany. The information furnished from these sources proved in several instances to be extremely valuable. The recommendations arrived at by the conference already mentioned as having taken place in London were explained fully to both the Military Attache and to the State Department officials with the Legation and were accepted and put into effect. Cooperation between the Military Attache's office and the office of our Legation was excellent and continued to be excellent during the remainder of the war. Considerable valuable information was also obtained from the interned personnel living at Schrirengus.

The following day a very strong wind came up which required the ship to remain at the dock for the next two days but by the morning of the 21st the wind had died down considerably and we sailed. It was cold and extremely rough. We anchored inside the mouth of the Thames late that night and very early the following morning proceeded to an anchorage off Gravesend where the passengers were landed by a tender.

When I arrived ashore I found that Captain Smith, the British Intelligence officer in charge of the control station, was ill but his assistant took me in charge and gave me an opportunity to listen to the examination of the passengers. The examination of these individuals was a long and very careful one. It had been found that many attempts at getting information as well as actual agents ashore had been made on several occasions. It was through this station that a message in invisible ink on the back of a would-be agent was discovered. Among the passengers on the ship on which I arrived were six women, three British nurses being returned to England, three other Englishwomen being repatriated. One of these women turned out to be a German and what happened to her I never knew.

I returned to London by train and shortly after my return Col. Solbert, our Military Attache from Denmark and Norway called. The following day at the Military Attache's offices where I had a desk, I met and talked with Solbert and Captain Robert W. Goelet. Mr. Doolittle from Tiflis came in and we had an extended conversation on Persia and Russia.

The following day Captain Yardley and I talked over the code and cipher situation in the Military Attache's office where considerable suspicion concerning one of the clerks had developed. In the afternoon I went to see Colonel R. A. Steel in charge of M.O.-5 which is the British Operations office for the Far East and Russia. Colonel Solbert went with me and we talked over with Col. Steel the situation in Russia in connection with the keeping open of the Trans-Siberia railroad for the Czechs. The British wanted the Japanese to push west of Lake Baikal in order to make a junction with the Czechs. I sent a cable concerning the matter at once.

On the 25th I met Colonel French by appointment and he went with me to see General Thwaites who was the new director of the Military Intelligence for the British having recently relieved General Macdonough who had been appointed Adjutant General of the forces.

Up to this time I have not mentioned the many courtesies extended to me purely as a representative of the Intelligence Section of the AEF. This courtesy consisted of luncheons and dinners to which I was invited given by our diplomatic and consular representatives in France, England,

Switzerland and Holland. Such courtesy was also extended by the Intelligence services of both France and Great Britain. In the case of Great Britain particularly the representatives and members of the intelligence service were extremely cordial and cooperative as they were from the beginning of the war to its end. While these courtesies had of course nothing to do with my mission I feel that they should be mentioned as showing the fine spirit of cooperation in which the intelligence service of the AEF was favored.

On Sept. 26th I had a long conversation with Colonel Turner on passport control and in the afternoon talked with Mr. Bell of our Embassy on the same matter. After dinner the next day, which I had with Colonel Solbert, we went to a meeting where I met with General Thwaites and the following British M.I. officers: Col. French, Col. Dansey, Col. Cornwall and the British Military Attache from Copenhagen. At this meeting we discussed many matters in which our two services were mutually interested, particularly with respect to policies and the possibility of the two services working together after the war.

The following day I discussed general intelligence matters in which the United States and Great Britain were interested with Colonel Dansey at his office and later I went to the office of our Consul General in London and discussed matters of passport control with him. In the afternoon Prof. Bernstadt came to see me to discuss the sending of information from enemy territory by means of signals. Later in the afternoon I was informed that Secretary of War Baker wish to see us at the house where he was staying in London and I went over and had a half hour's conversation with him. He asked me to return with him to Paris when he went in a couple of days.

On the 30th, Prof. Bernstadt again came in and after discussing the matter of signaling from enemy territory I sent him over to talk with Col. Dansey of the British Intelligence Service. As mentioned in the memorandum dated April 8, 1949, the intelligence service sent very few agents into enemy countries during the First World War. This was in response to a request by British and and French Intelligence services. Therefore, although we were of course vitally interested in the problem of assuring the safe entry and return of the Allied agents destined for enemy territory and in expediting the receipt of information gathered by these agents, the responsibility was not ours for providing the means by which these ends could be accomplished. As is well known the British and French both lost many of their very valuable agents while they were endeavoring to return from enemy territory, either shot by frontier guards or caught on the charged wires which lined almost our entire Western front. It must be remembered that the First World War up to its final stages was a war of position and trenches rather than movement and this made doubly difficult the problem of sending in agents and of providing for their safe return. Agents were injected into enemy territory in many ways, of course, in some instances the individual who undertook the service had lived in enemy countries for many years and remained there after war was declared. However, it was necessary to augment their number by additional trained agents and the getting of these individuals across the enemy lines was not an easy one. Some were dressed in the uniform of the Central Powers and accompanied an attack or a trench raiding party. Others were dropped in parachutes from airplanes at night and still others were able to enter enemy territory through neutral countries. Their return was even more difficult and barring those who in the early stages of the war were picked up by our airplanes and returned most of them had to depend upon their own wits in order to return to Allied territory.

The forwarding of information gathered by these agents in hostile territory was an equally difficult problem and many methods were used from first to last. I was told by the Chief of the British Intelligence, General Thwaites, that the most successful method employed by the British Intelligence was the carrier pigeon. He said that 85% of the pigeons sent into enemy territory returned with messages. The usual method of getting these pigeons into the hands of our agents in enemy territory was to drop them from airplanes at night in wicker cages provided with parachutes, at certain specified times and at places where known agents were quartered. It was necessary of course that the agents find these pigeons before daylight, destroy the parachutes and cages and release the pigeons with their messages since the discovery of carrier pigeons or their cages in the hands of an agent was his death warrant. The problem of rapid transmission of vital information from enemy countries to our own lines was considered so important that very well-known scientists of both sides of the Atlantic were engaged in the study of this matter and of producing methods during the latter months of the war. Whether this study continued after the end of the war I never knew.

After talking with Prof. Bernstadt, I went over to Scotland Yard office and paid a courtesy call.

On October 1st, I had another talk with Mr. Bell of our Embassy this time concerning the British Black List and the question of the omission of certain British firms from the list.

On October 2nd, I met the Secretary of War Baker at Victoria Station and went with him and his party to Southhampton sailing from that point at 10 A.M. for Boulogne. Col. Dansey joined us after we left London at the Secretary's invitation. At Boulogne, General Harbord's train was waiting for the Secretary and we all went aboard and proceeded to Paris. When we reached Paris I was met by Major Warburton and Lt. Munn and proceeded to Major Warburton's quarters.

The next morning Captain Walter Lippman came to the office of the Military Attache and I had a talk with him concerning propaganda. Captain Yardley also came in later having just arrived from London. Captain Voska also came in and reported on his recent trip to Switzerland and Italy.

On October 5th, Walter Lippman came in to tell me that he had seen Secretary Baker just before he left for the United States and that I was to take up the propaganda matter with General McAndrews, Chief of Staff, AEF.

Colonel Dansey and the British Military Control officer from Belgrade came in and after luncheon we discussed intelligence matters connected with the Bulgar and Swiss situation. Dansey returned to London that evening. Later in the afternoon Colonel Stickney came in to discuss postal censorship matters.

On October 7th and 8th Major Campanole and I went through the various sections of the Second Bureau including the counter-espionage section under Col. Walner whom I have mentioned before. While there we called on Colonel Gourgen, the head of the Second Bureau.

On October 9th Campanole and I by arrangement visited the French Intelligence office which is concerned with the instruction of prospective agents to be sent into enemy country. These offices consisted of a number of rooms in the Invalides and the school was run by two rather ancient professors from the Sorbonne. In these rooms were various uniforms and marking for the troops of the Central Powers, drawings and photographs of enemy airplanes and railroad trains with estimates of the number of troops and material which the railroads could transport and various other objects to be used in impressing on the memories of the potential spies under instruction and the various methods to be utilized by them in securing information in enemy territory.

In the afternoon, Campanole and I returned to the Invalides and went through the rooms containing various objects which might be useful in aiding Allied prisoners to escape. These objects consisted of maps, compasses, files, hacksaw blades and various other such objects so formed as to be capable of being concealed in food or other packages sent from Allied into enemy territory to our prisoners.

On October 11th I returned to Chaumont with Major Campanole and Lt. Ralph Hays who had been the private secretary of Secretary of War Baker during the first part of the war. We arrived at Chaumont at

THE FINAL MEMORANDA 73

6 P.M. After dinner I went to the G-2 office where I found Colonel Coxe who had recently come over from Washington and was not attached to the G-2 section of the AEF.

On October 13 Colonel Nolan returned from the front where he had been commanding combat troops in action. He arrived about midnight and we talked until breakfast the next morning, as it was necessary that he return to the front at noon of the 14th.

On the evening of the 14th, Captain Ogden Mills reported at headquarters. Mills was afterwards detailed as my assistant when I was the Intelligence officer with the American Section of the Peace Conference and it will be remembered that after the war he became the Secretary of the Treasury following Secretary Mellon.

On October 16th Colonel Conger returned to Chaumont from the front where he had been commanding troops. Both Conger and Nolan of course were members of the General Staff Corps and not ordinarily supposed to command troops; however, it was General Pershing's desire that all of his higher ranking staff officers should have active experience in the command of troops in combat which explains why these two intelligence officers had been serving with troops in the front lines.

On October 18th I was informed that Nolan had made arrangements for Coxe and myself to go to our front lines. That evening I had dinner with General Wagstaff, General Thwaites and Major Cornwall, all of the British service. I was to see something of General Wagstaff years later when I was sent to India on an intelligence mission by invitation of the British-Indian Military Service.

On the following day, General Thwaites came to the intelligence office and I took him to see the battle map which he was extremely anxious to see and then to Col. Moreno's counter-espionage section which he also wanted to see.

On October 21st the German reply to our peace note was received and it appears that the Germans were about ready to begin serious peace negotiations. I applied for a car to take Coxe and me to the front but was informed by the Quartermaster Department that there was none available but that I would be informed as soon as one came in.

Before I left for the front, Nolan told me that if I received a telegram recalling me to Chaumont not to be surprised because General Pershing had told him to tell me that as soon as Nolan was assigned to a brigade that I would be appointed G-2 in his place. I later received a personal note from General Pershing telling me that in October he had recommended my appointment as a brigadier general but that now that the Armistice had taken place the recommendation would not be carried out. This of course was in preparation for my appointment as G-2 to replace Nolan. This letter is appended hereto marked "Appendix E."

On October 23rd I left Chaumont at 10 A.M. accompanied by Colonel Coxe and proceeded to the headquarters of the First Army via Bar-le-Duc and talked with the assistant Army Intelligence officer, Major Catron, concerning the intelligence operations of the First Army and then proceeded to the headquarters of the Fifth Corps at Cheppy. The officers of the Fifth Corps were quartered in the old German dugouts. These dugouts were, of course, facing the wrong way but a little work made them fairly safe against artillery and light bombing attacks. Just as we reached Cheppy [a] heavy German anti-aircraft barrage started which resulted in the shooting down of two of our observation balloons. The Corps intelligence Officer was Colonel Russel and the commander was General Summerall. That night we had a rather lively airplane attack and the next morning we found an airplane "dud" bomb embedded in the earth directly above the dugout in which we slept.

The next morning Coxe, Russel and I proceeded to the headquarters of the 42nd Division and I had a talk with Major Judah, the intelligence officer of the Division. We then proceeded to the town of Exermont taking Major Judah with us and then on foot up onto Hill 272 where we had three observation posts, a Corps and two Divisions. There was considerable aircraft activity almost directly overhead and a good deal of artillery all along our front lines. We then visited a front line regiment commanded by Colonel Dravo and talked with his intelligence officer and then returned to Exermont where we re-entered our automobile and returned to Corps headquarters at Cheppy.

The next day the President's reply to the German note came in by wire and after it was typed Coxe and I took it down to the headquarters of the 42nd Division where we had a long talk with Major Judah, the Division Intelligence officer, on regimental and battalion combat intelligence work. Before talking with Judah we had a long talk with General Menoher, the Division commander. We returned to Cheppy after luncheon.

On October 26th, two British Intelligence officers, Colonel Sheridan and Major Glenn, came into Corps headquarters. Major Glenn was an instructor at the intelligence school at Langres. They continued their visit to our front lines the following day. The same day Coxe and I made some experiments with some of the message-carrying bombs which had been left by the Germans when they retreated from Cheppy. These bombs were used for sending messages from observation posts back to headquarters and from isolated posts to the main line. They were not very effective.

THE FINAL MEMORANDA

On the 27th a German plane was shot down near headquarters and the pilot was uninjured. He was brought into headquarters for interrogation by Lt. Szlapka, the interpreter.

On October 28th, as it was evident that the time had not yet arrived when our main attack was to take place, we decided to return to Chaumont and wait for word as to when the movement was to begin. During the time I spent with the Fifth Corps, I went into the organization and activities of the combat intelligence work pretty thoroughly. It was evidently proceeding efficiently. As I think I mentioned in my memorandum dated April 8, 1949, we found very heavy losses in combat intelligence personnel particularly those of the battalions and it was necessary to make an investigation as to the cause. Upon investigation it was found that battalion commanders had been making their trench raiding parties almost exclusively of intelligence personnel which accounted for the unusual heavy losses. Of course no such procedure as this was ever contemplated and strict orders were issued by General Headquarters AEF limiting intelligence personnel in any raiding party to two and specifying that they were to gather the information which was obtainable and return with it to our lines as promptly as possible. I found on this trip that in the Fifth Corps that those orders were being strictly carried out and the casualties among intelligence personnel were comparatively light. Coxe and I returned to Chaumont via the headquarters of the First Army where we saw a copy of the German reply to President Wilson's note.

After luncheon at the First Army headquarters mess, we proceeded to go over the intelligence set-up and particularly the interrogation of prisoners. At the prison pen at this headquarters we had introduced two Germans who posed as prisoners of war and who furnished our intelligence with considerable information gathered through conversations with the actual prisoners with whom they lived.

At this time it was decided to see if we could not make the Germans believe that we were setting up a Third Army in the Vosges. All during the war the lines in the Vosges area had been very indeterminate and it was comparatively easy for individuals to pass from the German lines into ours and vice versa. Neither the German forces nor ours were in much strength in the area so it seemed to the intelligence service that it might be possible to make the Germans move some of their divisions from their lines further north if they thought we were moving forces into this region. To this end, Colonel Conger proceeded to a town which would be a logical place for the location of the headquarters of an Army and went to a hotel. He took with him a few clerks and typewriters and dictated what purported to be a memorandum from Third Army headquarters making arrangements for the movement of troops from the north to occupy positions in the area. He also proceeded to set up a number of field radio stations which were directed to operate as if they were members of the occupying forces. After the typewriting of the memorandum mentioned above Conger dropped the carbons into a waste basket in his hotel room and left them there purposely, of course. Within a couple of days thereafter we found that the Germans were moving divisions to the south and eventually we discovered that they had moved several combat divisions in order to counter our supposed movement of troops into that area.

We reached Chaumont on the 29th and the next day Coxe and I both went down to Langres and both of us talked to the intelligence classes. In the evening Captain Robert Goelet came in from Holland for the purpose of a talk on passport control matters.

On October 31st I received a confidential message that the attack would begin on November 1st so Coxe and I left and proceeded back to the headquarters of the Fifth Corps at Cheppy. On the way up we saw Lt. Bourgeois of the French Army on the road. Bourgeois had been the liaison officer from the French to the Military Intelligence Branch in Washington and had had a mental breakdown and had been returned to France some months before. He now assured me he was well again and back on duty.

On November 1st, General Nolan came in to the Fifth Corps headquarters and the next day went over to the First Corps to observe intelligence operations there. That morning Coxe delivered some maps to the Second Division and in the afternoon I visited the Corps prisoners' cage and observed the questioning of prisoners. On the night of the third a copy of the Allied terms of surrender came in to Corps headquarters. About midnight the terms of the entente to Germany for the Armistice were telephoned up from First Army and also the fact that the Armistice with Austria had been signed about 3 P.M. The terms as reported were very hard for Germany but it looked as though she would have to accept. On the 4th Coxe again took an additional supply of maps to the First Division using our automobile because the Corps intelligence was short of transportation.

On November 5th Colonel Russel, the intelligence officer of the Fifth Corps, and I went down to the French Second Army to obtain some necessary maps. Corps headquarters were moved on the 6th but the G-2 remained at Cheppy. On Nov. 6th, Russel and I proceeded to the headquarters of General "Billy" Wright's division finding the roads almost impassable and choked with troops and supplies. We returned the same day to Cheppy.

THE FINAL MEMORANDA 77

It was evident that the heavy fighting was now over on the Argonne front and Coxe and I decided to see if we could get across the Meuse and see what the Second Army was doing before the Armistice took effect. We therefore started back for Chaumont on the 7th. However, our automobile broke down and we had to be towed into Claremont where we turned the car over for repairs. We found it was going to take until the next day to repair the car so we hitchhiked a ride in a car we intercepted on a corner and which landed us at Bar-le-Check where we waited until the next day for our car to catch up with us. Which it did the next day and we reached Chaumont about 2 P.M. Here we found Frederick Palmer still at luncheon with the intelligence mess. We were told that the terms of the Armistice had been agreed upon and would be signed that day or the next. It was therefore impossible for us to reach the Second Army before the fighting ceased and we therefore abandoned the attempt.

During the visits to the various organizations of the First Army, Coxe and I had been able to check quite thoroughly the operations of the combat intelligence service from the Army headquarters to the battalion. During the Argonne attack we were also able to check the efficiency of the service during movement which we had not been able to accomplish before this. Reports on our observations were made verbally to General Nolan and also in writing to General Churchill in Washington.

Captain Ralph Hayes and Mr. Keppel, Third Assistant Secretary of War, had dinner with us and the next day proceeded on to the Fifth Corps.

On Nov. 9th, immediately after breakfast, I had a long talk with General Nolan and Major Moreno on counter espionage matters. Nolan told me that he wanted me to go on down to Rome to attend to certain matters down there in connection with the office of the Military Attache even though the Armistice would end the fighting temporarily at least. On November 10th I saw "Billy" Mitchell who was then a brigadier general in the Air Corps. On the 11th word came from French GHQ that the Armistice had been signed at 5 A.M. that morning and would go into effect at 11 A.M.

While we had been receiving at AEF headquarters hints from time to time of what was going on in Russia, we had not received any definite information concerning the state of affairs there except of course that the Bolshevik government was being successful in its revolution. On November 11th a telegram from Godson, the Military Attache at Berne, told of a Bolshevik movement in Switzerland which threatened a strike on the part of the railroad men who were expected to refuse to transport troops. Rumors of similar trouble in Germany were also received and on November 12th a dispatch from Brussels told that the soldiers' and workmen's committee had taken over the civil and military government and that the Red flag was flying. Also a dispatch from Switzerland told of a general strike and that no trains had left Switzerland that day.

On November 13th I sent a cable to Churchill concerning conditions in Europe as affected by the Bolshevik revolution in Russia. A copy of which is appended hereto marked "Appendix F" and a letter of the same date and on the same subject which is appended hereto marked "Appendix G."

On November 18th Coxe and I proceeded by rail to Paris reaching there in the evening. Coxe went to a hotel and I proceeded to the quarters of Major Warburton who was waiting dinner for me. I obtained my reservations for Rome on the 20th and had luncheon with General Nolan and Colonel Coxe. At luncheon we discussed methods to be used in obtaining military information on the countries formerly belonging to the Central Powers by utilizing the visits of the agents of Herbert Hoover in connection with the providing of food where necessary. In this connection we hoped to use intelligence officers who were familiar with the country and who would accompany the agents of the Hoover Commission.

On the 21st I began an investigation of the rumors of misconduct which were apparently being circulated in certain French official circles concerning General Pershing and which had been privately reported to General Peyton March, Chief of Staff in Washington. It is unnecessary to say these rumors were without foundation and were soon squelched.

On November 22nd I was told that a cable had arrived from our Secretary of State, Mr. Robert Lansing, saying: "Mr. Baker promised me that Van Deman should be put in charge of all counter espionage for the Peace Conference." I thereupon went down to see Mr. Joseph Grew who had been appointed as the Executive Secretary of the American Section of the Conference to negotiate Peace, who said that he wanted me to take this job. However, I was under orders to proceed to Rome and there were other matters that had not been cleaned up in my original mission. I demurred from giving up the trip to Italy but when I got back to the office of the Military Attache I found a message from Major Magruder at Chaumont telling me that a cable had just been received from the Adjutant General in Washington directing the Commander in Chief, AEF, to detail me in charge of all counter espionage for the duration of the Peace Conference and giving me every assistance and directing me to report to General Bliss. I therefore canceled my reservations for Rome and proceeded to make arrangements to take over the new assignment with the Peace Conference.

Memorandum III

San Diego, California   April 10, 1951

MEMORANDUM

In order that there is no misapprehension concerning this memorandum, the introduction to the memorandum of April 8, 1949 and June 5, 1950 are repeated here.

> The following memorandum is in no sense to be considered an official document. Nor is it to be considered as a personal history of the writer. It is not for publication. It consists of certain incidents pertinent to the history and development of the Military Intelligence service of the United States Army which can now be recalled by the writer after nearly fifty-five years experience in intelligence work. It is more than possible that there may be some minor discrepancies in this work, since, with the exception of a few dates, the writer has had to depend entirely on his unaided memory, without notes of any kind, in its preparation. It has been written because very few of the persons connected with the early history of Military Intelligence in our Army are still alive and the writer believes it would be interesting for those now interested in that work to know something of its development as seen by one who was intimately connected with the incidents related.
>
> However, for the information contained in this memorandum the writer had access to a diary which he kept during his tour of duty in Europe which gave names of places visited and individuals contacted together with dates, but which gave practically no information concerning what had actually been done. He also had the help of various letters on intelligence matters received and written during this period.

In order that the position occupied by the writer may be clear the following portion of the memorandum of June 5, 1950 is repeated:

> On November 22nd I was told that a cable had arrived from our Secretary of State, Mr. Robert Lansing, saying: 'Mr. Baker promised me that Van Deman should be put in charge of all counter espionage for the Peace Conference'. I thereupon went down to see Mr. Joseph Grew

who had been appointed as the Executive Secretary of the American Section of the Conference to Negotiate Peace, who said that he wanted me to take over the job. However, I was under orders to proceed to Rome and there were other matters that had not been cleaned up in my original mission. I demurred from giving up the trip to Italy but when I got back to the office of the Military Attache I found a message from Major Macgruder at Chaumont telling me that a cable had just been received from the Adjutant General in Washington directing the Commander in Chief, AEF, to detail me in charge of all counter-espionage for the duration of the Peace Conference and giving me every assistance and directing me to report to General Bliss. I therefore canceled my reservations for Rome and proceeded to make arrangements to take over the new assignment with the Peace Conference.

R. H. Van Deman
Maj. Gen., U.S.A., Ret.

I reported to General Bliss for instructions on November 29th as required by the order of the Adjutant General in Washington and the Commander in Chief of the American Expeditionary Force, and was told to carry out the instructions received from Washington and Chaumont. On December 5th I received the further instructions from General Bliss which are appended hereto as Appendix A, page 3. [Published here as Appendix J - 3]

About this time our Ambassador at Paris had made arrangements to take over the Hotel Crillon and the office building at #4 Place de la Concorde to be used as quarters and offices by the American Section of the Conference to Negotiate Peace. I was assigned office space at #4 Place de la Concorde. This office suite was so arranged with two entrances that people desiring to leave the office without incoming visitors being aware of the fact could do so. I was also assigned certain office personnel consisting of two sergeants and a messenger detailed from the G-2, SOS.

It will be noticed that I was not relieved from General Pershing's staff and therefore was still responsible for the investigation of the intelligence services of the Allies on which I was directed to report. I therefore continued my investigation of the subject by means of interviews with various people many of these interviews, as was the custom, being held at social luncheons and dinners. In addition to this assignment I at once began the organization of the work I was expected to carry out as Intelligence Officer for the American Section of the Peace Conference and much of this was also necessarily accomplished by interviews with various and sundry people.

On November 30th I had an interview with Voska and Mr. Gordon Auchincloss secretary of Colonel House, and Mr. Joseph Grew, at Grew's office concerning the work which Voska had been carrying on in Austro-Hungary.

It will be remembered that at this time Herbert Hoover had been given charge of providing food and relief for certain devastated sections in Europe. We desired to send with Mr. Hoover's workers going into those areas certain intelligence agents who were familiar with the country but to this Mr. Hoover violently objected. However certain intelligence agents were sent on some of these missions and they reported conditions upon their return.

On Dec. 2nd I made an effort to obtain a complete list of the personnel of the American Section of the Conference to Negotiate Peace but was unable to do so at that time. That same day I had a confidential interview with Dr. Edward Benes of the provisional government of

Czechoslovakia concerning Voska. It had been reported that Voska was not in the confidence of Dr. Benes and his government but the Doctor assured me that this was untrue and that he had every confidence in Voska but he did not believe that Voska's education was sufficient to warrant his handling a political mission.

On December 4th Captain Ogden Mills reported for duty having been detailed as my assistant.

Some little time previous to this Mr. Moran, the head of the United States Secret Service, had come to Paris to make arrangements for the safeguarding of President Wilson during his contemplated visit. On December fourth with Mr. Moran, General William W. Hart (the American Provost Marshal in Paris) Mr. Auchincloss and certain others, I went to inspect the quarters which were to be used by the President. The palace of Prince Murat had been obtained for this purpose and we made a very thorough inspection on the entire premises and surroundings. Mr. Moran found the measures taken for the safeguarding of the President quite satisfactory as they were very thorough. For example the telephone was enclosed in lead and a part of the special American telephone exchange which was set up in the old bar room of the Hotel Crillon. The operators of the exchange were carefully-selected American girls and a part of the exchange had been arranged to allow me to listen in to any conversation at any time to see that instructions regarding security were being carried out.

On December fourth Sir Basil Thompson who was in charge of Scotland Yard called to assure me of his assistance whenever needed.

Due to the reputation of Maxim's Restaurant it had been placed off bounds for all American armed forces personnel in Paris. Hence, when it was discovered on December fourth that a trap door existed leading from one of the offices at #4 Place de la Concorde down to the second floor above the restaurant giving access to it, I ordered a padlock placed on the trap door and the keys thereof placed in the charge of a sergeant reported to be entirely reliable.

In addition to my other duties in connection with the Peace Conference I was detailed as a member of the Committee on Current Diplomatic and Political Correspondence of the American Section of the Conference to Negotiate Peace. The chairman of this committee was Mr. E. L. Dresel of the United States State Department. I do not remember the entire personnel of the committee although it can doubtless be obtained from the archives of the Peace Conference. As I remember it consisted of the two Dulles brothers, Adolph Berle, F. R. Dolbeare, E. T. Williams, J. H. Stabler, J. G. D. Paul, Major Royal Tyler and Major Delancey Kountze.

The principal function of the committee was to receive and and examine the various couriers as they reported from the different sectors of Europe and before they had made their report to the Commissioners. The committee usually met every morning.

On December sixth I took up the matter of the passes for personnel entitled to enter the Crillon and #4 Place de la Concorde.

On December seventh it was reported that a Socialist demonstration was to be pulled off on the arrival of President Wilson. Means to make sure that this demonstration did not interfere with the President's movements were taken with the aid of the French Surete and, of course, using our own forces where possible. As a matter of fact the demonstration did not materialize.

On December eleventh Captain Bertie Goolet together with Lts. Rose and Waldo from the Military Attache's office at the Hague arrived in Paris and the following day Inspector Ernest Hole of Scotland Yard arrived to be assistant to Sir. Basil Thompson.

On December twelfth Major Buckey, the Military Attache in Rome, together with the American Ambassador to Italy came in to discuss matters in that country. On the same day Senator Wadsworth came in and I had a talk with him on conditions in the United States.

On December thirteenth Voska came in with a letter from the Czecho-Slovak Council asking him to go to Prague. On the same day I checked on the mail system for the American Section of the Conference to Negotiate Peace.

On December fourteenth, President Wilson arrived in Paris. General Marlborough Churchill, chief of Military Intelligence in Washington, also arrived on the same ship and I discussed matters with him at length.

On December fourteenth I discovered while making a late evening inspection that there were no armed guards over the offices at #4 Place de la Concorde or the entire establishment of the Hotel Crillon after 4 P.M. The following day it developed that responsibility for the guards over these localities had not been properly placed and I discussed the matter with a representative from Captain Ward's office, G-2, SOS.

On December sixteenth I had an extensive conversation with Mr. Leland Harrison, head of the Secret Service of the United States State Department, and Joseph Grew concerning the collection and transmittal of Positive Intelligence as it was at that time called.

On December seventeenth it was discovered that the trap door leading to Maxim's Restaurant from the offices at #4 Place de la

Concorde which had been padlocked was open. This made it necessary, of course, to again padlock the door and remove the keys from the custody of the sergeant, which was done.

On December eighteenth I drafted a note of explanation to be sent to all the Peace Commissioners of the American Section explaining the necessity for the means guaranteeing security and the measures which had been taken to secure them. Later I made sure that a guard for the record room was provided.

On December 18th a memorandum similar to the one sent to the Commissioners was furnished to all personnel connected with the American Section of the Peace Conference.

On December 19th General Churchill, Colonel A. B. Coxe, (the Intelligence Officer at General Pershing's headquarters who served as liaison between that headquarters and the Peace Conference) and I prepared a cable to be sent to Colonel John Dunn (who was in charge of Military Intelligence in Washington during General Churchill's absence) discussing the reorganization of the Military Intelligence Section in Washington.

On December 20th I received approval for the permanent passes for the members of the press who were accredited to the American Section of the Conference to Negotiate the Peace. Among the accredited reporters was Mrs. Marguerite Harrison the widow of one of the editors of the Baltimore Sun. Mrs. Harrison had been quite helpful in many ways in the United States and when she arrived in Paris she came to me and offered to keep an eye on the various correspondents the previous records of some of whom were not too good. There were in the neighborhood of one hundred of these correspondents the complete list of which is undoubtedly available in the files of the Conference.

On December 21 the pass system for the offices at #4 Place de la Concorde and the Hotel Crillon was finally put into operation. For the next two days complaints concerning these passes were received from all sorts of sources and on the 24th the American Commissioners agreed to continue the system on a trial basis.

On December 24th Comdr. Gherdi of the United States Navy came to my office to report concerning the conditions on the Dalmation coast where he had recently been.

Colonel Sherman Miles came in to the office on the 31st to tell me that he was about to leave for the Balkans.

By the beginning of 1919 reports began to arrive from the intelligence officers of our occupying forces at Coblentz and from the Intelligence officers at the British Headquarters at Cologne to the effect that circulars were being distributed to both American and British forces on the Rhine which the intelligence officers, at least, believed were an invitation to mutiny by the troops. It was ascertained that these circulars were being prepared in Germany and an Intelligence Sergeant from my office was dispatched for the purpose of investigation. He ascertained and reported that these circulars were being prepared by one Robert Minor, a very well known and prominent American Communist. The Sergeant was instructed to see if he could get Minor to appear at the American or British bridgeheads in order that he might be picked up. But this the Sergeant later reported he was unable to do. While I was reading this last report from the Sergeant, Marguerite Harrison came into the office and I read the report to her. She offered to go to Germany herself and persuade Minor to come out with her in order that we might apprehend him in either British or American territory. For this purpose she was authorized to go to Germany which she did and during the period she spent in Berlin she also witnessed and reported on the Communist uprising there.

On January 3rd, Major John O'Laughlin, afterward the publisher and editor of the Army and Navy Journal, left for the United States. The next day Lt. M. Bourgeois of the French Service came in to see me. He had been the liaison officer in [sic] during the early part of the war. He had been returned to France because of mental disorders but it was apparent that he had entirely recovered when he called on me.

On January 5th Joseph Grew occupied his new office in the Hotel Crillon and I called on him and talked over matters of organization of the Peace Conference and similar subjects with him.

On January 6th I talked over with Robert Bliss of our Embassy in Paris the question of passes for the Crillon and for the offices in #4 Place de la Concorde.

About January eighth there was a report that the Allies were to prepare a force to be sent into Russia for the purpose of overcoming the present Russian set up and establishing a really democratic government.

On January 10th, Mr. P. A. Stovall, our minister from Berne, called and I talked over certain matters connected with intelligence in Switzerland.

On January 11th an effort was again made to obtain guards for the office rooms at #4 Place de la Concorde and this was finally accomplished.

On January 17th Comdr. Gherdi came to see me to talk over the people the American Commissioners were contemplating sending to Germany.

About this time I received a letter from Captain Bronson Cutting, the Assistant Military Attache in London, informing me that a letter which I had sent to him marked "Personal and Confidential" was opened by a secretary who had been a former code clerk of the London Embassy. She averred that this was by error and that she had not noticed the "Personal and Confidential" on the envelope. Previously there had been suspicion that this girl was not to be trusted and this was one of the reasons why it was deemed advisable to send coders to our Embassy in London from the United States. Bronson Cutting endeavored to investigate this matter but no very definite results were ever obtained.

I also received a letter from Lt. Col. Claude Dansey, of the British Intelligence Service, telling me that he was to be demobilized. This letter I answered at length thanking him for the very great service he had rendered to the United States Intelligence Services in enabling it to establish a really sound basis for intelligence work.

On January 17th Capt. Here, the assistant Military Attache at the French Legation at Copenhagen, came in with a letter from Capt. Solbert, our Military Attache to Sweden and Denmark. We had an interesting talk on Capt. Here's experience when he had been a prisoner in Germany.

On January 18th I had luncheon with General Sir William Wiseman and Colonel Arthur Murray, both of the British service, and talked on Bolshevism.

Coxe came in from Chaumont on January 20th and stayed with me. He told me that George Creel was making a trip through Germany and it was reported he had his name on the sides of his motor and was making speeches telling the people what the United States was going to do for them. Coxe returned to GHQ on January 23rd.

On January 28th I had a talk with the control officers to fix responsibility and authority of our men at Quay d'Orsey.

On January 30th and 31st several individuals were given clearance to engage in the work that Herbert Hoover was carrying on in the distribution of food in Poland.

For some time past there had been talk of the morale situation between the regular and temporary officers of the Army and I had written a letter on this subject to General Nolan on this subject saying:

AMERICAN COMMISSION TO NEGOTIATE PEACE

4 Place de la Concorde   Paris

December 23, 1918

General D. E. Nolan, G-2
General Headquarters
Amer., E.F., Chaumont

<u>PERSONAL</u> <u>AND</u> <u>CONFIDENTIAL</u>

My dear Nolan:

We have talked over the feeling of criticism and hostility existing against the officers of the Regular service on the part of Reserve and other temporary officers. Reports reaching me from many sources show that this spirit is rapidly increasing. Some of the criticisms are, as follows:

(a) That the Regular Army has placed its own officers in such positions that they have not suffered many casualties while, on the other hand, temporary officers have been placed where they would bear the brunt of the casualties.

(b) The transport service is not being utilized to send the army home but that both officers and men are being held on this side of the ocean unnecessarily.

(c) That temporary officers, particularly those in France, have not been given proper promotion.

(d) That Medical Officers (temporary) are being held on duty at hospitals where they have no patients and where there is nothing for them to do in spite of the fact that they want to get home to take up their work in civil life.

The talk along these lines is increasing more and more and becoming more violent and a good deal of it is being carried on before French people, who don't understand conditions, and an exceedingly bad effect is being produced on them, which, in turn, comes back through the large number of American civilians now here and is reacting very seriously against the Regular service.

I don't see how conditions can be remedied and am only reporting this to you so that you will be familiar with what is going on. I take it for granted that we are doing all that can be done under the circumstances to get the army home.

I do not think that disciplinary action against the people who are doing the talking would be advisable or would do the least good. But there is certain to be a reaction against the C. in C. and all this will be used against him by certain people at an opportune time and I feel that you, as a member of his Staff, should be kept informed.

Very sincerely,
R. H. Van Deman
Colonel, G.S.

HRVD
mck

By the middle of January there were rumors in Paris that there was a move on foot to remove General Pershing from command and replace him by an officer from the United States.

On January 31st Colonel William (Wild Bill) Donovan, Colonel Theodore Roosevelt, Jr., and Captain Harnwood met with Ogden Mills in my office to discuss and see if it would be possible to form an organization of temporary officers which would counteract the present ill feeling between officers of the regular Army and temporary officers.

On the same day I had a long talk with Colonel Menzies, of the British Intelligence service, on the possibility of cooperation between British and United States military intelligence services after the war. Menzies was very much in favor of such cooperation in order that tab might be kept particularly on the activities of the Soviet Government in all parts of the world.

On February 8th Colonels Donovan and Roosevelt again came into the office to continue the discussion of morale of temporary officers and their conflict with the regular Army officers.

On February 11th Nelly Bly, well known newspaper woman, appeared in Paris but refused to talk while in Paris. All during the war she was in Austria and it was believed she knew considerable about the Bolshevik organization and activities there.

On February 19th Comdr. Gherardi, U.S.N., came in from Berlin and gave me a detailed report on conditions there.

Many loyal Americans have been badly fooled by the propaganda put out by the Russian-Bolshevik set-up and a very excellent example of this is the case of William C. Bullitt who was in charge of the confidential records of the American Commission to Negotiate Peace and of the communications which passed between the Peace Commissioners and the

THE FINAL MEMORANDA

United States. Bullitt made a trip to Russia in February 1919 accompanied by Lincoln Steffens with whom he had earlier formed a friendship. This trip was made without the permission of the American Commissioners and upon their return they made a report giving an extremely rosy picture of what the Bolshevik government was accomplishing in Russia. This trip to Russia and the report on it forced the resignation of Bullitt from the American Section of the Conference to Negotiate Peace. Upon receipt of his report shortly after his return to Paris on March 26th, my office was directed to criticize this report and to call Bullitt's attention to the fact that the report contained many statements which could not be backed by facts. The subject of this criticism is contained in a letter prepared in my office and sent to Bullitt on April 1, 1919 and appended to this memorandum marked "Appendix B[2]."

Bullitt continued to hold this high opinion of the Soviet Union and its activities for many years during which time, in 1923, he married the widow of John Reed, the well-known American communist who is buried in Moscow near the wall of the Kremlin. While serving as our first Ambassador to the Soviet Union, Bullitt finally discovered what the Communist International really stands for.

One of our American couriers, Capt. Sargentisch, returned from Roumania on February 24th and I had dinner with him and he gave a detailed and decidedly unfavorable report concerning conditions there.

On March 3rd I had dinner with General Thwaites, the officer in charge of British Intelligence. The only other dinner guest was Laurence of Arabia who as usual was willing to talk about anything except his own part in the war. Later in the evening I had a talk with Hugh Gibson of the United States who had just come out of Germany and reported conditions to be very bad.

On March 10th I had a long talk with Colonel Drake of the British Intelligence service on the German-Russian-Japanese situation and the possibility of the British and American military intelligence services combining their efforts following the war.

On March 11th, Captain Foster, one of our couriers, made a report to the Dresel committee on conditions in Poland.

On March 17th Ogden Mills, my assistant, met with the committee consisting of Col. Theodore Roosevelt, Jr., Col. William Donovan and others for the purpose of discussing the advisability of forming a veterans organization before the troops returned to the United States. Later, of course, in the United States the veterans organization was formed as the American Legion.

On March 18th, General Churchill returned to the United States and his duties as Chief of Military Intelligence Division. On the same day Captain Yardley, who was the officer in charge of the code and cipher section of the Military Intelligence in the United States and who had been sent to Europe on a temporary trip by General Churchill, returned to the United States by way of Rome.

On March 21st, Lt. Col. Solbert, Military Attache at Copenhagen talked to the 11:30 session of the Dresel committee on conditions in the Baltic States.

On March 27th Major Henretin came in from Treves where he was attached to the advanced GH. He reported that he had an Intelligence Sergeant who had worked his way into the Bolshevik organization in Berlin posing as a deserter and who was really acquiring very valuable information concerning the activities of the Bolsheviks in Germany.

On March 29th the widow of Mr. Proctor of the Proctor and Gamble Company came into my office and reported her experiences and the treatment accorded her while serving with the Russian Red Cross for the previous year in Russia. She had finally managed to escape from Russia through the Ukraine. She was associated in Paris with a Colonel and several officers of the Czarist regime.

On April 3rd, Mr. Conger of the Associated Press came back to Paris from Berlin and confirmed our information that, if [the] present government failed it would be replaced by a radical socialist government with strong Bolshevik tendencies. He reported that it seemed likely that the German government will sign the peace treaty unless the terms included the loss of the territory west of the Rhine, the Saar coal fields and Danzig.

On April 10th William Bullitt appeared before the morning session of the Dresel Committee and stated that there would be a revolution in every country in Europe and that nothing we could do would stop it.

On April 13th General Dennis Nolan, G-2 of the AEF, and Col. Coxe called from Chaumont to discuss the demobilization of G-2, SOS. I urged the holding open of the Paris and Brest offices at least until the Peace Conference was over.

Mr. A. H. Frazier, Counselor of Embassy under Col. House, asked me to give him my ideas as to how the Military Intelligence should be handled for the League of Nations. I gave Mr. Frazier a rather long and detailed memorandum on this subject but it seems hardly worthwhile to repeat it in this report. It is of course on file in the archives of the American Section of the Conference to Negotiate Peace. In an interview

THE FINAL MEMORANDA

with Secretary of War Baker on April 16th he told me that he had intended taking me back to the United States with him on his return but he then thought he had better wait until he had reached the United States and talked with the Chief of Staff. In the meantime, I was to remain and carry out the instructions under which I was then acting.

On April 17th I had a conversation with Captain Ward and Lt. Robertson and on the 19th with Colonel A. Moreno, of Gen. Pershing's headquarters, both on the subject of the demobilization of G-2, SOS.

On April 19th I had a talk with Lt. Col. C. E. Dansey of the British Intelligence Service who had just returned from Germany. He said that the Germans were in a "blue funk" about Bolshevism.

On April 22th Colonel Charles Mason came in and reported on the trip he had made to Vienna and the Polish fronts.

On April 28th General Pershing inquired as to how serious the radical trouble which was expected on May 1st was believed to be.

Ogden Mills left by train on April 30th for Chaumont in order to discuss the proposition as to whether or not a veteran's organization should be formed in Paris or whether it should be delayed until the troops returned to the United States.

On May 2nd I wrote a letter in detail to General Churchill giving my opinion as to how a system of registering and keeping track of both officers and enlisted men who had worked with G-2 both in the AEF and in the United States should be handled. Unfortunately this arrangement was not carried out and as a consequence we lost touch with men who would have been of great assistance to Military Intelligence both during and in preparation for the Second World War.

I was directed to accompany Mr. Raycroft of the Red Cross on a trip which he was authorized to make over the battle fields of France and Germany. I left Paris with him on May 2nd and returned on the 11th.

On May 14th Mr. Thompson, our agent in Italy, camouflaged as a newspaper man, came in to report on the seriousness of the Italian situation over Fiume.

On May 15th, G-2, SOS in Paris was demobilized. This was most unfortunate because with the demobilization all the records of the office were returned to the United States. When the French and British Intelligence services inquired for information on Americans in Paris, we were then unable to supply the information as all those cards were kept in G-2, SOS.

William Treadwell who had been imprisoned by the Bolsheviks for a considerable time appeared at the morning session of the Dresel committee on May 17th and related his experience.

On May 19th, Colonel Sherman Miles who had been in the Balkans reported at the morning session of the Dresel committee to give an account of the situation as he found it.

At the morning session of the Dresel committee on May 21st we were informed that William Bullitt had resigned from his position in the American Section of the Conference to Negotiate Peace because of the disapproval of the American Peace Commissioners of his trip to Russia and his subsequent glowing report. In his letter of resignation he averred he was resigning because he did not agree with the terms of peace as proposed to the Central Powers.

At this same time Adolph Berle, Lt. G. B. Noble and Mr. S. E. Morison and others resigned from the Peace Conference over the terms of peace.

On May 31st Ogden Mills and Bertie Goelet left for the United States having been demobilized.

On June 1st Donald Thompson came in and talked of conditions in Siberia where he had recently been. Thompson is the only American who ever was allowed to photograph Stalin.

I was directed to accompany the Assistant Secretary of War Mr. Crowell on a trip which he desired to make over the battle fields and other places of interest connected with the war. Colonel William S. Graves gave me the itinerary the Assistant Secretary desired to cover on the 3rd of June.

On June 4th Colonel Coxe left GHQ on his return to the United States.

On June 5th I had luncheon with Colonel Dansey, Mr. Thompson, Colonel Volnaire, of the French Surete, Col. Menzies, Major Lamb and Major Gibson at the Traveler's Club at which general intelligence matters were discussed.

On June 6th I wrote the following letter to Churchill which is an excellent example of what happens to Army officers in the Military Intelligence.

June 6th, 1919

General Marlborough Churchill
Director of Military Intelligence
U.S. Army, Washington, D.C.

My dear Churchill:

Your very kind and characteristically straightforward letter reached me yesterday. I fully understand and appreciate just how you feel about going back to the artillery at this time. I feel a good deal the same way myself about coming back to Washington and taking up General Staff duty not connected with Intelligence for I have naturally lost touch with everything except that.

The Chief of Staff wants you to continue in your present position. That being the case, there is, of course, no place in Intelligence for me. I don't agree at all that you should be pushed out into some other place either for me or anyone else. I should resent that very much indeed. I tried to make that plain in my letter to you of some time ago. My position is simply this: if you are to be released and the Chief of Staff wants me to take your place, well and good, but both of these conditions must be fulfilled before the thing should be considered at all. Of course, it goes without saying that the Chief of Staff will see to it that these conditions do obtain so there is no use of our talking about it anyway.

Personally, I want to come home and am perfectly willing to go to troops at any time and any place. If I had a choice in the matter I would go to the Philippines. So much for that. Now about the Intelligence scheme with the League of Nations. I have been talking to several people on that subject and as far as I can gather no one seems to be impressed with the necessity for having any such service as part of the League of Nations.

How under the sun they expect to function without it, I can't imagine and am sure they will have to come to it in the end. Just now, however, they seem to have exceedingly vague ideas of what the organization of the League is going to be and also seem to have a feeling that they are not going to let military people have anything to do with it. I will certainly keep in touch with the matter as far as I am able to do so and if they finally decide to have a section in the League and you want me to take it on, you may be sure that I shall do all in my power to see that you get it.

In the meantime I suggest that you get in touch with Raymond

Fosdick and take the matter up with him. The Secretary of War can certainly tell you where he can be found. Now, then, there are one or two other things I want to talk to you about:

I had a very interesting luncheon yesterday with Colonel Dansey, Colonel Menzies, Major Gibson, Major Lamb (British M.I.) Mr. Thompson of Scotland Yard and in charge of the new Department of Political Intelligence of the British Government which has been created and Colonel Volnaire of the French 2nd Bureau. We talked on general intelligence matters and particularly on Bolshevism. Colonel Menzies spoke to me of a very warm friend of his who was coming to Washington as Assistant Military Attache by the name of Wallace. He was very warm in his praises of him and I hope you will have him looked up and do what you can for him.

You know of course who William Bullitt is and about his resignation from the Peace Commission. Bullitt is now in London and is consorting with the radical socialistic element there. I am having him watched rather closely and will let you know from time to time what he is up to. I am afraid he is going to develop into a dangerous man. Personally, I like Bullitt, but he is extremely radical and has been made much more so by his stay in Europe. He is also a disappointed and "disgruntled" man and such a chap is always likely to be dangerous if he is smart and Bullitt is that.

Now as to the so-called "suspect cards" which are in the hands of G-2, SOS. As Coxe will tell you, I recommended very strongly that these records be placed in the hands of the Military Attache at Paris. Those contain all that is known about undesirables in Paris, both American and others. This information does not exist anywhere else. Not a day passes but it is necessary to know something about one or more of these people contained in those records. Instead of turning the records over to the Paris Military Attache, they have been sent to M.I.D. and are now some place in transit and evidently unavailable. That means that neither the Military, the Peace Conference nor the Passport Bureau can check off any of these people. This is both dangerous and embarrassing for both the French and British have been calling on us for information concerning some of our "black sheep" and we can only tell them that we have no records. I have had no conversation now [sic] correspondence with Nolan but Coxe tells me that he objected sending the records to the Military Attache at Paris because he was afraid they would not be considered confidential. With all due respect to Nolan, I don't think that is a valid reason for putting the Intelligence Service in the position it is in now. The only records that the Military Attache in Paris has now is the lot from the Control Office at Bordeaux and these, of course, cover only the regular suspect cards and do not include the special information in regard to the Americans in France which is so vital to the Intelligence Service in Europe and to the Passport Bureau. Those records were "pied" in transit and it will take two weeks or more to straighten them out so they can be used. You can imagine what an outcry that is causing. Personally, I think the Paris, G-2, SOS records should be sent back to the Military Attache, Paris. He should, of course, be cautioned that they are extremely confidential and that no one expect specially designated officers in his office should have access to them. This is, of course, my personal opinion only and you must decide what should be done. Your telegram about the Polish-Jewish pogrom has just come in. As a matter of fact there have been no Jewish pogroms in Poland. There were about 32 Jews killed in Minsk some time ago but it was proved that they were killed because they were engaged in a Bolshevist plot and not because they were Jews. The Polish Government is fully aware that the Jews are engaged in trying to create the impression that the Poles are persecuting the Jews and have given very strict instructions on the matter. There is a group of Jews in Poland, assisted by certain Jews in the United States and by quite a number here in France who are making a distinct effort to create the impression that the Poles are going to massacre the Jews.

There is also very strong evidence to indicate that the Germans are also mixed up in the matter. Many of the items appearing in the U.S. papers originate in Copenhagen and are pure fabrications. The Minister in Poland, Hugh Gibson, has been directed to make a careful investigation of the matter and you will find that his reports are all on file in the State Department.

I hope I haven't tired you out with this long letter.

Most warmly your friend,

R. H. Van Deman
Colonel, General Staff

RHVD
mck.

On June 9th I accompanied the Assistant Secretary of War and his party on the journey of the battlefields in both Belgium and France and other points of interest, returning to Paris on the 13th.

It had been planned that as soon as Marguerite Harrison was able to persuade Robert Minor to appear at our bridgehead at Coblenz he would be arrested and tried by a military court for attempting to cause mutiny among the troops. To this end, Marguerite Harrison, still of course in Germany, was to report to our military intelligence officer at Coblenz when Minor would appear there. When Ogden Mills was demobilized and returned to the United States, a young Captain was ordered to my office as my assistant. As I knew nothing about the background or discretion of this officer and as the delay in bringing Robert Minor over on our bridgehead had been so great, when I was ordered to be out of Paris for a few days, I decided not to inform my assistant as to the plans for the arrest of Robert Minor. During my absence Marguerite Harrison informed the intelligence officer at Coblenz that Robert Minor would appear there and as was planned the intelligence officer at once informed my office in Paris.

This message was, of course, received by my assistant to whom as I stated above, I had not confided what the the plans concerning Robert Minor were. Apparently not knowing what to do in the matter, he informed our Embassy in Paris and the Embassy immediately demanded that Minor be turned over to them, which was done. Upon my return to Paris on June 14th Lincoln Steffens appeared in my living quarters at the Hotel Crillon and insisted that I give him the names of two Army officers who were known liberals. I asked him why he wanted the names of these officers and he said it was for the purpose of defending Robert Minor. I told him I would not give him the names of such officers and he finally departed. How he got pass the guards at the Hotel Crillon and into my living quarters I was never able to discover. As a result of all of the above Robert Minor was never tried and was sent back to the United States.

On June 19th Major Devenaux appeared before the morning session of the Dresel committee and reported on conditions in Estonia where he had been recently.

On June 25th Philip Patchen of the United States State Department came in to consult concerning the stolen dispatch from William Bullitt's safe in Paris which had turned up in Chicago. This safe contained all the confidential records of the American Section of the Peace Conference and its communications with Washington.

At the Dresel Committee conference on June 27th Lt. Cmdr. Bryant, of our Navy, reported on his observations in Turkey and Armenia.

On June 28th the Germans signed the Peace Treaty and the Assistant Secretary of War, Mr. Crowell left Paris the next day.

On July 1st I was informed by cable from Washington that I should

THE FINAL MEMORANDA 97

proceed to London for the purpose of assisting Consul General Skinner in a conference with representatives of the Allied Powers on the matter of passports following the war.

Leland Harrison came in on the same day to consult concerning the cable believed to have been stolen from William Bullitt's safe mentioned previously.

On July 5th I had a long talk with Anthony Czarnocki, correspondent for the Chicago Daily News, on Jewish Conditions in Poland.

On July 7th the Peace Commissioners discussed the measures that might be taken against the Bolshevik government under Bela Kun in Hungary.

On July 8th Mr. Poole, our Consul at Archangel, gave a talk on Russia before the morning session of the Dresel committee.

On July 9th Marguerite Harrison returned from Germany with a very interesting report on what she had seen of the Bolshevik uprising in Germany.

On July 14th ascertaining that General Pershing and his staff were to go to London I made arrangements with his Chief of Staff, General Harbord to accompany them and left that evening reaching Boulogne on July 15th. We proceeded to England on board a fast British destroyer and that afternoon I attended a meeting at the British Home Office with regard to passport control. Consul General Skinner was not present but the United States was represented by Consul Broy and Mr. Whelpley and myself. General John Pedder presided. There were no Italians or French present, four Belgians and several British amongst them Major Spencer, Colonel Kell, Colonel Menzies, Capt. Cummin and Mr. Thompson.

The proposition of the British was to continue the present passport system with its visa requirements indefinitely. This, of course, for the purpose of keeping check on the travel of undesirable persons, especially those of radical tendencies. In order to reduce to a minimum the inconvenience to citizens of the Allied and Associated Powers the British proposed that a zone comprising the United Kingdom, France, Belgium, Italy and the United States should be established, within which passports would be required to be vised only once. In other words that once a passport was issued to an individual, he would only be required to have it vised once for each country during the life of the passport.

In effect, this meant, of course, that the passport was to be a sort of certificate by the country issuing it that the individual is all right and the visa a certificate that the country making the visa is satisfied that the opinion of the country issuing the passport is concurred in. The idea was all right but, in order to make any such system effective, there would have to be a system of control, not only at the ports but along the entire land frontage of each country. It would require a very large number of men and heavy expense, especially in countries having long land frontiers, such as the United States. Unless the control system was effective the scheme would not work because the men we wanted to catch would slip through and we would only annoy and irritate the people who should be allowed to travel.

As far as the United States was concerned, the visa requirement ceased upon the declaration of the President that a state of peace existed and it would have required additional legislation and a special appropriation to undertake any scheme of the kind proposed. When Mr. Whelpley told the meeting this, they lost interest in the part the United States might play.

On July 16th at the British War Office I had a talk with the Assistant Director of Military Intelligence, General Bartholemew and Colonel Cribbon [and] Major Lampke also of the British service, concerning the possibility of cooperation between the British Military Intelligence and our own following the war.

On July 18th I attended a reception and luncheon for General Pershing at the Guild Hall in London. Later that day Raymond Fosdick came in to talk over an intelligence system for the League of Nations.

On July 22nd I returned to Paris and the next day my offices were moved from #4 Place de la Concorde to a set of rooms in the Hotel Crillon.

On July 26th I received a report from a Britisher connected with the biggest firm of metal merchants in Europe. He had been an officer in the British Intelligence Service during the war. He said that Japan had sold a large quantity of copper in England in the spring and now that she had bought all of that back at an advanced price and in addition was buying large quantities at the market price. Also that they were buying all the land in Australia that they could get. They were also getting in a considerable stock of mercury and antimony. This information was reported to Churchill in a cable followed by a letter with the details.

On July 25th I decided that I had better inaugurate a battle map covering the various small wars which were then going on. I realized that this was not my business but it was something which should be done and nobody else was doing it.

On July 25th I made a full report on the passport conference in London to M.I.D. in Washington, the full text of which will, of course,

THE FINAL MEMORANDA

be found in the archives of that organization. Also in the archives will be found a letter to Churchill on the 29th on Bullitt and the radical group in the Peace Conference. On August 2nd I was informed that I had been ordered back to the United States to report to the Chief of Staff.

On Aug. 4th I wrote a final report to Mr. Grew summarizing the work of my office which is appended hereto marked "Appendix A."* On the 6th I wrote a memorandum to him on controls which should be maintained at the Hotel Crillon after my departure for the United States. On August 12th I left Paris for Brest on route to the United States, sailing on the Prince Frederick Wilhelm on the 14th.

* Published here as Appendix J

PART II   THE BACKGROUND

WAR DEPARTMENT
Office of the Chief of Staff
Washington

War College Division
639-112

March 2, 1916

MEMORANDUM FOR THE CHIEF OF WAR COLLEGE DIVISION:

Subject: State of military information work in the War College Division, General Staff

1. In compliance with your verbal directions, I have made an examination of the subject of the state of the military information work in the War College Division, and herewith submit my report thereon. While I was not directed to examine into the cause for the present state of affairs nor to suggest a remedy therefore, I feel it my duty, as a member of the General Staff, to do so.

2. When the General Staff was organized, a well equipped, well organized, Military Information Division, with all its material, personnel and records, was turned over complete, and made a part of, the General Staff. It is unfortunate for the General Staff, perhaps, that this occurred. With the mass of information work already accomplished, with the many and intricate sources of information located and the machinery which brought it into the Military Information Division already created and put into running order, the necessity for military information work and organization was not brought home to the General Staff as it would have been had it not been able to take over and use the results of the seventeen years of labor and thought of the old Military Information Division. It would have discovered in the first months of its existence that facilities for information work would have to be created at once, and it would have realized the absolute necessity for a competent organization within itself to carry on this work. But, like money that "comes easy," it took what was given it and used it, but has never seemed to realize that the time would come when the reservoir would become exhausted. Things do not create themselves. They are the result of thought and labor, and if neither thought nor labor is expended, how can we expect results? With very minor exceptions, the military information now in the possession of the General Staff is either that collected by the old Military Information Division or has come to the General Staff as a direct result of agencies put into operation by it.

3. The question naturally arises as to what has become of the Military Information Division which was turned over to the General Staff in 1903.

Even a brief examination will reveal the fact that its personnel and material have been merged and scattered in the War College Division and that its functions have ceased to be exercised. To call a chair a table does not make it a table – it still remains a chair. And to call the personnel of the War College Division a <u>Military</u> <u>Information</u> Committee does not make it one.

4. We have on file partially prepared studies embracing military information on various countries called "Military Monographs." These are of two classes, the "Military Monographs" and the "Encyclopedic Military Monographs." The first is the completed study on the various countries of the world and is supposed to contain all the data of military value on that particular country which would be of use to the government in connection with the preparation of plans of invasion, or to the army in the field should it become necessary to invade. It should be prepared in the clearest and most condensed form and must contain nothing except what has been thoroughly studied and proven. The "Military Monograph" on each country is supposed to be kept up to date and in shape to be published, or at least furnished, in completed form, at short notice.

The second form of monograph is simply a collection of information on the various subjects covered by the "Instructions for Military Monographs" (WCD 5250, Dec., 1908). It is prepared in loose-leaf form and is supposed to form the basis for the preparation of the completed "Military Monograph."

5. In addition to this, there is on file in the Record Section a vast mass of information on military subjects. This information comes from various sources and is indexed and filed under various heads. I had almost said that this information was <u>collected</u>, but a very brief examination of the methods of the War College Division during the past few years will convince any one that the term would have been a most inaccurate one. It is not <u>collected</u> – it just comes in. A good deal of it is still coming in as the result of the labors of the old Military Information Division which went out of existence shortly after it was incorporated with the War College Division. But, even such information as does come in, is not studied and checked. It is indexed under various heads, as I have said, but the indexing is done by clerks without military knowledge or training. They are, therefore, utterly unable to study and digest, to check and prove, and re-check the various items of information of military importance which find their way across their desks. As far as any benefit to the government is concerned, the mass of this information might just as well be in Timbuctu. It will remain in the Record Section unavailable to the end of time.

6. The system employed at present in the War College Division appar-

THE BACKGROUND   105

ently contemplates that all information on a country is to be contained in one or the other of the Military Monographs. This point will be taken up later. The actual state of the monograph system is as follows:

Appended to this paper are two tables: Table A shows the present state of the "Military Monographs" of the various countries, and Table B that of the "Encyclopedic Military Monographs." A glance at these tables will show that for only three (3) countries have we complete "Military Monographs."

> Guatemala, 300 pages, completed in 1915.
> Mexico, published as W.C.D. publication No. 21 in 1915
> Salvador, 400 pages, completed in 1915
> Colombia, 450 pages, was partially completed in 1914.

The "Military Monographs" of four (4) countries are now being revised: Costa Rica, Cuba, Honduras and Nicaragua.

A very limited section of China has also been completed.

For the remaining forty (40) countries on which we are supposed to have "Military Monographs," we have nothing in completed form except partial and incomplete studies on various countries and special subjects, prepared by the members of the student classes of the Army War College, as a part of their course of instruction. This work is far from satisfactory. It is incomplete and a great deal of it has evidently been done in a purely perfunctory manner.

For the "Encyclopedic Military Monographs" which should cover forty-nine (49) countries, we have miscellaneous data on twenty-eight (28). Of these twenty-eight, five are now under revision. On the remaining twenty-one (21) countries we have nothing in the "Encyclopedic" form.

For sixteen (16) countries we have nothing under either monographic form.

Two officers on the Retired List are now engaged in work on several Central American countries (marked "Now being revised" in Table A).

The "Military Monograph" of Argentine Republic is being rewritten by an officer, now a member of the student class, who, at one time, was military attache in that country.

7. In the Map Section, which is, of course, most intimately connected with the subject of military information, things are in better shape since the carding has been kept up by a special clerk who has been especially trained for this particular work and who is under the immediate personal supervision of one of the best informed map man in the United States. But, even here, the topographical information contained in written re-

ports, the photographs which accompany reports and maps are not carded and the information furnished by them – often vital even from the map man's point of view – is very generally not available.

8. A rather large amount of map work has been done by our own officers covering reconnaissances in various countries. The countries which are of particular importance to us are, of course, our neighbors on the north and south – Canada and Mexico – since we might, at any time, be compelled to carry on military operations in one or both.

9. The state of the Canadian work is as follows:

The work, authorized by the Secretary of War in 1889, was begun by the Military Information Division in the summer of that year. There are a total of 74 sheets completed and 22, for which the field work has been completed, but sheets not yet drawn because of the drafting force being diverted to other work. These sheets are distributed as follows:

>Halifax to the eastern border of Maine:
>22 sheets drawn and field work for 14 additional.
>Field work in 1907.

>Quebec to Windsor (Detroit)
>37 sheets drawn and field work for 8 additional.
>Field work in 1893 to 1897.

>Sault Ste. Marie and vicinity:
>3 sheets drawn.
>Field work in 1907.

>U.S. Boundary to Winnepeg and vicinity:
>6 sheets drawn.
>Field work in 1907.

>Vancouver, Victoria and vicinity:
>6 sheets drawn.
>Field work in 1904.

It will be observed that the work covering the territory which would be of the first importance in case of military operations is between 19 and 23 years old, and that none of the field work is less than 9 years old. It will, also, be observed that the work was inaugurated by the old Information Division and simply continued under the General Staff. But what is particularly to be noted is that no field work of any kind has been done since the Military Information Division was absorbed by the War College Division, and thus lost its autonomy.

THE BACKGROUND 107

10. The status of the Mexican work is as follows:

There have been lithographed and published a total of 143 sheets covering various parts of the country. Of these, 126 sheets are re-published sheets of the "Carta General de Mexico," and 17 are so-called "provisional" sheets compiled in the Map Section from railway and mining maps and surveys. These published sheets are distributed as follows:

> El Paso to Chihuahua and vicinity:
> 26 sheets of the "Carta General" and 10 provisional sheets.
>
> Torreon and vicinity:
> 6 "provisional" sheets.
>
> Laredo – Matamoras – Monterrey:
> 33 sheets of the "Carta General."
>
> Tampico – San Luis Potosi:
> 32 sheets of the "Carta General."
>
> Vera Cruz – City of Mexico:
> 27 sheets of the "Carta General."
>
> Port of Mexico:
> 8 sheets of the "Carta General."

The territory covered by certain of these sheets, or parts of them, has been gone over by our own officers and certain corrections made and a limited amount of topographical data added. These sheets are included among those mentioned above. In the various groups they are as follows:

> El Paso to Chihuahua and vicinity: None
>
> Torreon and vicinity: None
>
> Laredo – Matamoras – Monterrey:
> 17 Sheets. Field work in 1907.
>
> Tampico – San Luis Potosi:
> 18 sheets. Field work in 1907.

Vera Cruz – City of Mexico:
23 sheets. Field work of 22 in 1906 and one short route in 1910.

Port of Mexico: None

Certain other "provisional" sheets are now under construction, but we have no data for them except railway and mining maps.

Large scale maps of some five cities have been compiled or are now being compiled from such data as exist in the Division, but none of them (with the exception of Vera Cruz) have been checked by actual observation.

Certain road and railway routes have been or are now being compiled from such data as are on file, much of the interior from the work of officers who were sent to Mexico during the years 1906 and 1907.

It will be observed that, with the exception of one very short route from a point on the coast south of Tuxpan to a point in the interior, and the work done in and around Vera Cruz by Army and Marine officers during the military occupation of that place, all of the field work which has been done by our own officers is over nine years old. And particularly will it be observed that all of the field work done was inaugurated by the Military Information Division before it became absorbed by the War College Division. Also that no field work of any kind (with the exceptions above mentioned) has been done since that time.

11. A limited amount of topographical work has been done in some of the South and Central American countries, but none of it since the absorption of the Military Information Division by the War College Division.

12. A good deal of work has been done in China, but this work was inaugurated and carried out by the Military Information Division at Manila, an organization which had and still has a large degree of autonomy and which has an officer directly in charge and responsible for its work.

13. A great many maps of various countries or parts of countries have been compiled in the Map Room from time to time as the necessity for them arose.

A very excellent map of Central Europe was compiled in the Map Room in 1915. This map has been lithographed and is available for distribution.

On the whole, the work in the Map Room is in very much better shape than that of any other branch of military information work.

THE BACKGROUND 109

14. Let us now see the condition of affairs for our own territory. The United States

The "Progressive Military Map" of the United States had its inception in certain work done by officers stationed in the Department of Dakota in 1893, carried on under the supervision of the Acting Engineer Officer of the Department, at that time H. C. Hale, 1st Lieutenant, 20th Infantry, and A.D.C. This particular work was only for the Department of Dakota, but in 1895 the Military Information Division took the matter up and in a memorandum dated May 25, 1895, proposed that a similar system be inaugurated in each Department. This memorandum was approved by the Secretary of War, and confidential instructions were issued to Department Commanders. The Military Information Division was given general supervision over the work in order to insure uniformity. The actual work in each Department was placed under the Department Engineer Officer or other officer detailed by the Department Commander for the purpose, and the actual field work was performed by officers serving in the Department and detailed by the Department Commander. The field work was to be entered on original sheets or tracings in the office of the Department Engineer, which sheets were then to be sent to the Military Information Division for record and reproduction and then returned to Department Headquarters. The work was to be confidential in character.

This system has been followed, with certain modifications, up to the present time.

Work on the Progressive Military Map was suspended by order of the Secretary of War in 1898 and was not resumed until 1904. In that year work was again taken up under the instructions of 1897 by authority of a memorandum of the Assistant Chief of Staff and approved by the Chief of Staff June 7, 1904, and detailed instructions were sent out by the Military Information Division to all Division Commanders.

In 1903 the subject of cooperation and coordination of work between the Interior Department and the War Department was taken up on the recommendation of the officer in charge of the Military Information Division and the Director of the Geological Survey. The recommendations made by these officials were approved by the Director of the Geological Survey, the Chief of Staff, the Secretary of the Interior, and the Secretary of War. A copy of this report, together with revised instructions for the preparation of the Progressive Military Map of the United States, prepared in the Military Information Division, General Staff, were sent to the commanders of the Geographical Divisions under date of March 8, 1905.

The Geological Survey also issued instructions to their topographers for carrying out the agreement. In these instructions aimed at furnishing to the Geological Survey the corrections made by the army topographers in the field and added to the atlas sheets of the Geological Survey published before the agreement between the two Departments was consummated and the noting of additional specified topographic details by the field topographers of the Geological Survey in all new work. Work under this agreement has continued to the present time. The data furnished by the Geological Survey are not always complete for the territory covered by the sheet and is usually done in a perfunctory manner. In many cases the information added to the sheets submitted was almost illegible and made the sheets totally useless for the purpose of reproduction. The vast majority of the data furnished would have to be redrawn on new sheets before it would be in shape to reproduce and make a legible map. This fact must be borne in mind when considering the diagrammatic sheet showing the state of the Progressive Military Map, since many of the sheets shown as containing military information furnished by the Geological Survey are not now in shape to be reproduced.

In order to reduce the number of officers on detached service a memorandum was approved by the Acting Secretary of War September 12, 1910, directing that "work on the Progressive Military Map of the United States away from the seacoast, except as hereinafter provided for along the Mexican and Canadian borders, be suspended indefinitely, that work of this character along the Canadian border be postponed until officers for the work become available, that work along the Mexican border be continued until completed, that work on the Atlantic, Pacific and Gulf coasts be prosecuted with vigor until completion, by officers of the Coast Artillery, that the work of mapping our insular possessions, at least in those sections where military operations are probable, continue."

Instructions to that effect were sent to Division and Department Commanders under date of September 24, 1910. In accordance with these instructions the work has been proceeding on both the Atlantic and Pacific coasts, under the immediate supervision of the Department Engineer Officers. On both coasts and particularly on the Pacific, the work has been enormously aided by organizations and officers of the Corps of Engineers detailed for the work by Department Commanders. Along the Mexican border work was prosecuted as rapidly as it was possible to do so with the officers available for the work. Since the dispatch to the border of the large number of troops which are now there, the work has been progressing very satisfactorily.

Attached to this memorandum is an index map showing the location of territory along the coasts and the Canadian and Mexican borders mapped under the various orders and arrangements which have produced such part of the Progressive Military Map of the United States as is complete in those sections.

15. In the Philippines a large area of the Island of Luzon has been mapped and the sheets lithographed, the field work having been done by organizations of the Corps of Engineers and line officers detailed for the work.

16. In Hawaii a large portion of the Island of Oahu has been covered, most of the work having been done in connection with the defense problems.

17. In Porto Rico the entire island was covered by officers of the Porto Rican Provisional Regiment from 1909 to 1913, and redrawn in the Map Room and is now ready for reproduction.

18. In 1911, because of the great shortage of officers available for map work, a further attempt to arrange for mutual cooperation between the War Department and the Geological Survey was made.

In a joint memorandum, signed by an officer of the General Staff appointed by the Secretary of War, and by the Director of the Geological Survey, and approved by the Secretary of War and the Secretary of the Interior, dated October 11, 1911, an agreement was entered into between the War and Interior Departments. Briefly, and in its essential features, this agreement was as follows:

The Geological Survey agreed to include on its atlas sheets certain essential topographic information of military value. It also agreed to concentrate its efforts, so far as practicable, on those unmapped portions of the United States along the coasts (particularly the Pacific coast), and the Canadian and Mexican frontiers, and for the future to comply, so far as practicable, with requests made by the War Department to map those areas of the United States which that Department might be desirous of having speedily mapped for military purposes. It also agreed to furnish to the Military Information Section of the General Staff, without cost, 100 copies of each military atlas sheet of its topographic map of the United States prepared under the agreement as soon as each sheet was completed, and additional sheets at cost of printing.

The War Department, on its part, agreed to secure additional appropriations from Congress from which the Geological Survey could be reimbursed for the additional expense to which it would be put for carrying out its part of the agreement.

In May, 1912, the Secretary of War informed the Secretary of the Interior that he had forwarded to the Secretary of the Treasury, for transmittal to Congress, an estimate of $97,000.00 for the purpose of reimbursing the Geological Survey for additional expenses incurred in securing such additional topographical data as were requested by the War Department, and engraving and printing the same on the atlas sheets. This estimate was stricken out of the appropriation in the House of Representatives.

On August 12, 1914, the Chief of the War College Division forwarded an estimate for a like amount to be included in the War Department appropriation for the same purpose. This estimate was returned by the the Chief of Staff under date of September 25, 1914, with the following memorandum:

"The Secretary of War directs that, owing to the necessity for extreme economy in the estimates of the War Department for the coming fiscal year, you be informed that he can not include this amount in his estimate. He further directs that steps be taken to avoid the incurrence of obligations along this line."

As it was obviously impossible for the War Department to carry out its agreement, the arrangement of 1911 came to nothing. The Geological Survey and the War Department, however, are still working under the agreement of 1905.

19. In addition to its regular work of carding and filing the maps coming into the War College Division and the work on the Provisional Mexican sheets mentioned above, the Map Room is engaged in completing a large scale Railroad Map of the United States. This map was begun in 1909 and, when nearly five-sixths completed, was stopped by the verbal order of the Secretary of the War College Division and not taken up again until August, 1915.

20. While we have fallen far behind in the performance of the duties which devolve on a General Staff in the matter of collecting and collating the information which must be gathered and digested in time of peace, we have been even more derelict in our study of and preparation for intelligence or information duties and organization with troops in the field in time of war. Our Field Service Regulations recognize these duties and, in a very general way, specify them as follows:

"The General Staff."

* * * * * * * * * * * * * * * * *

The third or intelligence section concerns itself with the movements and dispositions of the enemy, including exploration, reconnaissance, and the gathering and distribution of information; interpreters, newspaper correspondents, and various agents; relations with the enemy; flags of truce, deserters and prisoners of war; relations with the civil authorities of the occupied territory, requisitions, etc."

THE BACKGROUND

If there is one general principle on the observance of which the General Staff insists, it is that all training and preparation in peace must fit for war and war conditions. What has been done by the General Staff in the way of preparation and training for the duties devolving upon it as enumerated in the above quotation from the Field Service Regulations? And how can any preparation be made for it unless some sort of organization exists in peace whose business it is to study and make these preparations? For not only must the subject be carefully studied and plans made for carrying out the various necessary measures, but officers must be trained in the work and certain material must be provided in advance. If there is no organization provided in time of peace whose specific duty it is to attend to these matters, it is a foregone conclusion that they will not be attended to. It is hardly necessary to mention that we have no officer or group of officers in the General Staff to-day who are receiving any training in such duties or whose particular duty it is to even consider them.

20. In so far as I have been able to get at the facts, the foregoing is a brief statement of the condition now obtaining in regard to the collection, classification and preparation of military information by the War College Division.

A vast amount of work is necessary to bring even the information which is now on file in the Division into anything like the shape it must be placed to be available for use, and a great deal more work and study and planning must be done if we are to locate and obtain the information which will be imperatively necessary in time of war and which we are not getting now.

21. We are not getting the best results from the work of our military attaches because there is no system of efficient supervision and coordination of their work. Nor, beyond the fact that their reports are carded and indexed and a notice to officers on duty in the Division that a report on such and such a subject has been received, is there any system in operation whereby these reports are checked, omissions supplied, or doubtful points cleared up! This is one of the duties devolving upon a Military Information Division, and if there is no such organization, we can not expect that it will be performed.

22. Appended to this memorandum is a study of the subject of the collection, etc., of military information in our army as shown by the various orders, circulars, memoranda, etc., which have from time to time been issued on the subject. A consideration of this study will, I believe, force the conclusion that, while present conditions may be improved by certain changes which can be made within the War College Division, they can not be <u>cured</u> until a separate Division of the War Department

General Staff is created to which military information work shall be assigned, and the chief of which shall report directly to the Chief of Staff.

R. H. Van Deman
Major, General Staff

THE BACKGROUND   115

TABLE A   MILITARY MONOGRAPHS

COUNTRY	REVISED OR WORKED ON	DATE	NO. OF PAGES	COMMENTS
Alaska	-0-	-0-	-0-	
Antilles	-0-	-0-	-0-	
Argentine Republic	-0-	-0-	-0-	
Australia	-0-	-0-	-0-	
Austria Hungary	-0-	-0-	-0-	
Belgium	-0-	-0-	-0-	
Bolivia	-0-	-0-	-0-	
Brazil	-0-	-0-	-0-	
Canada	-0-	-0-	-0-	
Chile	-0-	-0-	-0-	
China	x	Apr., 1914	150	A small area in the neighborhood of Pekin
Colombia	x	Jan., 1915	450	Partially completed
Costa Rica	x	x	x	Now being revised
Cuba	x	x	x	Now being revised
Denmark	-0-	-0-	-0-	
Dominican Republic	-0-	-0-	-0-	
Ecuador	-0-	-0-	-0-	
France	-0-	-0-	-0-	
Germany	-0-	-0-	-0-	
Great Britain	-0-	-0-	-0-	
Guam	-0-	-0-	-0-	
Guatemala	x	Jan., 1915	300	
The Guianas	-0-	-0-	-0-	
Haiti	-0-	-0-	-0-	
Hawaii	-0-	-0-	-0-	
Honduras	x	x	x	Now being revised
India	-0-	-0-	-0-	

Italy	-0-	-0-	-0-	
Japan	-0-	-0-	-0-	
Liberia	-0-	-0-	-0-	
Mexico	x	1915	x	Published
Netherlands	-0-	-0-	-0-	
Nicaragua	x	x	x	Now being revised
Norway	-0-	-0-	-0-	
Panama	-0-	-0-	-0-	
Paraguay	-0-	-0-	-0-	
Peru	-0-	-0-	-0-	
Philippines	-0-	-0-	-0-	
Porto Rico	-0-	-0-	-0-	
Roumania	-0-	-0-	-0-	
Russia	-0-	-0-	-0-	
Salvador	x	1915	400	
Spain	-0-	-0-	-0-	
Sweden	-0-	-0-	-0-	
Switzerland	-0-	-0-	-0-	
Turkey	-0-	-0-	-0-	
United States	-0-	-0-	-0-	
Urugay	-0-	-0-	-0-	
Venezuela	-0-	-0-	-0-	

THE BACKGROUND 117

TABLE A   MILITARY MONOGRAPHS (Continued)

(Studies by War College Student Class. These studies are necessarily brief and incomplete.)

COUNTRY	REVISED OR WORKED ON	DATE	NO. OF PAGES
Alaska	Chap. I	1909-10	32
"	Monograph	Feb.,1914	98
Argentine Republic	Monograph	Apr.,1905	107
Austria Hungary	Monograph	Aug.,1906	45
Brazil	Chap. III	Jan.,1915	95
Canada	Chap. I	Feb.,1914	50
"	Chap. II	1910	20
"	Chap. III	Jan.,1915	95
Chile	Monograph	Nov.,1908	51
China	Chap. I	Mar.,1910	55
"	Chap. III	1910	36
Colombia	Monograph	Feb.,1910	56
Costa Rica	Monograph	Feb.,1910	28
Cuba	Monograph	Apr.,1910	49
Dominican Republic	Monograph	Jan.,1910	91
"	Chap. III	Jan.,1915	22
Great Britain	Chap. I	Aug.,1910	4
"	Chap. II	Jan.,1910	19
"	Chap. V	Jan.,1910	55
Haiti	Chap. I	1909-10	15
Honduras	Chap. I,II,IV	Feb.,1910	22
India	Monograph	Sep.,1907	640
Italy	Monograph	Mar.,1914	122
Japan	Chap. I & III	Apr.,1910	55
"	Chap. II	Dec.,1910	29
"	Chap. V	Apr.,1910	64
Nicaragua	Monograph	Sep.,1912	15
Panama	Monograph	1912-13	183
Philippines	Chap. I	Aug.,1910	12
"	(Mindanao)	Nov.,1915	250
Uruguay	Monograph	Mar.,1909	23
Venezuela	Monograph	Aug.,1905	299
"	Chap. I & III	Aug.,1908	376
"	Chap. III	Jan.,1915	20

118   THE FINAL MEMORANDA
TABLE B   ENCYCLOPEDIC MILITARY MONOGRAPHS

COUNTRY

Alaska	0	
Antilles	0	
Argentine Republic	675	
Australia	0	
Austria Hungary	55	
Belgium	10	
Bolivia	0	
Brazil	150	
Canada	100	
Chile	1000	
China	1100	
Colombia	250	
Costa Rica	-0-	Being revised.
Cuba	-0-	Being revised.
Denmark	0	
Dominican Republic	0	
Ecuador	0	
France	275	
Germany	375	
Great Britain	225	
Guam	0	
Guatemala	40	
The Guianas	0	
Haiti	282	
Hawaii	0	
Honduras	-0-	
India	0	
Italy	375	
Japan	400	
Liberia	25	
Mexico	-0-	Being revised.

Netherlands	0	
Nicaragua	-0-	Being revised.
Norway	25	
Panama	0	
Paraguay	0	
Peru	300	
Philippines	0	
Porto Rico	0	
Roumania	0	
Russia	75	
Salvador	50	
Spain	0	
Sweden	150	
Switzerland	0	
Turkey	0	
United States	0	
Uruguay	40	
Venezuela	-0-	Large amount of undigested matter.

WAR DEPARTMENT
Office of the Chief of Staff
Washington

War College Division
639-113 March 2, 1916

MEMORANDUM FOR THE CHIEF, WAR COLLEGE DIVISION:
Subject: Historical sketch of the steps taken by the War Department for the collection, classification and distribution of military information in the Army.

1. It is, of course, entirely unnecessary to point out the absolute necessity for the collection, classification, carding, filing and distribution of military information. Nor is it necessary to call attention to the fact that the mass of information and particularly that which will be the most necessary in war, must be obtained in peace.

2. These facts are so well known and recognized among military men the world over that it would be a waste of time to discuss the matter, since every officer who knows anything of General Staff duties realizes that the collection, classification and distribution of military information is the fundamental function of that body and that without it no General Staff duties worthy of the name can be accomplished. It is also everywhere, except in our service, fully appreciated that a highly trained and well equipped organization is necessary for the purpose of exercising these fundamental functions of a General Staff. This lack of a clean-cut, decisive policy in regard to keeping up such a trained personnel in our service is shown by the various orders, circulars and memorandums issued from time to time by the War Department.

3. That there was a necessity for work of this character was forced on the attention of our military authorities many years ago, long before the need of a General Staff was recognized, and steps were taken to provide the agency to accomplish the work as early as 1885. This agency took the form of a bureau which was established in the office of the Adjutant General of the Army. In 1889 this bureau was made a separate division of the Adjutant General's Office by the following confidential order:

"War Department,
Adjutant General's Office,
Washington, April 12, 1889

Confidential Orders:

1. A separate division under the personal supervision of the Adjutant General, to be known as the Military Information Division will be organized for the purpose of

obtaining and collecting such military data as may be deemed useful and beneficial to the Army at large.

*   *   *   *   *   *   *   *   *

The Division will occupy room 345, third floor, north wing, and all books, papers, etc., pertaining to this class of information will be transferred to it."

4. On March 18, 1892, the Secretary of War issued the following order which reorganized the Division and further prescribed its duties. Several duties were assigned to the Division by this order which did not properly pertain to a Military Information Division, but they were then so assigned because, at that time, there was no other organization in the Army to which they could be assigned. The essential duties, however, of a Military Information (or Intelligence) Division were set forth in the order and are still in force, although there is no distinct organization now in existence to carry them out:

General Orders,
No. 23

"Headquarters of the Army,
Adjutant General's Office,
Washington, March 15, 1892

I – The following orders of the Secretary of War are published for the information of all concerned:

War Department,
Washington, March 15, 1892

Orders:

The Division of Military Information heretofore created in the office of the Adjutant General of the Army is hereby reorganized as follows:

1. The division will be placed in charge of an officer of the Adjutant General's Department, to be selected by the Secretary of War.
2. In addition to its other duties the division will be charged with---

(a) The collection and classification of military information of our own and foreign countries, especially with respect to armed, reserved, and available strength, natural and artificial means of communication (rivers, canals, highways, and railroads); the manufacture of arms, ammunition, and other war material; supplies of feed, horses, draft animals, &, &.

(b) The preparation of instructions for the guidance of officers of the Army serving or traveling abroad, or acting as military attaches, and the arrangement and digest of information contained in their reports.

(c) The issuance to the Army of military maps, monographs, books, papers, and other publications, and the dissemination of valuable information on military subjects throughout all branches of the service.

(d) Correspondence with State authorities and militia officers on questions affecting the organization and armament of the militia of the several States and Territories and of the District of Columbia, and the reference to proper authority of questions for decision relating to tactical instruction, discipline, and equipment.

(e) The preparation of instructions to the officers detailed by the Secretary of War to visit the several encampments of State troops and to witness the movements and exercises of the militia, as well as the digesting, arrangement, and preservation of all reports that may be duly submitted by them.

(f) The study and preparation of plans for the mobilization and transportation of militia and volunteers and their disbandment, and for the concentration of the military forces of the United States at the various strategic points on or near the frontiers of the country.

3. The Division of Military Information will also have charge of a museum to be established for the proper care and preservation of such military relics as are now in the several bureaus of the War Department, or as may hereafter be obtained.

4. The officer in charge shall perform such other duties as naturally appertain to the division, or as may be hereafter assigned to him from time to time by the Secretary of War."

5. By Special Order, No. 210, Headquarters Division of the Philippines, Manila, P. I., December 13, 1900, a "Division of Military Information" was established in the Adjutant General's Office in Manila, and by direction of the Secretary of War was, on June 18, 1902, annexed to and made a part of the Military Information Division of the Adjutant General's Office in the War Department, Washington, by operation of the following instructions:

"War Department,
Adjutant General's Office,
Washington, June 18, 1902.

The Commanding General,
Division of the Philippines, Manila, P.I.

Sir:

I have the honor to communicate the following instructions of the Secretary of War:

With a view to increasing the facilities and rendering its operations broader and more effective, the Division of Military Information now existing in the office of the Adjutant General, Headquarters Division of the Philippines, is, for the purpose hereinafter set forth, annexed to and made a part of the Military Information Division, Adjutant General's Office."

* * * * * * * * * *

6. The following shows the character of the work required of the Military Information Division, Adjutant General's Office:

"Adjutant General's Office,
Washington, March 4, 1902.

The following statement of the organization of the Adjutant General's Office and of the class of work assigned to its several sections and divisions is made for official use and guidance:

* * * * * * * * * *

Military Information Division.

1. The collection and classification of military information of our own and foreign countries, especially with respect to armed, reserved, and available strength, material and artificial means of communication (rivers, canals, highways, and railroads); the manufacture of arms, ammunition, and other war material; supplies of food, horses, draft animals, etc.

2. The preparation of instructions for the guidance of officers of the Army serving or traveling abroad, or acting as military attaches, and the arrangement and digest of information contained in their reports.

3. The issuance to the Army of military maps, monographs, books, papers and other publications, and the dissemination of valuable information on military subjects throughout all branches of the service.

4. The preparation of instructions to the officers detailed

by the Secretary of War to visit the several encampments of State troops and to witness the movements and exercises of the militia, as well as the digesting, arrangement, and preservation of all reports that may be duly submitted by them.

5. The study and preparation of plans for the mobilization and transportation of militia and volunteers and their disbandment, and for the concentration of the military forces of the United States at the various strategic points on or near the frontiers of the country.

6. Charge of a museum to be established for the proper care and preservation of such military relics as are now in the several bureaus of the War Department, or as may be hereafter obtained.

7. Reports on professional subjects, prepared under Section 3, paragraph 11, of General Orders, No. 80, October 5, 1891, from this office, which may, for the dissemination of military information, be deemed specially valuable by Department Commanders, will, upon the consent of the authors, be forwarded to the Adjutant General of the Army with the view to publication by the Military Information Division."

7. The Act creating the General Staff Corps was passed February 14, 1903, and was promulgated to the Army by General Orders, No. 15, War Department, 1903. The duties of the General Staff are set forth in Section 2 of the Act, which is as follows:

<u>1903.</u>
General Orders,
No. 15.

"Headquarters of the Army,
Adjutant General's Office,
Washington, February 18, 1902

* * * * * * * * * *

Sec. 2. That the duties of the General Staff Corps shall be to prepare plans for the national defense and for the mobilization of the military forces in time of war; to investigate and report upon all questions affecting the efficiency of the Army and its state of preparation for military operations; to render professional aid and assistance to the Secretary of War and to general officers and other superior commanders, and to act as their agents in informing and coordinating the action of all the different officers who are subject under the terms of this act to the supervision of the Chief of Staff; and to perform such other military duties as may be from time to time prescribed by the President."

8. Referring to that part of the Act creating the General Staff Corps which enumerates the duties of the General Staff, it will be observed that every clause of this section prescribes the performance of duties which requires the previous collection and classification of military information before these duties can be performed. That the then Secretary of War, Mr. Root, recognized that the collection of military information was one of the functions of the General Staff, is evidenced by the following order:

> "War Department,
> Washington, August 6, 1903.
>
> Orders:
>
> The Military Information Division of the Adjutant General's Office, together with the records, files, property, and the persons now employed therein, are hereby transferred to the office of the Chief of Staff, to take effect August 15, 1903."

9. From the fact that this order prescribed that the Military Information Division, Adjutant General's Office, should be turned over to the General Staff Corps as a complete organization, with all of its "records, files, property, and the persons now employed therein," it is perfectly evident that the Secretary of War expected that the Military Information Division would continue to exercise the functions for which it was organized and developed during the years from 1885 to 1903, namely, the collection, classification, etc., of military information. And it is a matter of record that it did continue to exercise its proper functions after it was transferred to the General Staff and for several years thereafter, acting under its own chief who reported directly to the Chief of Staff.

10. This transfer also carried with it to the General Staff the annual appropriations by Congress, made for carrying into effect the purposes for which the Military Information Division was formed and developed. The Act in force at the time of the transfer – that of 1903 read as follows:

> "For contingent expenses of the Military Information Division, Adjutant General's Office, including the purchase of law books, books of reference, periodicals, and newspapers, and of the military attaches abroad, and of the branch office of the military information division at Manila, to be expended under the direction of the Secretary of War, six thousand six hundred and forty dollars."
>
> "For pay of the translator and librarian of the military information division of the Adjutant General's Office, one thousand eight hundred dollars."

THE BACKGROUND 127

This appropriation has been continued up to 1915, the only change in the wording of the Act being the change in designation of the "Military Information Division, Adjutant General's Office" to "Military Information Section, General Staff Corps" and an increase of the amount appropriated from $6,640.00 to $11,000. That Congress considers that this appropriation is made for the use of a specific organization for the purpose of military information work, I do not believe that anyone questions. That the various Chiefs of Staff so considered the matter is plainly shown from the fact that every order or memorandum which reorganized and prescribed the duties of the War Department General Staff has always been careful to retain, as a designation for one of its subdivisions, the name "Military Information Division" or "Section."

11. This is, perhaps, as convenient a place as any to give the various Acts of Congress appropriating money for the purpose of enabling the Army to carry on the work of collecting, classifying, etc., military information.

The first Act was in 1888, in which year Congress passed an act as part of the appropriations bill for military purposes. It read as follows:

> "For the pay of a clerk attendant on the collection and classification of military information from abroad, fifteen hundred dollars; and the officers detailed to obtain the same shall be entitled to mileage and transportation and also commutation of quarters while on this duty as provided for while on other duty."

Through the efforts of the Military Information Division, our first military attaches were sent abroad in the following year.

This appropriation was passed in the same form each succeeding year until 1894, when its form was changed to read as follows:

> "For contingent expenses of the military information division, Adjutant General's Office, and of the military attaches at the United States embassies and legations abroad, to be expended under the direction of the Secretary of War, three thousand six hundred and forty dollars."

In 1897 the section dealing with pay of the clerk was changed to read:

> "For pay of a clerk attendant on the collection and classification of military information, one thousand five hundred dollars."

The omission of the words "from abroad" allowed the clerk to be employed in all classes of military information "selection and classification."

In 1899 the section dealing with contingent expenses was changed to read as follows:

> "For contingent expenses of the military information division, Adjutant General's Office, including the purchase of law books, books of reference, periodicals and newspapers, and of the military attaches at the United States embassies and legations abroad, to be expended under the direction of the Secretary of War, six thousand six hundred and forty dollars."

In 1901 the section dealing with the clerk was changed to read as follows:

> "For pay of translator and librarian of the military information division of the Adjutant General's Office, $1,800.00."

In 1903 the appropriation was made to include the branch office at Manila by including the following words in the Act: "and the branch office of the military information division at Manila." The amount appropriated this year was increased to $10,000.00.

In 1905 the words "General Staff Corps" were substituted for the words "Adjutant General's Office" in both sections of the Act.

In 1906, in the section dealing with contingent expenses, the word "professional" was added before the words "books of reference," and the words "professional and technical" before the words "periodicals and newspapers."

In 1909 the word "Section" was substituted for the word "Division" just before the words "at Manila," in the section dealing with contingent expenses.

In 1910 the word "section" was substituted for the word "division" after the word "information" and before the words "General Staff Corps," in the section dealing with contingent expenses.

In 1912 the word "section" was substituted for the word "division" in the section dealing with the translator and librarian.

In 1913 the words "and the actual and necessary traveling expenses incurred by military attaches abroad under orders from the Secretary of War" were inserted in the section dealing with the contingent expenses.

In 1914 the same section was re-enacted and the amount was increased to $11,000.00.

In 1915 the section of the Army appropriation bill dealing with contingent expenses was changed to read as follows:

THE BACKGROUND 129

"For contingent expenses of the military information section, General Staff Corps, including the purchase of law books, professional books of reference, periodicals and newspapers; drafting and messenger service; and of the military attaches at the United States embassies and legations abroad, and of the branch office of the military information section at Manila, the cost of special instruction at home and abroad and in maintenance of students and attaches; and for such other purposes as the Secretary of War may deem proper; to be expended under the direction of the Secretary of War, $11,000.00"

Although the Military Information Section of the General Staff Corps and the Army War College are associated in the same subdivision of the General Staff, it should be noted that all the acts which appropriate money for contingent expenses appropriate expressly for the "Military information section, General Staff Corps." The Army War College has its own separate appropriation for expenses and maintenance. The appropriation acts are thus consistent in regarding them as two separate and distinct bodies, although both are now quartered in the War College building.

12. We will now go back and again take up the internal organization of the War Department General Staff.

By the following General Order the duties of the General Staff Corps were finally enunciated and the general organization prescribed under which the War Department General Staff was to begin work on August 15, 1903:

General Orders, No. 120	"Headquarters of the Army, Adjutant General's Office, Washington, August 14, 1903

* * * * * * *

Duties

3. The General Staff Corps, under the direction of the Chief of Staff, is charged with the duty of investigating and reporting upon all questions affecting the efficiency of the Army and its state of preparation for military operations. * * *

4. The General Staff Corps, under like direction, is further charged with the duty of preparing plans for the national defense and for the mobilization of the military

forces, * * * and incident thereto with the study of possible theaters of war and of strategic questions in general; with the collection of military information of foreign countries and of our own; the preparation of plans of campaign, of reports of campaigns, battles, engagements and expeditions, and of technical histories of military operations of the United States.

5. The officers of the General Staff Corps are committed the further duties of rendering professional aid and assistance to the Secretary of War and to general officers and other superior commanders. * * * They perform such other military duties not otherwise assigned by law as may from time to time be prescribed by the President.

* * * * * * *

War Department General Staff

8. To facilitate the performance of its duties the War Department General Staff will be arranged in divisions, each under the direction of an officer of the General Staff Corps to be assigned by the Chief of Staff. Each division will be subdivided into sections as may be directed by the Chief of Staff.

9. * * * * * * *

The distribution of duties to the several divisions and sections is regulated by the Chief of Staff."

* * * * * * *

13. On June 16, 1904, the following organization of the War Department General Staff was prescribed:

"War Department,
Office of the Chief of Staff,
Washington, June 16, 1904.

Memorandum:

Until further orders the distribution of business of the War Department General Staff will be as follows:

First Division

* * * * * * *

Second Division

(a) Military Information; collection, arrangement, and publication of historical, statistical, and geographic infor-

THE BACKGROUND

mation; War Department library; system of war maps, American and foreign; general information regarding foreign armies and fortresses; critical histories of important campaigns.

(b) Military attaches.

Third Division"

* * * * * * *

It will be noted that all the duties pertaining to the collection of military information were still assigned to a separate Division of the General Staff, acting under its own chief who reported directly to the Chief of Staff.

14. In June 1907, the Army War College building was ready for occupancy and the Third Division – the Army War College – was moved there from its temporary quarters in Jackson Place. During the time the Army War College had its offices at Jackson Place, it was found absolutely necessary to call on the Military Information Division, then located in the Lemon Building, for military information of every description. As the time approached for the War College to occupy the new War College Building, the President of the War College realized that it would be most inconvenient, if not impossible, to continue to utilize the Military Information Division as had been done while the War College occupied quarters at Jackson Place. He therefore recommended that the Military Information Division be moved bodily down to the War College building. This was strenuously objected to by the Chief of the Military Information Division, in which he was backed by the opinion of every General Staff officer then on duty in that Division. The views of the President of the War College, however, prevailed and in May, 1908, the Second (Military Information) Division was transferred with its personnel and material to the Army War College building. At the time the transfer was made the duties of the Military Information Division were as prescribed in the following memorandum:

"War Department,
Office of the Chief of Staff,
Washington, May 24, 1907.

Memorandum:

1. Until further orders the distribution of business of the War Department General Staff will be as follows:

First Division

* * * * * * *

Second Division

Military information; collection, arrangement, and publication of historical, statistical and geographical information; War Department library; system of war maps, American and foreign; general information regarding foreign armies and fortresses; preparation from official records of analytical and critical histories of important campaigns.
Military attaches.
Photographic gallery.
Issue of military publications, maps and documents.

Third Division (Army War College)."

*   *   *   *   *   *   *

The duties of the Army War College were defined by the following order:

"War Department,
General Orders,   Washington, May 28, 1907.
No. 116

1. Paragraphs 240 to 245, inclusive, of General Orders, No. 115, June 27, 1904, War Department, are revoked.
2. The organization and work of the Army War College will hereafter be regulated by the following provisions:
3. The purpose of the War College is to make a practical application of knowledge already acquired, not to impart academic instruction.
4. The objects of the War College are:-

(a) The direction and coordination of military education in the Army and in civil schools and colleges at which officers of the Army are detailed under Acts of Congress, and the extension of opportunities for investigation and study in the militia of the United States.

(b) To provide facilities for and to promote advanced study of military subjects and to formulate the opinions of the college body on the subjects studied for the information of the Chief of Staff.

5. The personnel of the Army War College shall be in part permanent and in part temporary.
6. The permanent personnel shall consist of a President, to be assigned to that duty by the Secretary of War, and the officers for the time being of the Third Division, War Department General Staff. The Chief and one other

member of the division shall be directors of the college. The Secretary of the college shall also be selected from the permanent personnel. The directors and secretary shall be designated in orders."

15. It will be observed that, as yet, there has been no interference or curtailment of the functions of the Second Division as an agency for the collection, classification, and distribution of military information. Also that up to this time there is a clean cut separation of duties between the Second and Third Divisions, that each is separate and distinct and acting under its own chief who reports directly to the Chief of Staff.

16. In the memorandum to which this paper is attached, attention was called to the fact that the collection and classification of the large amount of information in the possession of the General Staff, the cordial relations established between the Military Information Division and the State Department, the Navy Department, the United States Secret Service, and many other agencies necessary for the collection of military information, was only made possible by the fact that there was a distinct organization which was charged with military information duties. Attention is again called to that fact here. There was in existence a body of General Staff officers, small to be sure, but more or less trained in the work required of them. There was also a trained force of clerks, draftsmen, photographers, etc., whose activities were all expended on this work. It was possible, also, to handle the confidential work pertaining to the Division, so much of which is necessary and of such vital importance, directly and personally with the Chief of Staff or the Secretary of War, so that it was not necessary to put everything on paper in the form of memoranda or letters as afterwards became the case. It was possible to carry along a consistent policy in respect to information work and to train officers in the duties pertaining to such work.

The transfer of the Military Information Section to the War College building marked a backward step in the organization of the War Department General Staff. The Second and Third Sections were now to be merged into one and the majority of the conditions enumerated as absolutely necessary to the effectual accomplishment of military information work were vastly changed and some of them ceased to exist entirely. The new order of things went into effect under the memorandum, quoted later, dated June 27, 1908, Office of the Chief of Staff.

17. For a period after the consolidation of the Second and Third Divisions into the new Second Section, a semblance of a distinct organization for military information work was maintained. But it was only a semblance and the essential things which made it possible to fulfill the functions and duties devolving on the organization disappeared. Even

before the memorandum quoted was issued, all the records of the old Second and Third Divisions were consolidated into a single record section pertaining to the new Second Section. The clerks, typewriters, translator, librarian, draftsmen, photographers, etc., of the old Second Division were merged with the clerks of the old Third Division into one general body now pertaining to the Second Section. The custody of the records, files, library, photograph gallery, and all other material formerly pertaining to the Military Information Division passed to the Secretary of the new Second Section. The President of the War College became the Chief of the new Second Section and therefore the officer responsible for the performance of all the duties formerly pertaining to the old Second Division and the former chief of that Division ceased to have any authority over such functions. To effectually supervise and control the functions of the organization charged with information duties requires the undivided time and thought and attention of any one officer. Indeed, as experience as shown, if these duties are properly performed, that officer will find that he has more than any one man can handle. To charge, then, the Chief of the new Second Section with all the duties and responsibilities of the officer in charge of military information work in addition to those entailed by the supervision of the old Third Division, and to expect him to have time for all of the duties with which he was now charged was to expect the impossible. He would either have to pay particular attention to one class of duties to the detriment of the other, or find himself forced to perform all of his duties in a perfunctory manner. There are simply not enough hours in the day to make it possible to do the work.

18. The condition just described was brought about by the following memorandum, and the Military Information Division, as an efficient agency for the collection and classification of military information, passed out of existence. It is interesting to note that the officer who, as Chief of Staff, issued the memorandum which virtually emasculated the Military Information Division in 1908, issued an order, as commanding general, Western Department, establishing a Military Information Division in that Department in 1916:

"War Department,
Office of the Chief of Staff,
Washington, June 27, 1908.

Memorandum:

1. The following organization and distribution of business of the War Department General Staff is announced, and will be in force until further orders:

First Section

THE BACKGROUND   135

* * * * * * *

Second Section

Military information; collection, arrangement, and publication of historical, statistical, and geographical information; War Department library; system of war maps, American and foreign; general information regarding foreign armies and fortresses; preparation from official records of analytical and critical histories of important campaigns.
Military attaches.
Photographic gallery.
Preparation of non-technical manuals.
Issue of military publications, maps, and documents.
Collection and discussion of all obtainable data relating to strategic, tactical, and logistic features of future military operations, and formulation of complete working plans for passing from a state of peace to a state of war under such conditions as can be foreseen or may be assumed. Direction and coordination of military education in the Army, the militia, and in civil schools and colleges at which officers of the Army are detailed.
Plans for field maneuvers.
Permanent fortifications.
Submarine defense.
Field engineering.
Signaling, technical manuals, and logistics.
Military resources of the country."

* * * * * * *

19. In order to carry into effect the provisions of the foregoing memorandum, the Chief of the Second Section issued the following memorandum:

"Office Chief of Second Section
General Staff
Washington

June 27, 1908

Memorandum:

The Second Section of the General Staff having been created by paragraph 762 of the Army Regulations, (W.D. G.O. No. 128, 1908) and the duties hereto performed by the Second and Third Divisions of the General Staff having been assigned with certain modifications, to the Second Section of the General Staff, by memorandum from the Chief of Staff's Office dated June 27, 1908, the following executive staff and committees of the Second Section are announced and the following assignment of personnel and duties to the committees is made:

I

Executive Staff

Chief of Section:

* * * * * * *

Secretary of Second Section:

* * * * * * *

Chief Clerk of Second Section:

* * * * * * *

II

Military Information Committee

Chairman of Committee:

* * * * * * *

Members of Committee

* * * * * * *

To this Committee the following duties are assigned: Military information; collection, arrangement, and publication of historical, statistical and geographical information; War Department library; system of war maps, American and foreign; general information regarding foreign armies and fortresses; preparation from official records of analytical and critical histories of important campaigns.

Military attaches.

Photographic gallery.

Issue of military publications, maps, and documents.

* * * * * * *

VII

Correspondence

All letters and papers pertaining to the business of the Section, or to the business of the Army War College, addressed to superiors or to persons outside the Second Section, and all papers prepared for the signature of superiors, will be prepared under the supervision of the Chairman of each Committee; the originals of the former class will be initialed by the Chairman; and the duplicate copies of the latter class will show in the upper right hand corner the typewritten initials of the Chairman of the Committee, and will be submitted to the Chief of

Section with such written or verbal explanations as may be necessary.

Each Committee will keep a complete file and record of all its correspondence independent of the other committee. The copies of the correspondence and files of all matters pertaining to the office of the Secretary of the Army War College will be kept with the records of the Army War College Committee.

VIII
Vouchers

Vouchers for expenditures under the appropriations made by Congress for contingent expenses of the Military Information Division, General Staff Corps, and for all other expenditures which properly pertain to that Committee, will be prepared under the direction and supervision of the Chairman of the Military Information Committee in accordance with existing laws and regulations and submitted to the Chief of the Second Section for signature.

*   *   *   *   *   *   *   *

IX
Distribution of clerical force, messengers and employees
To the Military Information Committee."

(Here follow 39 names. The list includes draftsmen, typewriters, clerks, translators, librarian and personnel of the photograph gallery.)

20. It will be observed that the duties assigned to the Military Information Committee of the new Second Section by Section Ii of the above memorandum are the same as those assigned to the old Second (Military Information) Division by the memorandum of the Chief of Staff dated June 14, 1904. However, all authority to direct the work prescribed to be done, all control over correspondence, files, records, maps, etc., all power to direct the clerical force, in short all power to control the work or to plan for and initiate new work, was taken from the officer assigned in charge of military information duties. This fact is emphasized by Section VII of this memorandum.

It will also be observed that each Committee was directed to "keep a complete file and record of all its correspondence independent of the other committee."

This provision was intended to give each committee a certain degree of independence and initiative. An attempt to carry it out was made, but, as the clerical force was all under the control of the Chief of Section and as no clerks or typewriters were ever assigned to the Committee, the effort was abortive and was abandoned.

21. It would seem that the above memorandum was amply sufficient to render it utterly impossible for the officer immediately responsible for the collection and classification of military information to exercise his functions and to reduce the activities of the committee to purely clerical duties, but we will find that, ten years later, his functions were to be still further curtailed, and the work of the Committee on Military Information made still less effective. This was accomplished by the following memorandum:

"War Department
Office of the Chief of Staff
Washington
September 26, 1910

Memorandum

The following organization and distribution of business of the War Department General Staff is announced:

I. Mobile Army Division

All matters pertaining to personnel and material of the mobile forces, and such other subjects as are not otherwise assigned.

War College Division

(a) Collection and distribution of military information; War Department library; preparation of non-technical manuals; direction and coordination of military education; plans for field maneuvers; collation and discussion of all obtainable data relating to strategical, tactical and logistic features of future military operations and formation of complete working plans for passing from a state of peace to a state of war.

(b) Army War College

Coast Artillery Division

All matters pertaining to the personnel and material of the Coast Artillery forces.

II. Division of Militia Affairs

All matters pertaining to the Organized Militia.

III. Papers requiring the action of the Chief of Staff will be checked to the Chiefs of the above mentioned Divisions by the Secretary, General Staff, and all routine or

THE BACKGROUND 139

unimportant cases will be returned to him for submission to the Chief of Staff. Important cases will be submitted in person by Chiefs of Division."

22. The above is an additional step in the process which abolished the functions of any distinct body charged with that most important duty – the collection and classification of military information and all that that expression implies. The next step we will find in the following memorandum:

"War Department
Office of the Chief of Staff
Washington
February 3, 1912

Memorandum:

To further expedite the work and increase the efficiency of the War College Division of the General Staff, the following assignments of personnel to committees, and the duties of said committees are announced:

*   *   *   *   *   *   *

IV
Duties
War College Division

Military information; collection, arrangement, and publication of historical, statistical, and geographical information; War Department library; system of war maps, American and foreign; general information regarding foreign armies and fortresses; preparation from official records of analytical and critical histories of important campaigns.
Military attaches.
Photographic gallery.
Preparation of non-technical manuals.
Issue of military publications, maps, and documents.

Chief of Division and President of the War College:
The Chief of Division has supervision of all questions and matters of policy and administration, executive and professional work of the Division and the Army War College, the military attaches, confidential missions abroad, the War Department library, the photographic gallery, the distribution of documents, and considers and decides all important questions affecting the action or

recommendation of the Division, as well as signing of communications to equal or superior authority.

Papers, reports or recommendations upon subjects of special importance can be submitted to the Chief of Division in person with such verbal or written explanations as may be necessary, but all papers or routine matters of office work will be submitted to the Secretary.

* * * * * * *

V
Committees

Committee on War Plans:

The Committee will collate and discuss all obtainable data relating to strategical, logistical and tactical features of possible future military operations, and will formulate complete working plans for passing from a state of peace to a state of war under such conditions as can be foreseen or may be assumed. The Committee will be charged with the coordination of technical and non-technical manuals with the Field Regulations and with each other, and will keep the Secretary of the War College Division advised of the Committee's needs as to maps, appropriate to its studies.

(Here follows a list of a General Staff officers and the temporary personnel of the Army War College).

Committee on Military Information:

The Committee is charged specifically with the following duties:

(1) The preparation and maintenance of military monographs. These monographs will be prepared in accordance with a general form approved by the President of the War College. In its monographic work the Committee will have the assistance of such officers of the War College as may be available for that duty.

(2) The direction and coordination of military education in the Army, the militia, and in civil schools and colleges at which officers of the Army are detailed.

(3) The preparation and maintaining of a system of military maps, American and foreign.

(4) The preparation from authentic sources of histories of important military events.

(5) The compilation and editing of important articles on military subjects for publication to the Army, either as War Department Documents or in the service journals.

THE BACKGROUND 141

(6) The furnishing of information to officers entitled thereto, and the preparation for transmittal to military posts and headquarters, of monthly lists of books and subjects carded in the War College library.

(7) The arrangement, carding, classification and filing of publications, periodicals, newspapers and of the carding of the reports of the military attaches abroad, as well as the miscellaneous information received in the division, for ready reference."

(Here follows a list of 10 General Staff officers.)

* * * * * * *

23. Of the above duties assigned to the Committee on Military Information, (1), the first clause of (6), and (7) are essentially functions of a Military Information (or Intelligence) Division. The other sections are not necessarily so, although (3), (4) and (5) might be assigned to such a division or section if there were no other agency to perform such work. The other duties enumerated in this section have no relation whatever to military information work. But, in addition to the fact that the body charged with the above duties has no power to control its own work or to initiate new work, is the fact that no officer or group of officers is charged with the duty of <u>obtaining</u> military information other than military attaches or military observers in time of war. As has been said before, the most necessary and essential kind of information, the information without which no war plan can be made that is worth the paper it is written on, does not come in of its own accord or as a matter of routine. It must be actively sought and traced out and proved up. Other agencies than those in the War Department and other men than those occupying chairs in the offices of the General Staff must be put to work. To find these agencies and men and to put them to work and keep them at it along the proper lines requires no small degree of thought and planning by a strong, permanent central authority. Yet, in this assignment of duties, this vital element is not mentioned.

But this is not all. Section (7) requires the "arrangement, carding, classification, and filing of publications, periodicals, newspapers, and the carding of the reports of the military attaches abroad, as well as miscellaneous information received in the Division, for ready reference."

One would naturally suppose that this work was to be done by officers, whose professional knowledge would make it possible to do it in an efficient manner. This, however, is not the case. It is done by civilian clerks, who, however zealous and efficient as clerks, can not be expected to have the expert knowledge possessed by the trained and experienced officer. It is not even made the duty of any officer or group of officers to supervise this work. This is work of the utmost importance and should be done, not only by officers, but by officers especially trained in military information work, since the information received must be digested and checked and proved and re-checked before it is of any value whatever. To use information which has not been through this process is not only a waste of time – it is positively dangerous.

24. This omission to provide the agencies for the very foundation of General Staff work is undoubtedly not intentional. It is simply the result of the lack of familiarity with the details and functions of military information work.

25. But the above are not the only handicaps on military information work that we find in this memorandum. The following section takes away from the already emasculated Military Information Committee all the agencies usually employed to obtain information and vests their control in this Chief of Division. If the Chief of Division had no other duties to perform except this, the arrangement could not be criticized. But it is simply a physical impossibility for one man to attend to the many and various duties imposed upon him as Chief of the War College Division and take over and perform these others in addition. Here is what this section says:

> "Chief of Division and President of the War College:
> The Chief of Division has supervision of all questions and matters of policy and administration, executive and professional work of the Division and of the Army War College, the military attaches, confidential missions abroad, the War Department library, the photographic gallery, the distribution of documents, and considers and decides all important questions affecting the action or recommendation of the Division, as well as signing of communications to equal or superior authority."

26. If it were only a matter of _supervision_ there would be little criticism of the above section of the memorandum. But read in connection with the remainder of the memorandum it will at once be seen that it is not only _supervision_ that is involved. For in no place do we find that any other officer, other than the Chief of the War College Division, is charged with any of the duties mentioned in the above paragraph. That it is not only supervision, it is _all_ of the duties which pertain to the subjects mentioned that devolve on the Chief of Division, at least in so far as the initiation of work is considered. The effect of such a provision was, of course, to make it impossible for the Committee on Military Information to inaugurate any work; they could only do what was assigned them by the Chief of Division. It made it absolutely impossible

for the Committee to carry on a continuous policy in the work or to train officers in information work.

27. That just the results that were to have been anticipated were realized is evident from the following letter from the Chief of Staff:

> "War Department
> Office of the Chief of Staff
> Washington
>
> January 20, 1913
>
> Memorandum for the Chief, War College Division:
>
> There have been brought to my attention from time to time certain statements concerning the Military Information Section, which I think the following fairly well embraces. This is sent to you because I know you are anxious to get this section on the best possible basis, and I think you will find in it some valuable suggestions; at least, I send it to you for what it is worth. I am inclined to think we can shale [sic] out a good deal of dead material, and get the work on the line which I indicate below.
>
> There seems to be lack of organization and coordination of the work. Undoubtedly much valuable work is done, but a great deal (if not the major part) is wasted and the effects lost to the army through the lack of crystallized results.
>
> 1. There seems to be a lack of continuity about the work. The section's work does not go forward continuously. An officer may spend months of a year or so on a particular subject or line of work and when the time comes for his relief another officer is assigned to that subject who has no previous training or familiarity with it; it therefore takes him months to get up to the point where his predecessor left off – the time so spent being waste effort, except in so far as the officer himself is concerned – the problem or line of work being in the meantime at a standstill.
>
> In other words the section does not seem to be sufficiently self perpetuating. It is not training up a set of officers to carry the work forward uninterruptedly.
>
> 2. All reports coming in from officers in all parts of the world are carded and filed as if all were of equal value. These reports are generally sent around to the members of some committee to read, but they do not seem to be

empowered to make any comments thereon. It seems as though there might be a committee of censors to throw out reports that are of a temporary nature and prevent the permanent records becoming clogged by so much dead wood; at least they might express their opinion as to a report being "good," "indifferent," "of permanent value," "of temporary interest only," etc., etc. If the report is saved the committee's appraisal of the same should be noted on the card index. An officer looking for information on a given subject ought to be able to tell something from the card index as to the value of the report and thus what reports he wants to consult; this would save a great deal of time not only for himself, but of the clerks', which is otherwise spent in hunting up and looking over reports that turn out to be of no value to the particular subject under investigation.

3. * * * * * * *

4. Military monographs are for the most part in a very incomplete stage. * * * * * * *

5. As said above, most of the monographs seem to be in a very incomplete stage; in most cases this is probably for lack of accurate or trustworthy information, but no one seems to be specially charged with seeing that efforts are put on foot to obtain this needed information.

6. There is lack of coordination with other departments of the government. Much information that is useful is to be had from consular and other reports that are continually coming into the State Department. A tactful officer detailed for that work could easily justify his time; he could make himself persona grata to the State Department by helping to fill out gaps in their information that might be supplied from the War College Division, having due regard to confidential matters, of course.

Of course, more could be obtained from the Navy Department than from the State Department if satisfactory arrangements were made for a regular exchange of information, by means of an officer charged with the duty of keeping up this relation."

7. (In substance, this section suggests a wider field of work in China and Japan through the Military Information Division in Manila and the embassy in Japan and the legation at Peking.)

(Sgd.) Leonard Wood
Chief of Staff

THE BACKGROUND 145

28. In reply to the above the Chief of the War College Division submitted a memorandum dated January 27, 1913. In his comments the Chief of the Division very plainly indicates that the difficulties encountered by the War College Division in handling matters connected with military information are just those which I have pointed out in this paper, although he does not express it in exactly the same way. In paragraph 2 of his memorandum we find the following:

> 2. All questions of any importance are considered by committees and if they are questions of more or less permanence, these committees are permanent ones. There are, for example, the committees of each arm of the service, composed of all the officers of that branch of the service, a committee on schools, a committee on equipment, a committee on the reorganization of the army, which are permanent or semi-permanent in nature. For special subjects, special committees are appointed, such as for field regulations, service manuals, etc.
>
> * * * * * * *
>
> It would not be practical to educate one officer to take the place of another, as the head of a sub-committee must naturally be the officer of the highest rank assigned to that committee.
>
> * * * * * * *
>
> 3. As to the question of censorship of information coming in, this has been done by the officer in charge of the library. There has been discussed in the committee a number of times the question of the desirability of appointing a separate committee on the subject of censorship. Up to the present time this has not been considered desirable but the subject has not been neglected.
>
> * * * * * * *
>
> The officers of the War College class are at present engaged in preparing monographs on various countries.
>
> * * * * * * *
>
> 4. It is a fact that the monographs are not in as satisfactory a state as could be desired. This fact has been admitted here for several years past and efforts have been made to correct it. It has not been possible to do this satisfactorily on account of the small number of officers and the numerous changes that have been made. During the last two or three months the situation in that respect has improved and it is hoped that we will be able to place the monographs in better shape.

5. As to the statement in paragraph 8 in the memorandum that no one is charged with seeing that efforts are being put on foot to obtain other information. This is not strictly a fact, although it may be admitted that new information on various subjects may be needed. However, requests are sent constantly to military attaches and others to obtain information on special subjects."

* * * * * * *

29. The above reply, read in connection with the letter itself, make it perfectly clear where the trouble lies. The conditions complained of in the letter obtained because there was no proper organization for handling matters connected with military information. The explanation in the reply to the letter of the Chief of Staff of the manner in which the business was handled in the War College Division make it perfectly evident that all initiative must come from outside the Division – that there is no organization or especially designated group within it whose function is to study the needs of the army and the government with respect to military information and formulate plans for the accomplishment of the desired ends. The criticisms made by the Chief of Staff in 1913 could be made today. Nothing of a permanent nature was done to remedy the conditions mentioned. Nor could anything have been done as matters stood then and still stand today, because the fundamental, basic trouble lies in the lack of organization.

30. The following memorandum gives the duties assigned to the War College Division and describes the manner in which the routine work of the Division is performed:

"Washington, May 3, 1915.

Memorandum for the Chief of Staff:

Subject: Names of officers on General Staff work at the Army War College, their specific duties and the different committees organized.

1. On January 4, 1915, the names of the officers on General Staff work at the Army War College were as follows:
(Here follow the various sub-committees into which the War College Division is divided and the names of the officers assigned to them.)

* * * * * * *

VII. Military Information and Monographs. (Here follow the names of the officers on this committee.)

Distribution of General Staff Work.

The General Staff officers enumerated above, together with the attached officers, constitute the personnel of what is known in the Army Appropriation Bills as the "Military Information Section, General Staff Corps. "This is the legal designation of one section of the War College Division, General Staff; the other section is designated the "Army War College," which will be referred to later. It is the primary function of the Military Information Section to do current General Staff work. As papers requiring General Staff action come into the War College Division, they pass over the desk of the senior General Staff officer, who supervises the work of the section, assigning the papers to individuals and committees for report. He reviews these reports before he lays them before the Chief of the War College Division for signature. He presides at called meetings of the various committees of which he is chairman and at those of the Military Information Section in full committee, except on some special occasions when the Chief of Division is present. These duties require the constant attention of this senior General Staff officer and he should not be hampered with outside work not pertaining to this section of the General Staff, as Colonel Treat now is, as explained in paragraph 5 of this memorandum.

* * * * * * *

Army War College

6. The purpose of the Army War College is to train officers of recognized ability and experience in the functions of higher command, and in General Staff duties appropriate to the higher grades."

* * * * * * *

31. The following memorandum gives briefly the duties of the War College Division under the two sections, Military Information Section and Army War College:

"War Department
Office of the Chief of Staff
Washington
November 6, 1915

Memorandum for the Chief of Staff:

Subject: Duties of the War College Division and

assignment thereto of individual officers.

1. Herewith is a memorandum from the Chief of Staff, dated November 3, 1915, directing the submission of a brief statement of the duties of the War College Division, its subdivisions and the assignment of individual officers thereto. The following statement is submitted accordingly:

Establishment.

The division was established under the designation "War College Division" in accordance with a memorandum from the Office of the Chief of Staff, dated September 26, 1910, and is housed in the War College building.

Composition.

The division is composed of two distinct bodies: (a) the Military Information Section, General Staff Corps; and (b) the Army War College, both of which are recognized by Congress in that separate appropriations are made for each. Both are accommodated in the Army War College building where they have been located, the former since June, 1908, and the latter since June, 1907, and each has its own distinct functions and duties.

Duties.

These duties are briefly stated as follows: (a) Military Information Section. Collection and distribution of military information; War Department library; preparation of non-technical manuals; direction and coordination of military education; plans for field maneuvers; collection and discussion of all obtainable data relative to strategy and tactics of future military operations; and formation of complete working plans for passing from a state of peace to a state of war. Also, system of war maps, American and foreign; military attaches; military publications; photographic gallery; preparation, from official records, of analytical and critical histories of important campaigns.

(b) Army War College. Development of officers of recognized ability in the functions of higher command and in the duties of the General Staff in the higher grades."

32. The organization under which we are working today is specified in

THE BACKGROUND 149

the "Manual of the War College Division, General Staff," dated August 10, 1915. This manual is a compendium of all rules and regulations in force relating to the present organization of the War College Division.

33. Let us see, now, just how this organization of the War College Division works practically in so far as military information work is concerned.

The explanation given in the memorandum to the Chief of Staff of May 3, 1915, gives this very exactly. All of the General Staff officers on duty at the Army War College, together with the attached officers, "constitute the personnel of what is known in the Army Appropriations Bills as the 'Military Information Section, General Staff Corps'. This is the legal designation of one section of the War College Division."

34. That expresses it exactly. It is a "legal designation" and nothing else and the designation was probably used because it was necessary to do so in order to utilize the appropriation made by Congress for the purpose of handling matters connected with military information work. That the duties of this section are not primarily related to military information work is emphasized by the following: "The primary function of the Military Information Section is to do current General Staff work." And that is precisely what the Section does – "current General Staff work" (and much which is not General Staff work at all). As explaining how this "current General Staff work" is performed, the memorandum continues: "As papers requiring General Staff action come into the War College Division, they pass over the desk of the senior General Staff officer, who supervises the work of the Section, assigning the papers to individuals and committees for report." Now, although General Staff work embraces military information work, it also embraces a vast amount of work which does not pertain to military information at all. On the other hand, military information work embraces much which is not current work but which must be inaugurated within the organization which handles it. The memorandum continues: "He reviews these reports before he lays them before the Chief of the War College Division for signature." But who attends to the various duties pertaining to the "collection, classification," etc., of military information and the many other and various duties connected with work of this character? Who is to do the planning for future work and who considers the many important questions which arise in this connection? The senior General Staff officer could not do it even if it were assigned to him unless he neglected his other duties, as is pointed out by the memorandum: "He presides at called meetings of the various committees of which he is chairman and at those of the Military Information Section in full committee * * *. These duties require the constant attention of this senior General Staff officer and he should not

be hampered with outside work not pertaining to this section of the General Staff, as Colonel Treat now is, as explained in paragraph 5 of this memorandum." Nor even if he had the time, could he carry out the work, since we will find that some of the most important of the agencies created to carry on military information work are removed from his supervision, and their control vested in the Chief of Division, namely, "the military attaches, confidential missions abroad, the War Department library, the photographic gallery," as we will find in the memorandum of February 3, 1912.

As a matter of fact, the designation "Military Information" no better describes the duties really performed by this Section of the War College Division than does the term "War College," the duties performed by the Division as a whole.

35. If then, as is evidently the fact, the senior General Staff officer, who is charged with the supervision of all the work of the so-called Military Information Section, General Staff Corps, is not able to attend to actual military information work, who does it? On what group of officers does the duty devolve? The only possible group in the Division which might be expected to look after it is the Committee on "Military Information and Monographs." The chairman of this committee is the Chief of the Division and one of its members is the secretary of the Division. The reason for this is that these officers have charge of the military attaches and observers and direct their work. While this arrangement is good as far as it goes, these officers, due to numerous and pressing additional duties, cannot give the time and attention required to various other important phases of military information work. Nor can the remaining members of the committee do so, there is not one of them who is not assigned necessarily to one or more additional committees which have to consider other and entirely different subjects.

The consequence is that the General Staff cannot digest the information that is being collected and put it in shape for use, and are utterly unable, through lack of proper organization, to keep up a constant flow of the kind of information we need for planning military operations intended primarily for our own defense.

36. From the point of view of military information, we are not prepared for military operations even in our own country and we are doing nothing to remedy the condition. The work that was done by the Military Information Division of the Adjutant General's Office and the Second (Military Information) Division of the General Staff was excellent in character and large in amount when the number of officers and facilities available are considered. Under the present system we are unable to digest the mass of information coming in from abroad much less to

THE BACKGROUND 151

develop our information service at home. It would seem, then, that the sooner we abandon a system which is not giving results and return to one which did, the better it will be for the government, the General Staff and the Army at large.

But there are additional reasons why this should be done and done speedily, as will appear from what follows:

37. Any one who has anything to do with military information work realizes that work of this character can be handled only by trained men – officers and clerks alike. The work does not require any particular brilliancy of intellect but it does require training and experience, thought and planning, and hard, plodding work. Since we have no means of training General Staff officers in our Army except through actual service in the General Staff Corps, it is only by performing the duties connected with military information work that this instruction and experience can be gained. There is no text-book or other source of information to which officers can go to learn how to perform duties of this character. If, then, there is no organization of the General Staff which does work of this character, how can the younger officers be expected to acquire the knowledge of methods necessary to enable them to handle military information work?

38. To accomplish results of lasting benefit, to establish methods of collecting information which will work automatically over a period of years, to establish permanent or semi-permanent agencies for the collection of information, requires coordination and "team-work" which can only be obtained by organized effort. It requires an established policy and a policy which will impress itself on the work from year to year.

39. A large percentage of military information work is, necessarily, confidential in character. This is true even of many matters handled by military attaches as matters of routine, and serious trouble is likely to ensue unless they are so regarded. Much of the information absolutely essential in war must be obtained in the country to be operated in before even a suspicion of war arises. A great deal of this is of such character that it can not be obtained through our regularly accredited military attaches, and other means must be sought. Whether this is accomplished through officers of our own army who are sent into the country in question, or through agents already residing there, it must be regarded as highly confidential.

But it is not only matters connected with foreign countries that require secrecy in their handling. Certain information in our own country can not be obtained unless you can convince the persons who furnish it that the information and the source from which it comes are to be considered as confidential. If they are not absolutely convinced of this, the information will not be forthcoming, no matter how essential it may be to the government and the army.

40. Matters of this nature must be handled personally. They can not be treated as mere matters of routine which pass under the eyes of many people. Indeed it often happens that certain matters should not be committed to writing at all. In many of these cases the matter must be taken up directly with the Chief of Staff or with the Secretary of War and sometimes with the President. This is essential in time of peace and it is especially so in time of war. It is, therefore, not only important but essential that the officer who is charged with military information duties deal directly with, and be responsible to, the Chief of Staff.

41. It transpired a short time since that the Quartermaster Corps was engaged in collecting information with regard to the railroads of the United States with a view to preparing the data for use in case of war. This is, of course, essentially the work of the Information Section of the General Staff. But since that Section is not organized exclusively for information work and since it has been the specific duty of no one to study the subject in question, it naturally has not been done. However, as such information was vitally important to the Quartermaster Corps, and as they knew it was not being collected by the General Staff, it is hardly to be wondered at that they took it up. Information concerning not only railroads but concerning many other classes of industry should be collected by the General Staff. We should be engaged on that work now. If there had been a properly organized Military Information Division in existence, that work would have been begun as soon as it became evident that it was going to be essential to the government.

42. Mention has been made in the memorandum to which this paper is attached, of the organization of the Military Information or Intelligence Division with the forces in the field in time of war. The importance of General Staff work in the field has increased enormously during the present European war. Just what the organization and duties of the General Staff of the various belligerent powers are, in detail, we do not yet know because the entire subject is guarded with great care. We do know, however, that the powers and duties of the General Staff in all of the warring nations are much greater than ever before. We also know that the organization of the various Intelligence Departments is most complete. For one of these nations we have the organization and assignment of duties of the General Staff in the field. In this organization the General Staff with the troops in the field is divided into four primary divisions, each reporting directly to the Chief of Staff of the unit to which it is attached. The second in order named of these divisions is the

THE BACKGROUND 153

Intelligence Division. The duties which it is called upon to perform are many and intricate and call for a high degree of previous training. They also make a very close and intimate relation with the home Intelligence Department absolutely necessary. If all this has been found to be necessary in Europe, it will be found to be equally necessary in this country.

43. But, beyond defining the duties to be required of the Intelligence Section in the field in our Field Service Regulations, we have done nothing in this direction to prepare for war conditions. And, naturally, as we have no organization in time of peace whose duty it is to train officers and others for such duties, we have no trained personnel. For the same reason we have none of the material which will be necessary immediately upon the outbreak of war and no plans for its preparation.

44. To sum the whole matter up in a single sentence, we are no better prepared, in so far as organization for intelligence duties in the field are concerned, than we were the day the General Staff was created, and so far as military information is concerned we are not so well prepared since much of the information on hand at that time, particularly the topographical data pertaining to our neighbors on the North and South, has not since been corrected or added to and is now so old as to be practically worthless.

45. Does it not seem that the time has come when the General Staff should take steps to correct this condition of affairs? The power to do this is within the General Staff itself – as is also the obligation. Both are placed there by Congress in the Act which created the General Staff Corps. It will not answer to say, when we are tried and found wanting, that Congress did not furnish us the means to accomplish the desired results, because we have not used the powers we have.

46. From all of the above considerations, and many others not possible to enter into in this paper, I am forced to the following conclusions, if we hope to have more effective General Staff work in the future:

(1) That the Military Information Section, General Staff Corps, must be re-established as a separate unit of the War Department General Staff and freed from all those duties which do not pertain to military information work. (2) That this Section must have an independent organization and that its chief must be responsible directly to the Chief of Staff. (3) That it must have its own personnel of officers and clerks, draftsmen, photographers, and other assistants. (4) That it must have its own records and files. (5) That it must handle all matters connected with military information work and it must not be required to consider matters not connected with its legitimate duties.

47. The question of where such an organization should be housed is a secondary matter. Without doubt it would be much more convenient for the Chief of Staff, and would make for efficiency, if it were located near the office of the Chief of Staff. In time of war or public danger this might become imperative. But in ordinary times of peace other sections of the General Staff, notably that whose duty it is to consider and prepare war plans, and also the Army War College in its educational capacity, could utilize the services of the Military Information Section to very great advantage. For this reason it would, perhaps, be best to house it in the War College building. There is no more reason for claiming that two or more separate sections of the General Staff could not work under the single roof of the War College building than there would be to claim that those now housed in the War Department building could not function as distinct entities.

48. It is futile for us to try to delude ourselves with the idea that the General Staff has taken the place in the regard of the Army and of Congress that it was hoped and believed it would. The Army at large is certainly no more than lukewarm in its support; the various bureaus of the War Department can not be said to be enthusiastic; and there is a distinct spirit of hostility developing in Congress. This is not pleasant to contemplate. The General Staff Corps has now been in existence for 13 years. There is a wide-spread feeling that it has not accomplished all the good that it was expected to accomplish – that it has not entirely fulfilled the functions for which it was created. This feeling may be erroneous or there may be reasons why it was impossible for the General Staff to fully carry out its functions. But whatever has caused the feeling, it is there. This being so, is it not time that we were examining into the matter and finding out if, after all, the cause for this feeling does not lie within ourselves? I believe that if any cause for the feeling of dissatisfaction be found, if it develops that we really have not been doing all that should have been done, that one of the primary causes will be found in our lack of a proper internal organization.

49. In presenting this paper for consideration, I desire to say that it is not done in any spirit of carping criticism or faultfinding. It is merely a presentation of the facts as I see them and is presented because I believe it to be my duty, as a member of the General Staff Corps, to point them out for the consideration of higher authority. With that accomplished, my duty and obligation in this connection cease.

R. H. Van Deman
Major, General Staff

PART III   APPENDICES

Appendix A

Colonel Dennis E. Nolan June 4, 1918
Assistant Chief of Staff,
G-2, G.H.Q., A.E.F., FRANCE

My dear Nolan:

.... I am having the papers, listed in your memorandum of April 19th, gone over here and if there are any others which we know of and which it would seem desirable to have, we will let you know. For the present, you may consider that the matter is on a satisfactory basis as it now stands.

You will no doubt be very much surprised, as I was, to learn that I was to attempt to take charge of the work which Van Deman has built up. I am sure if I had known I was to take any serious part in intelligence work, I should never have attempted to leave your section last July in the hope of obtaining more active duty. If I had remained with you from July until now, I should be much more qualified to go on with the things here. It only shows that we never know what is good for us when we make decisions about our own careers.

After you have had an opportunity of talking things over with Van Deman, you will realize, in spite of his modest description of the work here, that he has performed miracles in building up an intelligence service which is as good as anything which I saw in England or in France. As time goes on and American imagination and originality begins [sic] to get in its work, I am sure that we shall have a better intelligence service than anybody else.

I do not know the plans of either the Chief of Staff here or the Commander-in-Chief, A.E.F., but I sincerely hope you will arrange to let Van Deman come back after he has obtained a thorough grasp of the European end of things, so that he can go on with the work here. I am willing to do everything that is humanly possible to "carry on" in his absence, but it is impossible for an amateur, no matter how well-intentioned, to equal the work of a professional like Van Deman.

It is unfortunate that our paths have been so divergent for the past ten months, but you may be certain that I shall do everything possible to get us together again and you can trust implicitly on my good faith and loyalty in sending you from this side of the water any officers, men or equipment which you may ask us for and in backing you up to the limit in everything.

Very sincerely yours,
M. CHURCHILL

Appendix B[1]

WAR DEPARTMENT
OFFICE OF THE CHIEF OF STAFF
WASHINGTON

MEMORANDUM No. 64   August 28, 1918

1. Under the provisions of General Orders No. 80, War Department, current series, the Military Intelligence Branch has been made a division of the General Staff and designated as the Military Intelligence Division. The officer in charge has been designated as the Director of Military Intelligence and as Assistant Chief of Staff.

2. The Military Intelligence Division is charged with the following duties:

Cognizance and control of military intelligence, both positive and negative.

The maintenance of estimates, revised daily, of the military situation, the economic situation, and of such other matters as the Chief of Staff may direct and the collection and dissemination of military intelligence.

Cooperation with the Intelligence Sections of the General Staffs of allied countries in connection with military intelligence.

The preparation of instructions in military intelligence work for the use of our forces.

The supervision and training of personnel for intelligence work.

The organization, direction and coordination of the intelligence service.

The supervision of the duties of military attaches.

Obtaining, reproducing, and issuing maps.

The translation of foreign documents.

The disbursing and accounting for intelligence funds.

Cooperation with the censorship board and with intelligence agencies of other departments of the government.

Direct communication with department intelligence officers and intelligence officers at posts, camps and stations and with commands in the field, in matters relating to military intelligence is authorized.

APPENDICES

3. Colonel Alexander B. Coxe, General Staff, is announced as executive assistant to the Director of Military Intelligence. He is charged with the following duties:

Action for the Director of Military Intelligence during his absence.

The coordination of the activities of the several branches and sections of the Divisions.

The viseing of all communications prepared for the signature or personal attention of the Director and all communications involving internal or external policy.

The coordination of the control of military intelligence, both positive and negative.

The insuring of cooperation with the Intelligence Sections of the General Staffs of allied countries in connection with military intelligence.

The supervision of the organization, direction and coordination of the intelligence service.

The insuring of cooperation with the Censorship Board and with the intelligence agencies of other departments of the government.

4. Captain Birch Helms, Infantry, U.S. Army, is assigned to special duty in the office of the of the Director of Military Intelligence.

5. In order to insure proper coordination of the duties assigned it, two branches are formed in the Military Intelligence Division. These are designated as the Positive Branch and the Negative Branch.

Colonel John M. Dunn, General Staff, is assigned to duty as chief of the Positive branch.

Colonel Kenneth C. Masteller, General Staff, is assigned to duty as chief of the Negative Branch.

6. The Positive Branch is charged with the following duties: The maintenance of estimate, revised daily, of the military situation, the economic situation and of such other matters as may be directed.

The collection and dissemination of military intelligence.

The preparation of instructions in combat intelligence work for the use of our forces.

The supervision and training of personnel for positive intelligence work.

The supervision of the duties of military attaches.

The obtaining, reproducing and issuing of maps.

The translation of foreign documents.

The preparation of codes, the solution of enemy codes and ciphers and the examination of documents for secret writing.

7. The following sections are assigned to the Positive Branch:

M.I.2; M.I.5; M.I.6; M.I.7; M.I.8; and M.I.9

8. The Negative Branch is charged with the following duties:

The supervision of the Censorship.

The preparation of instructions in counter espionage work for the use of our forces.

The supervision and training of personnel for counter espionage work.

The organization, direction and coordination of the negative intelligence service.

The stimulation of military morale.

9. The following sections are assigned to the Negative Branch:

M.I.3; M.I.4; M.I.10; and Military Morale Section

10. Major Arthur G. Campbell, Coast Artillery Corps, is assigned to duty in charge of the Administrative Section (M.I.1). This section is charged with the following duties:

The coordination of the activities of the several subsections of the M.I.1.

The viseing of all communications prepared in M.I.1 except routine communications not requiring the signature or personal attention of the Executive Assistant.

The coordination of the work of all liaison officers.

The supervision of action on all communications received from the office of the Chief of Staff or the Secretary of War and the preparation of replies to the same.

The disbursing of and accounting for intelligence funds.

The procurement of all supplies necessary for the Division.

Providing for the appointment of commissioned personnel for intelligence duty.

APPENDICES 161

Arranging for the induction of enlisted men for intelligence duty.

Employing civilian personnel.

The supervision of all matters relating to the Corps of Interpreters and Corps of Intelligence Police.

The supervision of the recording and filing of the papers and documents of the Military Intelligence Division and the Maintenance of the register of suspects.

The supervision of clerks, messengers, guards, watchmen and other employees.

The editing, publishing and distribution of all summaries, reports, rosters, etc. Printing, mimeographing and lithographing. Photographing and photostating.

The supervision and maintenance of the library of the Military Intelligence Division.

By command of Brigadier General Churchill.

A. B. Coxe
Colonel, General Staff
Executive Assistant

Appendix B[2]

Office of Negative Intelligence
Department, April 11th, 1919

Mr. Wm. C. Bullitt,
American Commission to Negotiate Peace,
#4 Place de la Concorde, Paris, France.

My Dear Mr. Bullitt:

I have read with great interest your report on Russia, more particularly, as you know, for the last three months it has been my duty to study conditions in that unfortunate country, and, to summarize the various reports which deal with Bolshevism and its manifold activities.

If I may take the liberty of speaking perfectly frankly, I am somewhat afraid that your report, as it stands, might produce an impression on the minds of those who have not studied the Russian situation in detail which would not be strictly in accordance with the facts as they exist in that country. I am more particularly impressed with this danger as in my conversation with you yesterday, your explanatory statements coincided almost exactly with the many reports which I have seen on Russia whereas your report, as it stands without explanatory statements, would lead the reader to a different conclusion. For instance, you state that "Russia today is in a condition of acute economic distress. The blockade by land and sea is the cause of this distress and the lack of the essentials of transportation is its gravest symptom." This statement standing alone might well lead one to believe that the lifting of the blockade would of itself relieve the distress and permit a resumption of normal economic life.

The fact is, however, that irrespective of the blockade, it is highly problematical whether under the present Soviet Government, which has systematically destroyed the entire economic and industrial structure as it existed, the resumption of normal industrial activity is possible. Lenin in speeches has repeatedly stated that the Russian workman must now exercise the strongest discipline and self-restraint and has expressed doubts as to his ability to do so. You, yourself, stated that the factories were now being operated at a loss. Responsible reports indicate that the industrial chaos is indescribable even in those factories which continue to attempt to work. It is quite true that there are no locomotives or cars but granted that there were, is there any proof that committees of workmen, and Russian workmen at that, are capable of operating great transportation systems even if they impress, under duress, the services of so-called railroad experts?

Again you state on page two that loafing by the workingman during work hours has been overcome. This is contradicted by a number of reports which state that there have been numerous strikes and sabotage and, as already stated, Lenin, himself, has complained of the unwillingness and inability of the Russian workman to exercise the necessary self discipline to put in a normal day's work.

You state that the power of judgment has been taken away from the Committee for the Suppression of Counter-Revolution which now merely accuses suspected counter-revolutionaries who are tried by regularly established legal tribunals. Isn't it a fact that the Government reserves the right, and would not hesitate to use it of re-establishing the Extraordinary Commission; and, what is the character of the regularly established legal tribunals? Is there a semblance of constitutional guarantees and is "the right of life, liberty and the pursuit of happiness" as we Americans conceive it even partially recognized?

You state the Soviet form of Government is firmly established. How has it been established and on what does it rest today? Is it by force of arms or can it be said to have the popular support of the great majority of the Russian people? As I recall it, you, yourself, commented upon the absolutely undemocratic character of the Russian Soviet form of Government. Certainly no more ingenious scheme has ever been devised to permit control by a minority under the disguise of democracy.

On Page five you state that the only ponderable opposition to the Government comes from the more radical parties. Isn't it a fact that all opposition parties, with the possible exception of the social revolutionaries, and every other form of political organization was totally destroyed by the Bolsheviks? Were they not all wiped out by the Bolsheviks' terroristic methods and is there any reason to believe that if terrorism and dictatorship were taken away, strong opposition parties would not at once spring up?

The statement as to the small number of people that have been killed do [sic] not agree with the documents in this office which indicate that compared with the Russian revolution the French was a rather tame affair. The White Book on Bolshevism, recently issued by the British Government, is particularly enlightening on this point.

In so far as your conclusions are concerned, I would respectfully suggest that I have seen no evidence in the many reports which I have read which indicates "that the Lenine [sic] wing of the Communist Party is as moderate as any Socialist Party which control Russia." The Lenin Government is not, in any sense, democratic or representative. It is a tyranny of a minority which has been imposed by force of arms. Could it continue to exist were repressive measures removed is something that no man can affirm or deny, but, certainly the fact that the present government carefully suppresses all contrary expressions of opinion and systematically destroys any at [sic] organized opposition makes legitimate the conclusion that it entertains some doubt as to its popularity with the majority of the Russian people.

As to point two: Is it not a fact that the Soviet leaders have declared they would make peace only in order to better wage war on capitalistic governments?

As to the third point: Even assuming that the blockade is lifted, has Russia the capacity to pay for the goods and materials sent her and is it possible for an inefficient communistic government, struggling with the chaos which it has created to resume economic relations with the World, which may still be described as capitalistic? Isn't it a fact that Lenin, himself, admits that it is not possible and that the World must become communistic or Russia itself capitalistic?

Finally, wouldn't such a peace as you recommend merely give immense prestige and moral support to the existing Soviet Government without corresponding benefit to the rest of the World. If, as the Bolsheviks contend, their conception of society cannot exist side by side with the present social structure, why should existing society lend moral support to an organization which, by its very nature, must destroy it or cease to exist?

Yours sincerely,

(s) R. H. Van Deman

R. H. VAN DEMAN
Colonel, G.S.

Appendix C

September 4th, 1918

Colonel M. Churchill,
Chief, Military Intelligence Branch,
Executive Division,
Washington, D.C.

My dear Churchill:

During the past two or three days I have had several long talks with the men in M.I. 5 who are running the Passport and Post Control work. The weakest link in the whole chain now is the U.S. Canadian situation. I of course do not know what Post Control we have succeeded in establishing in the U.S. The system when I left the U.S. was somewhat complicated and not at all satisfactory. Since that time there has been some legislation but I do not know just what, nor what measures have been taken to tighten up examinations at the Ports. The British tell me that they have never been able to get the Canadians to establish anything like an effective control because they said that until the U.S. did so, it was useless to attempt it, which of course is true. What is happening now is that people are coming into Canada from the U.S., and then sailing to England without any sort of control. Of course the British can send them back, but a proper control would be much more satisfactory from every point of view. If we have not established a satisfactory Port Control, I suggest that the matter be taken up at once.

Just here I was interrupted by a call from the Office of the Naval Attache, and found McCauly there. We had a long talk along the lines above mentioned. McCauly tells me that the arrangement which was in force before he left, was that the Customs people agreed to examine and search all incoming neutrals and such Americans as were "regarded" as suspect and that a representative of M.I.D. and C.N.I. should be present. They would not agree to examine or search Americans (other than suspects) because of the complaints that would be made through Congressmen of such action. So far as outgoing passengers were concerned (and these are the ones the British are particularly interested in) I don't know what the Control is, except of course the arrangement which we had with the State Department on Passports. That of course duly included new or renewed passports and did not cover visas of old passports nor the examination of neutrals or Allies who had had their passports vised by neutral or Allied Consuls. This whole situation should be taken up as I am sure you will agree. Until a satisfactory system is actually put in force by us, it would be useless to try to get the Canadians to do anything. However, when we have succeeded in getting an efficient system, it might help if you would write a semi-official letter to the Canadian D.M.I. at Ottawa and tell them what we had done and what great assistance it would be to the common cause if Canada would establish a similar one, pointing out how undesirables pass from the U.S. into Canada and so get to Europe without control.

Of course the situation is not particularly good in connection with travel to and from Spain. Just how that is being handled I don't know, but if undesirables are allowed to get to Spain by sea the possibility of getting into France across the Franco-Spanish frontier is pretty good, due to the laxity of the French control. This is something against what we and the British are up against all the time, and it is necessary to back up the French in their control of circulation, not only on the Frontiers, but within the S.O.S. areas as well. We have lately put our own officers at four points along the Franco-Spanish frontier, working with the French, and things ought to be better shortly. If we can get it tied up as tightly as the Franco-Swiss Frontier, I will feel that we are in pretty good shape. However, an efficient control at U.S. ports over people going to Spain, would help enormously.

While we are on the subject, don't forget the control of passengers sailing direct for France. While we have Port Control officers working with the French at French ports, control at U.S. ports would also help. To show how important this matter of control is, General Foch sent a personal letter to the French Franco-Swiss border control service the other day, in which he thanked them for the excellent work they had done, and said that he considered their work had been mainly responsible for the fact that the Germans had not been able to get even a hint of the beginning of the Franco-American offensive in July.

Now the Western and Northwestern situation needs looking after. If we had proper control at Vladivostok and the Chinese ports, it would not make the situation quite so bad. But, barring a British Port Control at Yokohama and one at Shanghai and Hong Kong, we have no control at Asiatic Ports. The British have only recently put in their man at Yokahama and did so with a good deal of fear and trembling as to what the Japanese would say. As a matter of fact it pleased the Japs to death. Now, if we can get one of our own men at Yokohama working with the British and one of our own at Nagasaki, Vladivostok, Chin-kiang-tao and Tientsin (or Tang-Ku) I think we could stop this influx of Bolsheviki and other undesirables into the U.S. These Port Control officers might be created as I suggested for the men for the Consular offices in the various cities – in Switzerland – [sic] take Reserve or National Army officers and have the Secretary of State give them a commission as a vice-consul or consular agent and put them into the Consular offices as cover.

All this of course is only to give you the situation as it appears over here and you must use your judgment as to what had best be done to accomplish the end in view.

Am still waiting for the convoy for Holland. They tell me that it will sail within the next three or four days, but the Admiralty say they don't know themselves the exact date and wouldn't tell if they did. I am most anxious to get this trip over and get back to France so that I can get the [sic] work with troops, for I feel that I could get down to Spain and Italy as soon as possible.

Had a letter from Buckey the other day, urging me to come as soon as possible as he needed help in many ways.

Major Riggs has just come into my office; just arrived from Archangel. He is sent over by Ruggles and the Ambassador to see the British here, General Pershing and the Supreme War Council at Paris. A report by Riggs will come along to you by cable, which you will have received before this letter reaches you. This will be repetition of one sent from Murmansk which he was in doubt about having gotten through. I will see him in the morning and get the situation as he knows it.

Will write you again in a day or two about the O.N.I. situation and particularly about McCauley.

Give my love to all the people in the Office.

Yours sincerely,
R. H. Van Deman

Appendix D

September 5th 1918

Colonel M. Churchill,
Chief, Military Intelligence Branch,
Executive Division,
Washington, D.C.

My dear Churchill,

I have been intending to write you for some time, on the connection which should be established between our various I.O.'s and the Naval I.O. on board Naval Transports and arrangements which should be made on ships which are not under the Navy, and therefore have no I.O.'s permanently on board. You may have gone into all this, but as I know what you are up against in that office in the way of work, it is not improbable that you have not, so I will tell you what my investigations along this line have brought out and what I think should be done, this last being suggestions of course.

After questioning a lot of Divisional and Regimental I.O.'s, I find that there is seldom or never any connection between them and the Naval I.O. aboard ship on the voyage over; there undoubtedly should be. On the Naval transports and those run by the Army (if we have any of the latter) there is no ship's I.O. and therefore our C.E. control on the crew is almost nil. In this connection I have talked over the subject of continuing the Divisional C.E. system after the arrival of our troops in France. At first there was some doubt in the minds of our people at G.H.Q. as to the necessibility [sic] of this, because they believed the loss of personnel would be so great that the system could not be kept up. However, after explaining to them that it was the business of the man in charge of each echelon to see to it that new men were selected as soon as one dropped out, they changed their attitude. They all agreed that the system has given most excellent results in the U.S., and would continue to do so if the personnel could be maintained in France, so I think we may consider that G.H.Q. will favor the keeping up of the system in France. Now to return to the principal subject of this letter.

There should be an Intelligence Officer at each Port of Debarkation. I take it that the I.O. at Hoboken can cover not only Hoboken, but the Bush Terminal and the sailing point in Brooklyn. If he is not doing that now, he should do so. As soon as he is notified that an organization is scheduled to sail (and he should be given this promptly) he should get in touch with the I.O. of the organization – Divisional

APPENDICES 169

C.E.O. if possible – and take him to the Naval I.O. on the ship on which he is to sail. On the ship on which Division Headquarters sail, this Division C.E.O. should be the one in touch and on those ships of the convoy carrying other units of the Division, the senior C.E.O. should be put in touch with the Navy I.O. There should be an interchange of information between the troop C.E.O. and the Navy I.O. and any men under the least suspicion among either troop or crew should be known to both. This connection should be kept up during the entire voyage and upon arrival at the Port of Debarkation, the Port Control officer (who is of course a C.E. officer under the S.O.S.) should at once get in touch with the troop C.E.O. and the Naval I.O. Upon the arrival of a Naval transport at an American Port, the I.O. there (C.E.O.) should get in touch with the Naval I.O. This will tie up the C.E. service so far as the Naval Transports are concerned.

    Now, what arrangements can be made on the British ships and on the Naval transports, is not so clear. I think the I.O. at Hoboken should be put on this job and see what can be done. If anything needs action by the British M.I. let Slocum know what is wanted, and there will be no trouble whatever in getting the necessary instructions issued. In any case, the object to be accomplished is of course to make certain that a perfect system of C.E. information and cooperation is established at the Port of Embarkation during the voyage and upon arrival in France or England.

    In carrying out this scheme as well as in all the Port Control work, cable communication will often be necessary between the various Port Control officers on both sides of the Atlantic. I do not think it would be advisable to give these officers authority to cable each other directly. The congested state of the cables makes it of course, necessary to keep down cables to the lowest possible limit, and as many of our Port Control officers are inexperienced, I believe the line of cable communication should be as follows: From Port Control officers in France to the Chief of the S.O.S. C.E., Service – Colonel Ward – in Paris, and then through the M.A., Paris, to M.I.D. From Port Control Officers in the United Kingdom to the senior S.O.S., C.E. officers in England – now Captain Turner in London, and then through the M.A., London to M.I.D. From Port Control officers in the U.S., to M.I.D., and then to the Chief of the S.O.S., C.E., service in Paris through the M.A., Paris, or the M.A., London, depending as to whether the case pertains to France or the U.K. This will cover the signaling of suspects sailing, as well as other matters which may require communication between C.E. officers on both sides. Port Control officers in the U.S. should be authorized to communicate directly with each other, sending a copy to M.I.D. and the same arrangement should be made on this side of the ocean, a copy going to G.H.Q.; I can attend to this end of the line on this.

As you of course know, our C.E. service, which was ....

Very sincerely,

R. H. VAN DEMAN

Appendix E

AMERICAN EXPEDITIONARY FORCES
OFFICE OF THE COMMANDER-IN-CHIEF

France, Nov. 29, 1918

My dear Colonel Van Deman:

It gives me great pleasure to inform you that on October 20th I recommended you for promotion to the grade of Brigadier General, basing my recommendation upon the efficiency of your service with the American Expeditionary Forces.

The War Department discontinued all promotions to the grade of General Officer after the signing of the Armistice, and I regret that you will not therefore receive the deserved recognition of your excellent services.

Sincerely yours,

(s) John J. Pershing

Colonel R. H. Van Deman
Asst. Chief of Staff, G-2
G. H. Q., A. E. F.

Appendix F

CABLEGRAM TO CHURCHILL

(through Yardley at Paris, November 13, 1918)

S E C R E T

In view of the evident attempt of Bolshevists and affiliated elements to bring about widespread trouble, consider it most important that passport control is strictly maintained. Suggest that you keep in close touch with Department of Justice and urge on them importance of watching this matter in United States and keeping you informed. Vital that we here be kept informed of any developments of this kind in United States and names of Americans now in Europe identified with revolutionary movements and of departure of such persons for Europe. Whole matter should be kept as quiet as possible.

VAN DEMAN

Appendix G

November 13, 1918

Brigadier General M. Churchill,
Director, Military Intelligence,
Military Intelligence Division,
Washington, D.C.

My dear Churchill:

I have just asked Yardley to send a cable to you in the special code he brought with him to Europe.

Long before this reaches you will have received reports from here and from Switzerland, Italy, Holland and other places showing that the Bolshevik elements and those associated with them are beginning their propaganda. There is no use telling you what this movement means or what its objective is – a world-wide social and political revolution. In other words, the fulfillment of the dream of the Internationalists. If they are able to carry out their plans, we all know what will happen.

From our standpoint (Intelligence) the first thing to be done is to ascertain how far this propaganda has permeated our troops and next to take any measures possible to eradicate what exists and counteract future efforts of the Bolshevik-Internationalist group. This we have started to do by means of our troop Counter Intelligence organization. The results will be sent you promptly as obtained. We are undoubtedly going to have a very difficult period to get through from now until we can demobilize. Every possible effort should be made to get our troops home and demobilize just as rapidly as possible. Under the most favorable circumstances, it is going to be in the neighborhood of a year before this can be done. To maintain discipline in our forces over here during that period is going to be a most difficult task. It would be under the most favorable conditions but with this revolutionary business on there is no telling what may happen. Italy, particularly northern Italy, is ready to blow up; Austria-Hungary has practically gone to pieces now; Belgium appears to have been taken over; the conditions in both France and Poland are most dangerous; Holland is honeycombed as is also Sweden; the condition of Russia you know. So, take it all in all, it looks as though we might be entering on a period of even greater danger to the civilization of the world than the one through which we have just passed. We will watch this end of it to the best of our ability and I suggest that M.I.D. watch the developments in the United States. We should keep the other in touch with the situation. To prevent the circulation of revolutionary agents, we should keep our passport control in force and the closest watch must be kept on all the well known agents of these people both here and in the U.S.

It seems to me that the Intelligence Services of all of us should take this work over, in close liaison with the civil services of the various governments. It is perhaps hardly a "War activity" but if an attempt to spread anarchy and revolution over the world is to be made, it seems to me we must use every means at our disposal to fight it.

Don't think I am an alarmist. But I can not help thinking that things look most dangerous for the future. Please let me know what your views are on this subject and what developments have come to light in the United States.

Most sincerely,

(s) R. H. Van Deman

Colonel, General Staff

Appendix H

August 13, 1918

My dear Churchill:

The two letters, one mailed from Washington and telling me of the probable changes of General Staff organization and the other from New York, were duly received while I was in Switzerland.

I was certainly delighted to know that the Intelligence was at last to be made a division and have been waiting anxiously to see the actual order. You are to be congratulated in being able to put it over.

I got back from Switzerland on the evening of the 9th of August, and have just finished my report, a copy of which will be sent to you at once. The report is rather brief but will give you an idea of what the general conditions there are and what is needed. I was in Switzerland from July 25th and to August 9th, and went pretty well over northwestern and northern Switzerland, in order that I might see local conditions for myself and also talk to the Consuls and Vice-Consuls who have been doing intelligence work under the direction of the Military Attache. I also saw and talked to all the officers of the Allied Intelligence Services and think I have established a basis on which we will be able to get better and more effective cooperation, locally, particularly in counter-espionage work. I also went to the office of these services and was shown the entire working of their offices without reservation of any kind. I had intended to come back by way of Evian-les-Bains, Annemasse and Bellefort and go through the French Services at those points but the increasing spread of the "Spanish Greppe" caused the French to quarantine against Switzerland and so I came out the same way I came in, by Pontalier. I went over that station as I went down and also met there at luncheon the Chief of this whole French border service who came over from Bellefort to meet me. The Pontalier station is important as it is the point through which the Allied courier service passes between France and Switzerland, and because through it nearly all of the passenger traffic between these two countries now passes. We have one officer there who is very closely associated with both the French and British services there. Annemasse (just east of Geneva) is the station through which all the "Repatries" come through from Germany into France. The French have an exceedingly good service there and we have an office closely associated with them. The British also have a station there. A great deal of information is gotten from the "Repatries" which is freely interchanged among all three services. Also the Boche frequently attempts to get his agents through in this way and has to be checked.

Evian-les-Bains, on the French side of Lake Geneva and about due south of Lausanne, is a French and British station. We also have an office there closely in touch with the French. Here the work is mainly counter-espionage. Agents are instructed for work in Switzerland and most of the work on secret-writing and ciphers [which] gets into the hands of the Secret Service in Switzerland is sent here.

Bellefort is the headquarters of the entire service for this frontier and both the British and us [sic] have offices here. To this point is sent all the information from Switzerland (French Service) and is checked before being sent to Paris and French G.H.Q. Here also comes all the information from Alsace and Lorraine and further back in Germany. This is the prize service of the French and they do some really remarkable work. For instance, the French had the entire plans for the German offensive of July 15th twelve hours before the attack developed and were able to open up with their artillery an hour before the German artillery was to begin. The excellence of this service is due, of course, to the fact that the French have their permanent agents in Alsace. Nearly all the French officers engaged in this service are Alsatians and most of them are serving under names not their own for the simple reason that they are deserter officers from the German Army. I shall go down there and go through the Service again just as soon as I get back from the North.

An Intelligence School has been established at Langres which is doing some good work. I went over it today. Nolan expects to be able to develop a duplicate lot of instructors and to be in a position to send them over to the U.S. if needed. I suggest that it would be a most excellent plan to establish a similar school at Washington and ask Nolan to send this lot of men over as soon as you are ready for them. You can then have your divisional and regimental intelligence officers at Washington instead of having to send men around as you are now doing. Incidentally, the officer in charge of the School at Langres spoke of the almost universal inability of reserve and National Army officers to read a contoured map, and suggested that every intelligence officer intended for duty with troops be given a thorough course in map reading. I heartily concur in this suggestion.

I didn't get back in time to see either Lippmann or Blankenhorn, both of whom are up in London. Will see them either there or when they return here. Major O'Laughlin was with me in Switzerland and made a very comprehensive report on the propaganda matter of Switzerland which is on Nolan's desk now. I hope he can go with me to Holland, and, if I go, to Denmark and Sweden as well, in order that we have reports from the same man on the whole proposition.

Yours most sincerely,
(s) R. H. Van Deman
Colonel, General Staff

Colonel Marlborough Churchill, G.S.,
Chief, Military Intelligence Branch
Washington, D. C.

Appendix I

October 15, 1918

My Dear Harrison:

I have been trying to get an opportunity to write you for a long time but have been so constantly on the go that I could not find it. As I am now back at G.H.Q. for a few days, I shall try to get this letter written. The general subject is that old and much-discussed subject of Passport Control. I have gone into this subject personally in France, England, Switzerland and Holland and have gone over the situation with our Military Attache from Copenhagen (who covers Denmark and Norway) whom I asked to have ordered to London to meet me on my return from Holland. Within the next two months I hope to be able to look into the subject in Madrid and Rome. However, I feel very sure that about the same conditions will be found in Italy and Spain as in the countries I have already seen.

It is, of course, perfectly evident that the "control" of travel to and from the United States of all classes of persons, and travel of persons holding U.S. passports between the countries for which the passport is granted is a wartime necessity. It is imposed to prevent, as far as possible, the circulation of enemy agents and other classes of persons whose actions may be dangerous to the United States or the nations with which she is associated in the prosecution of the war. To allow the unrestricted travel of enemy agents is to aid the enemy in the prosecution of the war and therefore to add to the number of killed and wounded of our forces and to the prolongation of the war. the control of travel is, therefore, imposed as a military necessity.

The issuing of passports and the granting of the passport visa is under the control of the State Department. The administration of these functions is performed by its agents. The only reason for associating the military arm in this work is because the military arm is primarily charged with the prosecution of the war and because that arm, through its Intelligence Service, has sources of information concerning suspect persons and enemy activities which are not available to other branches of the Government.

With the subject of control at ports of the United States this letter has nothing to do. I am only here considering the issue and visa of passports in foreign countries.

What I have said above as to the reasons for the association of the military arm of the Government in connection with this function is shown by the wording of the "Confidential Instructions for the Guidance of Officials connected with the Administration of the Act of May 22, 1918" (Public No. 154), and in Supplement No.1, dated June 5, 1918, of the General Instruction No. 535, of July 26, 1917.

These instructions require (at least I take it from the wording of Section 1 of Supplement No. 1 that such is the case) all applications for visa to be submitted to the Military or Naval Attaches, or both, for examination as to whether, from the standpoint of <u>enemy activity</u>, the applicant is of such character that the visa should be denied.

This rule holds for all countries where we have Military and Naval Attaches except in France where the State Department has authorized the formation of a Passport Control Office. In this office the Military representative is an officer detailed from the Counter-espionage Service of the Services of Supply of the A.E.F., and the duties of the Military Attache in this connection pass to him, although the Military Attache is in close liaison with the office.

The establishment of this office has facilitated very much indeed the Passport Control work. The system is working well and with the arrival of a State Department official who really understands the situation will leave little to be desired.

I am sure you know enough about conditions in France to know that the establishment of this office was a necessity and that it opens to the State Department sources of information concerning suspect persons which could not be made available in any other way. In addition to that, it frees the Ambassador from the necessity of withstanding the pressure from people who desire visas which he would be subjected to were the matter administered by the Embassy. I understand, unofficially, that the Ambassador has asked that he be authorized to overrule the decisions of the Passport Control Office. I hope this authority will not be granted, not only from the standpoint of Passport Control but because the functions of Passport Control should not in any way be associated with diplomatic functions. It is essentially a military matter, imposed because the military situation demands it. The organization of the Passport Control Office also simplified the control of travel, opened up sources of information concerning suspect persons which could only be done by such a system and in every way made for efficiency and coordination.

As you know, England is Base No. 3 of the Service of Supply, A.E.F. and has, therefore, representatives of the counter-espionage service of the S.O.S., A.E.F. The situation is practically identical with that in France. A Passport Control Office should, therefore, be established in England along the same lines as the one in Paris. Everyone is in favor of this except the Consul General in London. The intelligence service, the Military Attache and the Embassy have all urged this course but up to date nothing has been done. Under the heading of "England" you will find a further consideration of the situation in England.

After studying the question personally in France, England, Switzerland and Holland and talking at length to both civil and military officers from several other countries, I have come to the conclusion that the safest, quickest and best way to handle this question is by establishing a Passport Control Office in each country on lines similar to the one established in Paris. The office should not be located at the Embassy or Legation. I believe it should be in a separate building but not too distant from the offices of the Military and Naval Attaches. In this office should be an officer representing the Military authorities to whom all applications for visas should be referred, together with all information concerning the individual in the hands of the consular authorities, including that obtained at the time the formal application was made. It will then be the duty of the military representative to assure himself that there is no objection to the visa from the military standpoint.

It should be clearly kept in mind that the only interest the military authorities have in this matter is to assure themselves that no person who will be dangerous to the military interests of the United States is allowed to travel, but that the actual visa is a function under the control of the State Department. On the other hand, instructions in Consulates and to Embassies and Legations should forbid a visa when the military authorities have recommended that such should not be granted, unless such recommendation is overruled by Washington. In addition to this, the instruction should state specifically that the military authorities will not be required to give reasons for recommending a refusal of a visa. This is necessary because, very often, to disclose these reasons is to warn not only the person whose visa is refused but others connected with him as to what information the military authorities have in their secret files. Obviously this is not only most undesirable but would make it possible for enemy agents who believe they are suspected by our authorities to verify their belief and so make it much more difficult for us to deal with them.

The status of the passport control in the countries of which I have personal knowledge is as follows:

FRANCE: There is a Passport Control Office established in Paris by direction of the State Department. In this office there is an officer belonging to the Counter-Espionage Service of the Services of Supply to whom all applications for visa are referred. It is this officer's duty to examine into the record of the applicant through all the sources of information at his command (which means all the information in the

APPENDICES   181

hands, not only of our Intelligence Service, but of all the Allied Services as well) and to inform the official in charge of the office if, in the opinion of the Intelligence Service, a visa should be withheld.

It is my understanding that this office is under the direction of the State Department and not directly under the Consular Department. From the military standpoint, it is immaterial whether the office is controlled by the State Department or by the Consular Department, the essential thing being that the military authorities must have the right to negate any application for visa and that no authority short of the State Department at Washington shall have authority to overrule their recommendation. This office is working well and is accomplishing the object sought.

ENGLAND: No Passport Office has been established in England up to the date of this letter. The establishment of an office along the same lines of the one in France has been recommended by both the military authorities and by the Embassy in London but so far without result. I believe this is due to the attitude of the Consul General who feels that his prerogatives are being interfered with. As I have tried to point out in the first part of this letter, this is not necessarily the case. A Passport Control office could be established directly under the Consul General, if that should be considered available [sic], instead of under the State Department as has been done in Paris. But, frankly, however the office is established, I do not think the objection of the Consul General on the ground that his prerogatives are being interfered with should be allowed to interfere with the safeguarding of the interests of the United States and the protection of our troops. The arrangement in England at this time is not satisfactory and I earnestly recommend the establishment of a Passport Office along the same lines as the one in Paris. Whether it is under Consular or State Department is immaterial from the military standpoint. As England is Base No. 3 of the S.O.S., the military representative in the Passport Office should be a representative of the Counterespionage Service of the S.O.S. and not a representative of the Military Attache's office.

SWITZERLAND: Conditions in neutral countries differ in a great many ways from those in France and England. In neutral countries the only military representation we have is the office of the Military Attache. His office is furnished with the Intelligence suspect lists and he is in direct cable communication with the Military Intelligence Division in Washington and the Intelligence Section of the A.E.F. He is also in close liaison with the Intelligence services of all the Allied governments. His office is, therefore, the one to be represented in the Passport Control Office, if one is established, which, in the interests of efficiency and economy of effort, I believe should be done in all neutral countries. At present the passport control matter is being fairly well handled, the office which attends to the work being in the office of the Military Attache, although not a part of his office, and the examination of applicants for visa are made by the Military Attache's office. I suggest that a Passport Control Office be established here along the same lines as in Paris, but that the military representative be designated by the Military Attache from among his assistants.

HOLLAND: The situation here is not satisfactory. Under instructions of the Minister, the visa of passports has been taken over by the Legation and an office established in the Legation building. The office itself is well-run and its records are in good shape. However, I believe it is a mistake to have this work performed by the Legation. It is the duty of the Legation to foster friendly relations between the country in which it is located and the United States. Often the refusal of a visa is regarded as a hardship and frequently brings violent protests for the applicant and his friends who often are influential citizens or officials of the country. If the Passport Control Office is under the Legation, these protests are made to the Minister or the Charge d'Affaires which is a condition which should not obtain. The day I left The Hague, there were five or six persons two of whom were high Dutch officials, in the Legation protesting against the refusal of visas to their friends and demanding the reason. It would be better in every way if a Passport Office were established, as suggested for Switzerland. In Holland there is a Naval Attache and his office should also have a representative in the Passport Control Office if he so desires.

DENMARK & NORWAY: I have not visited these countries personally but have talked at length with the Military Attache as well as the Naval Attache accredited to them. All applications for visa are submitted to the Military and Naval Attaches and the object sought, viz., limitation of travel by suspected persons, is apparently being fairly well accomplished. However, the efficiency of the work is very much dependent on the personal force and energy of the Military Attache. This is faulty organization and I recommend the same procedure as for Holland.

SWEDEN: I have neither visited this country nor talked to the Military Attache. I have, however, talked to the Military Attache from Copenhagen who is familiar with conditions in Sweden. From what he tells me and from what I know from other sources, I have no hesitancy in saying that it would be advisable to establish the same system in Sweden as that recommended for Holland.

ITALY: I have not yet been to Italy, although I expect to go there in the not distant future. As we have no troops (at least not enough having

APPENDICES

a special commander) in Italy, I believe that, for purposes of Passport Control, we should treat Italy as we do a neutral country. Unless I find that conditions there are very different from what I think they are, I suggest that Italy be treated as recommended for Holland.

SPAIN: I have not yet visited Spain. However, Spain is a neutral country and should be treated as recommended for Holland.

GREECE: I have not visited Greece and do not expect to do so. Nor do I know much as to passport conditions there. However, we stand very much in Greece as we do in Italy and I recommend the same arrangement there as for Holland.

JAPAN: We are in the same position with regard to Japan as we are with regard to Italy. The British Intelligence have recently established a Passport Control Office in Yokohama, in close liaison with the Japanese Intelligence Service and the arrangement was welcomed by the Japanese – rather to the surprise of the British. I believe, therefore, that we should do practically the same thing and that Japan should have a Passport Control Office as recommended for Holland. It is really, so far as we are concerned, in the same position as Italy, except that, due to the attempts of the Bolsheviks to come from Russia to the United States, and vice versa, it is of considerable importance from a Passport Control standpoint.

SIBERIA: There should be a Passport Control Office at Vladivostock the Military representative in which should be from the Intelligence Service of the Commander-in-Chief, U.S. Troops in Siberia. In other words, the same arrangement as in France and England.

CHINA: Due to the fact that enemy agents may endeavor to pass in and out of Siberia through the northern ports of China, we should have passport control there. We have, of course, troops in China but not on the same footing as those in France, England and Siberia. I suggest, therefore, that a Passport Control Office be established for China as for Holland. The office should be either in Peking or Tientsin.

CUBA: Cuba should be treated, for purposes of Passport Control, as is a neutral country and should have the same organization as Holland.

OTHER COUNTRIES: All other countries, whether neutral or belligerent, in which we have Military or Naval Attaches or both, should be organized as Holland.

This has been a long and doubtlessly tedious letter, but I felt that I ought to give you my views as to the whole subject if I wrote at all. And I felt that I should write and give you the benefit of the information that I have gained by seeing conditions at first hand and the general conclusions that I have drawn from the experience. So please consider this letter in that light. It is not an official communication in any sense. I am going to send a copy of it to General Churchill, merely in order that he may know what my personal views are on the subject. If you feel disposed to consider the matter at all, won't you let Mr. Carr see this?

I wish very much that I could <u>talk</u> this matter over with you instead of writing for I could save you much of the time that it will take you to read this letter. But of course that cannot be.

Please don't think that there is any friction between the Consular and Military representatives. Except for the one case in London, there is complete accord in trying to accomplish the object sought, and this letter is only written as suggesting a method by which I believe that object can be accomplished with the least expenditure of time and money and most efficiently.

Most sincerely,
(s) R. H. Van Deman

Mr. Leland Harrison
State Department, Washington, D.C.

Appendix J

Paris, France
August 4th, 1919

From: Colonel R. H. Van Deman, General Staff
Negative Intelligence Department

To: Secretary-General, American Commission to Negotiate Peace.

Subject: Report

As I have been directed to proceed to the United States and report to the Chief of Staff, I submit the following report of the activities of the Negative Intelligence Department, in compliance with request contained in memorandum issued by the Administrative Officer of the American Commission to Negotiate Peace.

Under date of November 20th, 1918, the following cable was received by the Commanding General, A.E.F. -

    X X X X X X X X X X X X

November 21, 1918

No. 222-R
November 20th

Confidential

PERSHING
AMEXFORCES

    X X X X X X X X X X X X

PARAGRAPH 2. Direct Colonel Ralph H. Van Deman, if available, to report to General Bliss to take charge of Contre [sic] Espionage Service until conclusion of peace negotiations. Place at his disposal such Intelligence Personnel as may be necessary and give him necessary facilities for carrying on this work. If this officer is not available, recommend another officer for the duty.

HARRIS

In compliance with this order, the following instructions were issued:

GENERAL HEADQUARTERS
AMERICAN EXPEDITIONARY FORCES
GENERAL STAFF, SECOND SECTION

November 27th, 1918

FROM: A.C. of S., G2
TO: Colonel R. H. Van Deman, General Staff
SUBJECT: Instructions

1. In compliance with confidential instructions from the WAR Department you will proceed to Paris, France, reporting upon arrival to Brevet General Tasker K. Bliss for instructions, and take station in that city.

2. In order to enable you to carry out the instructions of the WAR DEPARTMENT, you are authorized to call upon the Second Section, General Staff, these Headquarters, or any subsection or office thereof, for such assistance as may be required to carry out your instructions.

3. You are also authorized to consult with the Commanding General, U.S. Troops, District of Paris, and the Provost Martial [sic], who will render such assistance as may be necessary for the carrying out of your duties.

4. Copy of this letter is being furnished the Commanding General, U.S. Troops, District of Paris, and, the Provost Marshal General, for their information and guidance.

(Signed) D. E. Nolan,
Brigadier General, G.S.
Chief of Section

The following instructions were also issued: -

AMERICAN COMMISSION TO NEGOTIATE PEACE
#4 Place de la Concorde
PARIS

December 5th, 1918

FROM: GENERAL TASKER H. BLISS, U.S. ARMY
TO: Colonel R. H. Van Deman, General Staff
U.S. Army
SUBJECT: Instructions.

APPENDICES

1. Having reported to me for instructions in compliance with Paragraph 2, Confidential Cable No. 225 [sic], from the WAR DEPARTMENT, dated November 20th, 1918, and with Paragraph 1 of letter to you from the A.C. of S., G-2, GHQ., A.E.F., you are hereby instructed, as follows:

2. You will satisfy yourself that the proper measures are being taken for the safeguarding of the records and the buildings occupied by the offices and personnel of the American Commission to Negotiate Peace; that efficient protection is assured to the persons of the Commissioners at all times; that the personnel employed in and about the offices and quarters of the Commission, including clerical personnel, orderlies, messengers, couriers, telephone operators, house servants, laborers, etc., is loyal and trustworthy; that the lines of communication are properly safeguarded, and, that in general, all other measures in connection with Negative Intelligence duties relating to the work of the Commission which may from time to time be necessary or advisable [to] be taken.

3. To carry out the above instructions, you will avail yourself of the authority granted you in letter from the AC of S, G2 GHQ, A.E.F., dated November 27the 1918, already mentioned in Paragraph #1 of this letter.

4. In discharge of your duties you are authorized, when necessary, to correspond directly with any Department, Bureau, Office or person.

(Signed) Tasker H. Bliss
Brevet General
U.S. Army

The above instructions were issued in order that the agencies already in existence might be utilized thus avoiding the expense and time necessary to form a special organization for the American Commission to Negotiate Peace. This plan has worked out very successfully. (The entire personnel used by the Negative Intelligence – Contre [sic] Espionage – Department has been drawn from the A.E.F. and the work has been carried out with practically no expense to the Commission).

The organization of the Department began immediately upon the receipt of the orders and instructions quoted above.

The office force consisted of three enlisted men detailed from the enlisted personnel attached to the Commission, Sergeant Wm. W. McKinnon as Stenographer and Chief Clerk and Sergeant Lawrence F. Hansel as File Clerk. There was also one Private detailed as Orderly. This was the only personnel furnished by the Commission. On May 22nd, 1919, the two men above named were transferred to the Corps of Intelligence Police as Sergeants, leaving only one Private from the personnel detailed to the Commission.

On December 2nd, 1918, Captain Ogden L. Mills, Jr. was detailed from the office of G-2, S.O.S. as my assistant in the office work. He was demobilized on or about the first of May, 1919 but continued voluntarily to perform the same duties until his return to the United States on May 31st, 1919. I cannot give too high praise to Captain Mills for the manner in which he handled the work entrusted to him. Upon the departure of Captain Mills, Lieutenant P. H. Moseley came into the office as my assistant, performing these duties in addition to those developing [sic] upon him as officer in charge of the Library of G-2, GHQ., which had been loaned to the Commission. He has been most faithful and efficient.

Insofar as the Commission is concerned, the work of the Negative Intelligence Department consisted in preventing interference with the operations of the Commission by outside agencies. To accomplish this, certain specific steps had to be taken:

(a) The records of the Commission had to be safeguarded.

(b) The persons of the Commissioners and of the working staff protected.

(c) Measures taken against possible espionage by any and all outside agencies.

To accomplish these objects, it was, of course, imperative that the personnel employed by the Commission should be trustworthy; that persons known to hold disloyal sentiments and those of anarchist or terrorist tendencies should be denied admission to the buildings and that constant and close supervision should be kept on all persons entering the buildings whose sentiments and affiliations were not known, and that the communication system – telegraph and telephone – should be closely supervised to prevent "tapping" and "cutting in." This meant that all orderlies, messengers, telephone operators, hotel employees, clerks, typists, laborers, etc. had to be carefully investigated before being employed. It also meant that we must know what persons were admitted to the buildings, where they went to those buildings and when they left. Also, due to the unusual conditions following the long war. it was necessary to assure ourselves as far as possible that no evil intentioned persons were allowed to loaf about the entrances of the buildings. To accomplish this a system of passes had to be established and a carefully worked out plan of supervision over persons admitted to the various offices and rooms whose characters were not known. This work was carried out by a carefully selected body of Intelligence Police Sergeants belonging to the G-2 (Intelligence) Section of the SOS, under the direction of a small group of officers trained in Intelligence work, also belonging to G-2 SOS. These men were simply assigned to this duty under authority of the above quoted orders and instructions and the funds of the Commission were not drawn on. The original force consisted of three officers (1st Lieutenants Colwell, Brevoort and Hornblow) and thirty-five Intelligence Police Sergeants. This force was later increased to seven officers and sixty Intelligence Police Sergeants and was then gradually reduced as the requirements of the work permitted. Upon the demobilization of G-2, SOS., A.E.F., the force of officers and Intelligence Police Sergeants was transferred to G-2, GHQ. and detailed to duty under my supervision. Major Cooper was in charge of this group and has so continued to this date. The force on duty now consists of six officers, two Army Field Clerks and thirty-five Intelligence Police Sergeants.

For the purpose of "Pass Control," the entire personnel of the Commission, including orderlies, messengers, house servants, etc. were furnished passes bearing their photographs. This pass admitted them to the Crillon or to #4 Place de la Concorde or to both buildings at any time. A second series were issued to Press Correspondents, some of whom were authorized to attend a morning meeting with the members of the Commission. All passes were issued by authority of the Commission and upon the written statement of the Personnel Offices that the individual was entitled to the pass. The "Press Passes" were issued only upon a written request from the "Press Bureau" with a statement that the Executive Committee of Correspondents had considered the individual's name and were convinced that a pass should be issued.

From time to time passes were issued to certain officials of the Allied Governments and to persons not members of the Commission but whose duties required them to visit the Commission.

All General Officers of the Army and all high officials of the Government, as well as high officials of the Allied Governments, were admitted on recognition without passes of any kind. With those exceptions, every person not holding a pass was required to apply at the desk in the Reception Room of the Hotel Crillon or in #4 Place de la Concorde where an "In and Out Pass" was issued bearing the name of the individual and the office which he wished to visit. This pass was delivered to the I.P. Sergeant at the door when the individual left the building. As a record was kept of these passes, when issued, it was always possible to know whether or not any person not having a permanent pass was in the building.

In addition to the Sergeant stationed at the various doors of the building and those at the Reception Desks, a certain number were detailed to circulate throughout the buildings during the entire twenty-four hours for the purpose of observing persons moving about and to check up on anyone acting in a suspicious manner. As everyone within the buildings (except the class mentioned above) was required to have in their possession at all times either a permanent pass or an "in and out" pass, it was possible to check up on unauthorized people within the buildings.

In addition to this, watch was kept on offices and living rooms to see that important and confidential papers were not left lying about when the rooms were unoccupied. A certain amount of supervision was exercised over the telephone to see that conversations on particularly confidential subjects were not indulged in.

In addition to the forces actually detailed for duty with the Commission, the closest liaison was maintained with G-2, GHQ., G-2, SOS., Military Intelligence Division in Washington, the Military Attaches all over the world, the Department of State, the U.S. Secret Service and the Intelligence Services of the Allied Powers. By these means it was possible to detect the presence of suspicious persons in Paris and so be warned in advance should they attempt to enter the buildings.

As a special precaution, I.P. Sergeants were stationed as guards in the Records Room and the Map Room at all hours.

Supervision over all wastepaper was maintained, the contents of the wastepaper baskets being burned daily under the direct supervision of an I.P. Sergeant. All discarded files of offices which were closed were destroyed under supervision of I.P. Sergeants.

At the request of the French Surete General, two I.P. Sergeants were detailed to sit with their agents at all plenary meetings of the Peace Conference at the Palais d'Orsay and at Versailles.

At the request of Mr. Moran, Chief of the U.S. Secret Service, certain specially selected I.P. Sergeants were detailed for duty in the houses occupied by the President – the Murat House and that on Etats Unis.

As the Central Powers maintained an Espionage Personnel in France and particularly in Paris, it was necessary to make sure that uniformed members of the Commission Personnel were warned when they were approached by individuals who were definitely suspect. This was done by myself personally and in the most quiet and confidential way possible.

The above, in a general way, covers the measures taken in connection with the protection of buildings, records and personnel.

The larger subject of general contre-espionage [sic], it is hardly possible to report on in detail. It is perhaps sufficient to say that it was carefully covered. In this work very great assistance was rendered by the British Intelligence Service and to a lesser extent by the French Second Bureau. The mass of the work was, however, accomplished by our own Intelligence organization – the Military Intelligence Division, General Staff; G-2,

APPENDICES

GHQ., AEF., G-2, SOS., AEF, our Military Attaches and by Special Agents from various Sections.

In addition to its regular work of contre-espionage [sic], the Negative Intelligence Department took up at the request of the Secretary General the subject of "Bolshevism" and its allied activities. All cables, reports, etc. reaching the Commission on this subject were routed to the Negative Intelligence Department and our Military Attaches were directed by the Military Intelligence Division, General Staff, to send to me directly all information obtained by them in this connection.

Beginning with December 12th, 1918, the Negative Intelligence Department issued a daily bulletin giving a resume of the information on "Bolshevism" and kindred activities coming into the office during the past twenty-four hours. It also issued a monthly resume on the subject covering every country in the world in which agitation of this character appeared.

Before closing this report, I want to express my appreciation of the very excellent work done by the Officers and Intelligence Police Sergeants who have been acting under my immediate supervision during the past eight months and a half. Their work has called for intelligence, tact and self-sacrifice. I believe that the thanks of Commission is due to these men for the manner in which they have performed their work.

On my own behalf, I desire to express my appreciation of the uniform kindness and courtesy I have received from every member of the Commission personnel. I am especially indebted to Mr. Joseph C. Grew, the Secretary-General, for his hearty and sympathetic support in connection with every phase of the work revolving on me.

>Respectfully submitted,
>
>(s) R. H. Van Deman
>
>R. H. Van Deman, Colonel, General Staff
>In Charge, Negative Intelligence Department

RHVD
mck

RAYMOND Lt